AUDITING THE RISK MANAGEMENT PROCESS

AUDITING THE RISK MANAGEMENT PROCESS

K.H. SPENCER PICKETT

WILEY

John Wiley & Sons, Inc.

Library of Congress Cataloging-in-Publication Data:

Pickett, K.H. Spencer.
   Auditing the risk management process / K.H. Spencer Pickett.
    p. cm.
   Includes index.
   ISBN 0-471-69053-8 (cloth)
   1. Auditing, Internal.   2. Risk management—Auditing.   I. Title.
   HF5668.25.P529 2005
   658.15′11—dc22

                                                           2005000043

Printed in the United States of America

10 9 8 7 6 5 4 3 2 1

ABOUT THE INSTITUTE
OF INTERNAL AUDITORS

The Institute of Internal Auditors (IIA) is the primary international professional association, organized on a worldwide basis, dedicated to the promotion and development of the practice of internal auditing. The IIA is the recognized authority, chief educator, and acknowledged leader in standards, education, certification, and research for the profession worldwide. The Institute provides professional and executive development training, educational products, research studies, and guidance to more than 80,000 members in more than 100 countries. For additional information, visit the Web site at *www.theiia.org*.

*This book is dedicated
to the memory of Jenny Topham*

CONTENTS

PREFACE

Auditing New Horizons is a new series of short books aimed primarily at internal auditors, but which will also be useful to external auditors, compliance teams, financial controllers, consultants, and others involved in reviewing governance, risk, and control systems. Likewise, the books should be relevant to executives, managers, and staff as they are increasingly being asked to review their systems of internal control and ensure that there is a robust risk management process in place in all types of organizations. Each book provides a short account of important issues and concepts relevant to the audit and review community. The series will grow over the years and

Figure P.1 The Auditing New Horizon Book Series

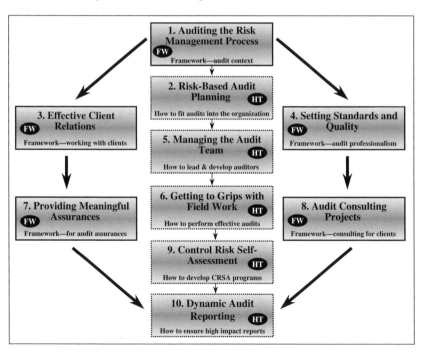

John Wiley & Sons, Inc., is working alongside the Institute of Internal Auditors, Inc., to ensure that each new title reflects both current and emerging developments. The framework for Auditing New Horizons is illustrated in Figure P.1.

FrameWork (FW) books set out various models, supported by reference material that can be employed to ensure best practice pointers can be assessed for their impact on current practice. HowTo (HT) books use similar models but focus more on checklists and worked examples that can be employed to implementing aspects of relevant underlying frameworks. Each book is immersed in the Institute of Internal Auditor's Professional Practices Framework in terms of their published standards, advisories, and assorted guidance. Because the books are fairly succinct, reference to other sources will need to be limited. There are no detailed case studies taken from well-known companies in this book series because of the fast-changing pace of business, where current material quickly falls out of date. The books do, however, refer to many short examples of what happens in different organizations as a way of illustrating important points. The dynamic nature of the governance, risk, and control context means that some new book titles for the Auditing New Horizons series may change over the coming years. We hope that readers find the series both interesting and stimulating and that this series will provide a reference source that adds value to internal auditing, external auditing, and other review functions.

LIST OF ABBREVIATIONS

BASEL: Committee on Banking Supervision

CAE: Chief Audit Executive

CEO: Chief Executive Officer

CFO: Chief Finance Officer

COSO: Committee of Sponsoring Organizations

CRO: Chief Risk Officer

CRSA: Control Risk Self-Assessment

CSA: Control Self-Assessment

ERM: Enterprise Risk Management

H&S: Health and Safety

IIA: Institute of Internal Auditors

IS: Information Systems

IT: Information Technology

KPI: Key Performance Indicators

OECD: Organization of Economic Cooperation and Development

PPF: Professional Practices Framework

PR: Public Relations

RA: Risk Assessment

RI: Risk Identification

RM: Risk Management

RO: Risk Owner

SEC: Securities and Exchange Commission

SIC: Statement on Internal Control

1

WHY RISK MANAGEMENT?

> The internal audit activity should assist the organization by identifying and evaluating significant exposures to risk and contributing to the improvement of risk management and control systems.
>
> IIA Standard 2110

INTRODUCTION

Internal auditing has grown tremendously over the years to reflect its new high-profile position in most larger organizations. It has shifted from back-office checking teams to become an important corporate resource. The focus on professionalism and objectivity has driven the new-look auditor toward high-impact work that can really make a difference. The key development that has underpinned this change relates to the shift from enforcing controls on employees to using an assessment of risk to empower management and their staff to establish meaningful controls over their business. This move from must-do to want-to control cultures has allowed employees more scope to innovate and experiment.

Unfortunately, in the past, robust risk management processes have not always been in place. The rapid change programs of the 1980s and '90s meant that many organizations were likened to speeding trains that would leave behind anyone who was not bold enough to jump on board and hang on for dear life. Investors expected quick returns, while competition was about being the first to bring new or improved products to the marketplace—or at least give that impression. The resultant crashes and scandals that rebounded throughout the last decade underpinned the lack of clear direction or ethical values that could be described as the much-needed rail signals and brakes—to continue our train analogy.

Reckless trading against the backdrop of the cutthroat competition of the 1990s continued into 2000 and beyond, before the regulators started to get tough. The old governance models of a select board of high achievers

1

gathered around a powerful CEO, whose only accountability was to publish financial accounts that had been reviewed by a friendly auditor, could not cope with the new business dynamic. In this type of environment, regulations were seen as obstacles to be sidestepped. Corporate lawyers were often used to design roadmaps to allow the executive teams to weave a path through legal provisions and industry-specific regulations. Societal concerns came to a head in 2002, with the publication of the Sarbanes-Oxley Act, to enshrine personal responsibility at the top of each company to adhere to the rules and demonstrate that this is the case. The link between risk management and corporate governance has been explored by the Institute of Internal Auditors (IIA):

> Risk management is a fundamental element of corporate governance. Management is responsible for establishing and operating the risk management framework on behalf of the board.[1]

In the past, control frameworks have helped in setting standards, but they often acted as basic benchmarks to be checked off against and often ended up as just checks in the Compliance Box, something that is done and then filed away—until the same time next year. Nowadays, the new focus is firmly on risk—to the business, executives, and stakeholders. Several societal concerns appear at the forefront of this idea of risk, including the risks that:

- Published accounts are misleading.
- Performance information is fudged.
- Regulatory disclosures are not supported by sound evidence.
- Senior executives are making uninformed assertions about the adequacy of controls over financial reporting and compliance procedures.
- The corporate asset base is not properly protected from waste, loss, attack, or natural disaster.
- The corporate reputation militates against customer loyalty.
- Operations and processes are inefficient and inflexible.
- The wrong people are being promoted and recruited.
- The organization is failing to meet the changing expectations of customers, the marketplace, and stakeholders generally.

Attempts to address these issues have led organizations in the direction of Enterprise Risk Management (ERM). That is a wholesale approach to identifying and managing risk across all aspects of the business—from a strategic standpoint. As each risk changes in impact and urgency, so does the organization respond to ensure that any damage is limited and opportunities are exploited through using gaps in the market thrown up by new risks. In fact, the main feature of a successful enterprise is its ability to anticipate and deal with global risks more efficiently than other similar organizations. In this scenario where the stakes are so high, the role that is carved out by the internal auditor becomes all the more important. If ERM is to be a key driver for success, the various parties that affect the ERM framework that is built to address risk across the business become a fundamental concern. Where each party has a clear role, there is a need to discharge the precise responsibilities of each of these roles. Any shortfalls may lead to problems. The choices made by the Chief Audit Executive, in the context of the audit approach to ERM, are likewise important, and nothing should be left to chance.

If organizations faced no risk, there would be no need to employ internal audit staff. The organization would always be in complete control, and there would be no need to review, adjust, realign, or even implement internal controls. The auditor exists because plans do not always go as intended, and things don't always appear as they really are. The auditor is needed to ensure that the organization understands its risks and has taken steps to both handle foreseeable problems and seize potential advantages. Advising, helping, cajoling, and issuing warnings are all tools that may be employed by the auditor to put risk on the agenda and ensure that it is given proper consideration. This combination of effort to achieve a risk-smart workforce means that the auditor is fast becoming what some now refer to as a critical friend to executives, management, and employees generally.

Before we launch our first model, we need to outline the formal definition of *internal auditing* from the IIA:

> Internal auditing is an independent, objective assurance and consulting activity designed to add value and improve an organization's operations. It helps an organization accomplish its objectives by bringing a systematic, disciplined approach to evaluate and improve the effectiveness of risk management, control, and governance processes.[2]

As is clear from this definition, internal auditing is firmly rooted in the risk management, control, and governance agenda. Dave Richards, President of the IIA, presented at the IIA's Enterprise Risk Management and Control Self-Assessment* Conference in Las Vegas, Nevada, on September 9, 2004, which is reported as follows:

---

*Control Risk Self-Assessment (CRSA) is also called Control Self-Assessment (CSA); the two terms are interchangeable.

Richards highlighted key ERM and CSA trends, including legislative movements around the world emphasizing the need for risk management as well as signs that internal auditors are becoming more proactive in the use of risk-assessment processes. Although CSA has not been fully embedded in many organizations, he said ERM is becoming known as a key ingredient to good governance, and internal auditors should promote its adoption and progression. In Richards' closing comments he encouraged the audience by saying, "It couldn't be a better time to be in the internal audit profession," and challenged participants to advocate risk management processes within their organizations while keeping internal audit standards and basic principles at the forefront of their audit activities.[3]

This sets the challenge: To help and support management as they struggle with establishing good risk management in the organization, while ensuring that the rigorous provisions of audit standards are retained. *Risk management* is defined by the IIA as:

A process to identify, assess, manage, and control potential events or situations, to provide reasonable assurance regarding the achievement of the organization's objectives.[4]

Enterprises include all public and private-sector organizations, and *enterprise risk management* is described as:

A structured, consistent and continuous process across the whole organization for identifying, assessing, deciding on responses to and reporting on opportunities and threats that affect the achievement of its objectives.[5]

We will also be devoting some time to a landmark document on ERM, which was launched by the Committee of Sponsoring Organizations (COSO) on September 29, 2004. COSO consists of five major professional associations in the United States and was formed in 1985 to sponsor the National Commission on Fraudulent Financial Reporting. All further references in this book to COSO ERM relate to the 2004 COSO ERM framework. Further information on COSO and their publications can be viewed on their Web site at *www.coso.org*. COSO provides the following commentary in its foreword to ERM guidance:

The need for an enterprise risk management framework, providing key principles and concepts, a common language, and clear direction and guidance, became even more compelling. COSO believes this Enterprise Risk Management—Integrated Framework fills this need, and expects it will become widely accepted by companies and other organizations and indeed all stakeholders and interested parties.[6]

RISK MANAGEMENT FRAMEWORK MODEL: PHASE ONE

Our first model looks at the way risk management resides in an organization. We start at the top of an enterprise with the position of the CEO and the board and the way they respond to the pressure to ensure good corporate governance in Figure 1.1.

Figure 1.1 Risk Management Framework Model: Phase One

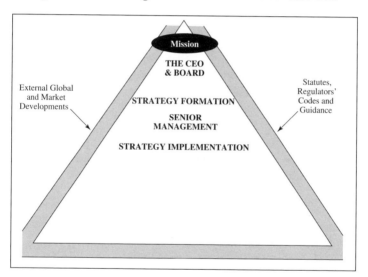

Each aspect of the model is described below.

External Global and Market Developments

Risk is inherent in the way global events shift in the economy, including changing interest rates, international developments, and the fluctuating movement of capital. Meanwhile, markets are constantly changing as consumer demand alters and competitors enter or leave the marketplace. Public-sector services are also affected by constant changes in the demands and expectations of society. This sense of uncertainty has been summed up by COSO:

> Enterprises operate in environments where factors such as globalization, technology, restructurings, changing markets, competition and regulation create uncertainty.[7]

Statutes, Regulations, Codes, and Guidance

Governance codes and company legislation can be generic or industry specific, and they create additional demands on enterprises—normally in response to heightened expectations from society, or as a result of corporate scandals that revealed a need to tighten up on existing regulations. The most famous of the more recent laws arrived several years ago in the guise of Sarbanes-Oxley, with the resulting impact on companies listed on the New York Stock Exchange and NASDAQ. An assortment of local state laws also add to the compliance framework within which enterprises must operate. Some professions, such as law, medical practice, and accounting, provide various codes of conduct and specific regulations that must be adhered to by their practicing members. Within this context, governance is about the way organizations conduct themselves and administer their affairs. The IIA's definition of *governance* is:

> The combination of processes and structures implemented by the board in order to inform, direct, manage and monitor the activities of the organization toward the achievement of its objectives.[8]

Most significant organizations understand the need to respond properly to the wider demands of society as expressed through the regulators. The foreword to the COSO ERM addresses this important point:

> The period of the framework's development was marked by a series of high-profile business scandals and failures where investors, company personnel, and other stakeholders suffered tremendous loss. In the aftermath were calls for enhanced corporate governance and risk management, with new law, regulation, and listing standards.[9]

Business performance goes hand in hand with regulatory performance, as described by one large retail company:

> Our size and global reach present extraordinary opportunities, but also present additional complexity in dealing with an ever-changing variety

of laws and regulations. Keeping pace with changes in the regulatory environment is a challenge for management, but we are committed to do so. We continually monitor our legal and regulatory performance, and will upgrade internal systems or change the way we do business when necessary in order to assure compliance.[10]

The Mission

The risk management framework is driven by what the organization is trying to achieve, which, at its highest level, is the overall mission. For example, the mission of the Ford Motor Company is stated as:

> We are a global family with a proud heritage passionately committed to providing personal mobility for people around the world. We anticipate consumer need and deliver outstanding products and services that improve people's lives.[11]

Meanwhile, the company's future vision is:

> To become the world's leading consumer company for automotive products and services.[12]

Many corporate governance codes argue that corporate objectives should be enriched by ensuring that they also address wider societal concerns:

> In addition to their commercial objectives, companies are encouraged to disclose policies relating to business ethics, the environment and other public policy commitments.[13]

The reality of private, public-sector, and not-for-profit environments means that there can never be total certainty that the mission will always be fully achieved and make the vision a reality. Risk is about this lack of certainty, and it has been defined as follows:

> Risk is the chance of something happening that will have an impact on objectives. Therefore, to ensure that all significant risks are captured, it is necessary to know the objectives of the organization function or activity that is being examined....Organizational success criteria are the basis for measuring the achievement of objectives, and so are used to identify and measure the impacts or consequences of risks that might jeopardize those objectives.[14]

The CEO and Board

The driving force for the enterprise is the CEO and board of directors. This is where the key decisions are made regarding the strategy that will transform the mission into firm results. The IIA defines a *board* in the following way:

> A board is an organization's governing body, such as a board of directors, supervisory board, head of an agency or legislative body, board of governors or trustees of a nonprofit organization, or any other designated body of the organization, including the audit committee, to whom the chief audit executive may functionally report.[15]

The board formulates strategy and employs executives, managers, staff, and appropriate resources to implement this strategy. The need for sound boards has been remarked on in the past:

> The three main problems at Enron were that the company had an accommodating and passive board, an unhealthy drive to meet earnings targets and—probably the most damaging quality—a penchant for hiring only the best and brightest and rewarding them lavishly if they proved they could innovate, innovate and innovate. Unfortunately, the dark side of innovation is fraud.[16]

Moreover, the board has a key role in overseeing the risk management process. COSO ERM has provided some direction in clarifying this role by suggesting the following oversight responsibilities:[17]

- Knowing the extent to which management has established effective enterprise risk management in the organization
- Being aware of and concurring with the entity's risk appetite
- Reviewing the entity's portfolio view of risk and considering it against the entity's risk appetite
- Being apprised of the most significant risks and whether management is responding appropriately

Strategy Formation

Our model suggests that the context for the development of a formal strategy is found within the global market forces and the relevant regulatory framework for each individual organization. One short example of strategy formation comes from CalPERS, the California Employees' Retirement System, which provides retirement and health benefits:

> Our Strategic Plan provides our organization with a road map for meeting the retirement and health benefits needs of more than 1.4 million members and participating employers. It guides our business relations and interactions. Our business philosophy is straightforward. We are customer-focused, and our decision-making process is guided by value and quality.[18]

Senior Management

The next aspect of the model relates to senior management (i.e., the people who sit in the firing line to get the job done). The corporate strategy will result in various objectives that will need to be delivered to ensure that the organization is successful (i.e., the overall mission is achieved). Senior management run the business lines and are responsible for meeting key performance targets, commonly known as Key Performance Indicators (KPIs). COSO ERM builds on this theme and goes on to locate key responsibilities to senior managers:

> Managers guide application of ERM components within their sphere of responsibility, ensuring application is consistent with risk tolerances. In this sense, a cascading responsibility exists, where each executive is effectively a CEO for his or her sphere of responsibility.[19]

Strategy Implementation

Managers are responsible for ensuring that their staff, systems, and budgets are applied to delivering the set strategy. They do this by breaking down the longer-term corporate strategy into more manageable shorter-term chunks that are handed out to their workforce and associates. The workforce is in effect the engine room of the organization. Empowering organizations allow people to make decisions on the front line and flex their responses to the needs of customers and clients. In terms of implementing solutions, the responsibilities of senior management have been outlined in the banking operational risk management framework, BASEL:

> Senior management should have responsibility for implementing the operational risk management framework approved by the board of directors.[20]

RISK MANAGEMENT FRAMEWORK MODEL: PHASE TWO

So far we have described an overall corporate arrangement that has a basic view of setting strategy and then implementing the various aspects of a more detailed plan to keep the workforce busy and productive. This rather one-dimensional version of the way businesses operate needs to become much more layered and colorful. The additional dimension that has emerged over the years relates to the need to isolate and understand risk. Our model is further enhanced in Figure 1.2 in recognition of this fact.

Figure 1.2 Risk Management Framework Model: Phase Two

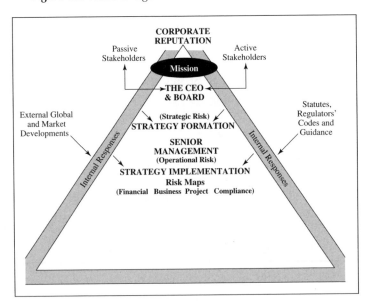

Each new aspect of the model is described below.

Active Stakeholders

Over the years we have come to accept the role of stakeholders in corporate life. Active stakeholders have a direct influence over an organization, and in incorporated companies, this relates to shareholders who can vote on the board members and what they are paid for their services. Investors, lenders, associates, partners, bankers, employees, and other parties each have an important influence on the organization. Likewise, institutional investors have a major role in holding a batch of voting shares in many large enterprises, whereas public-sector organizations are beholden to their public to ensure they deliver and deliver well. *Stakeholders*, in the context of risk management, are described in the Australian/New Zealand risk management standard:

> Those people and organizations who may affect, be affected by, or perceive themselves to be affected by a decision, activity or risk.[21]

Passive Stakeholders

There is a growing band of stakeholders that sits just outside of direct interfaces with specific enterprises, and this is what we mean by passive stakeholders. Local communities, the media, environmental groups, and people who are concerned about the behavior of large organizations may have no obvious influence over the board, but they do have some collective sway in the way the organization is seen by others. Increasingly, such pressure groups are able to influence businesses that are behaving badly or have not made a full assessment of their impact on local communities. The Australian/New Zealand risk management standard has something to say on this matter:

> Communication and consultation are important considerations at each step of the risk management process. They should involve a dialogue with stakeholders with efforts focused on consultation rather than a one-way flow of information from the decision maker to other stakeholders.[22]

There is an emerging theme based around the concept of corporate social responsibility that is starting to enhance the importance of all types of stakeholders.

Strategic Risk

Our model places strategic risk firmly on the corporate agenda. The risks from changing markets and the risk of failing to comply with various laws and rules, or meeting the needs of stakeholders, may mean the stated mission will not be achieved. Strategy takes on board these diverse risks and ensures that they are addressed in such a way as to achieve the set objectives. This link is clearly defined in the Australian/New Zealand standard:

> Organizations that manage risk effectively and efficiently are more likely to achieve their objectives and do so at lower overall cost.[23]

The concept of strategic risk emphasizes strategic solutions. All organizations need to consider several matters that are encompassed in ERM:[24]

- Aligning risk appetite and strategy
- Enhancing risk-response decisions
- Reducing operational surprises and losses
- Identifying and managing cross-enterprise risks
- Providing integrated responses to multiple risks
- Seizing opportunities
- Improving deployment of capital

Many big risks confront all sorts of organizations, and global terrorism, rapid technological change, and the availability of good staff cannot always be underwritten by insurers. Many organizations have now moved toward internal insurance arrangements in the form of good risk management systems to reinforce the need for a sustainable business base. Returning to COSO ERM, several events may affect an organization, which can be classified as either external or internal factors:

- External factors:
  - Economic
  - Natural environment
  - Political
  - Social
  - Technological
- Internal factors:[25]
  - Infrastructure
  - Personnel
  - Process
  - Technology

Operational Risk

Strategy is a high-level concept that eventually gets filtered through to front-line operations. These operations need to address risk to the more detailed objectives that form the basis for the work of most middle managers and the actual workforce. Operational risk affects the day-to-day operational objectives, and each entity must deal with the important task of aligning operations across the entity:

> Enterprise risk management over operations focuses primarily on developing consistency of objectives and goals throughout the organization.[26]

International banks have already recognized the importance of operational risk management, and the Committee on Banking Supervision, Bank for International Settlement, have prepared guidance on operational risk management for the banking community. BASEL Principle One deals with the importance of operational risk:

> The board of directors should be aware of the major aspects of the bank's operational risks as a distinct risk category that should be managed, and it should approve and periodically review the bank's operational risk management framework.[27]

Risk Maps (Financial, Business, Project, and Compliance)

The next factor that we need to add to our model relates to the way generic risk is structured to fit the way the organization sees the world. There are many and varied perceptions of risks to an organization. We have broken down risk into various categories of financial, business, project, and compliance risk. In this way, a map can be drawn as to how these different types of risk run up, down, and through the organization. The COSO ERM viewpoint is that risk may be categorized as follows:

> Within the context of an entity's established mission or vision, management establishes strategic objectives, selects strategy, and sets aligned objectives cascading through the enterprise. This enterprise risk management framework is geared to achieving an entity's objectives, set forth in four categories:[28]
>
> 1. *Strategic.* High-level goals, aligned with and supporting its mission
> 2. *Operations.* Effective and efficient use of its resources

3. *Reporting.* Reliability of reporting

4. *Compliance.* Compliance with applicable laws and regulations

Risk maps attempt to track the way strategic and operational risk affects different parts of an organization. The Australian/New Zealand standard describes the way risk affects all parts of a business:

> Risk management can be applied at many levels in an organization. It can be applied at a strategic level and at tactical and operational levels. It may be applied to specific projects, to assist specific divisions or to manage specific recognized risk areas. For each stage of the process records should be kept to enable decisions to be understood as part of a process of continual improvement.[29]

RISK MANAGEMENT FRAMEWORK MODEL: PHASE THREE

Our model continues in Figure 1.3. Each new aspect of the model is described below.

Figure 1.3 Risk Management Framework Model: Phase Three

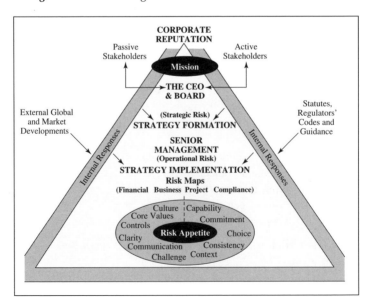

Risk Appetite

The concept of risk appetite appears next on the model, as it holds a central role in all risk management frameworks. As such, it warrants its own chapter, which appears later in the book (Chapter 4). Here we focus on 11 Cs that are important to understanding the way risk is perceived by an organization. Before we launch into these Cs we need to make clear that, in essence, risk appetite creates an unwritten contract between an organization and its stakeholders regarding the balance between exploiting opportunities and protecting the business and its reputation. If management moves too quickly to seize an opening, it may lose out in the long run. If it is too slow, it may also miss out in the long run. The concept of risk appetite runs across many risk standards, and for banks, risk appetite is seen as a major consideration:

> Banks should have policies, processes and procedures to control and/or mitigate material operational risks. Banks should periodically review their risk limitation and control strategies and should adjust their operational risk profile accordingly using appropriate strategies, in light of their overall risk appetite.[30]

Capability

Our first C relates to the capacity within an organization to understand and manage its risks. A short example will illustrate this point.

CASE STUDY

The Cost of Low Capability

In one not-for-profit organization, there was no system of risk management in place and no record of how important decisions are made or plans approved. In fact, the one person who raised the issue was ridiculed or ignored by colleagues. A main feature of the corporate culture was poor role definition and the lack of clear objectives. The organization suffered for many years from fragmented teams and a reputation for vague and ill-defined services.

Commitment

The next C concerns the need for people to buy into the risk management concept (i.e., a commitment from the top that runs through the workforce), as in the following example.

Board-Level Sponsorship

In one public-sector body, a board-level Control Risk Self-Assessment (CRSA) sponsor is used to oversee the CRSA process and ensure that it is both effective and challenging. This person has to be satisfied that the risk workshops are well designed and that CRSA is being applied to the best effect within key parts of the business. The success criteria are defined as changed behaviors from staff as they take more ownership for their business processes and products.

Choice

Risk appetite resides in the choices that are made or not made on issues that have a significant impact on the success or otherwise of the business and is about the level of risk that remains after controls have been put in place. Decisions should be made based on the acceptability of this level of risk, described as follows:

> Residual risk is the risk that remains after treatment options have been identified and treatment plans have been implemented. It is important that stakeholders and decision makers are aware of the nature and extent of the residual risk. The residual risk should therefore be documented and subjected to monitor and review.[31]

Consistency

The next C suggests that the organization should apply a consistent approach to the way it manages risk (i.e., it fits with the way people behave at work):

> The risk management process should be customized for the organization, its policies, procedures and culture taking into account the review process.[32]

Context

Risk appetite should be seen within the context of the way an organization operates and deals with its customers and other stakeholders. Establishing the right context is therefore a prerequisite to establishing the right risk appetite:

> Communication and consultation are intrinsic to the process of risk management and should be considered at each step. An important aspect of "establishing the context" is to identify stakeholders and seek and con-

sider their needs. A communications plan can then be developed. This plan should specify the purpose or goal for the communication, who is to be consulted and by whom, when it will take place, how the process will occur, and how it will be evaluated.[33]

Challenge

Risk management should not lead to a bunker mentality in which people become obsessed with a multitude of risks that have a remote bearing on the business. It should lead to an empowered workforce that is able to take charge of its priorities and decide what works best at the sharp end, as demonstrated in this example.

CASE STUDY

The Risk Management Challenge

In one commercial company, risk management was sold as a chance for each local office to secure some degree of autonomy from head office control. So long as they adhered to the basic control and compliance systems, they were free to implement local initiatives after they had been formally risk-assessed. Some managers performed risk assessments using a team approach, whereas others carried out a basic review, or analytical survey. Team-based CRSA workshops were designed to last less than an hour at a time. Internal audits would help these local managers understand and meet the set criteria, as well as reviewing their efforts. Risk maps and detailed registers were compiled by the chief risk officer (CRO) from regular interviews with the managers. The really good managers performed well, whereas poor ones did not last long. The middle range received a great deal of support from the CRO and chief internal auditor in understanding their risks.

Communication

The corporate risk appetite can only be understood if people around the organization understand each other and their priorities. If the board has a view on what is acceptable behavior, it will need to paint this image for its stakeholders and employees, to support a common understanding of risk appetite:

Communication between an organization and its external stakeholders allows an organization to develop an association with its community of interest, and to establish relationships based on trust.[34]

Clarity

Clarity of objectives, clear accountabilities, and clear risk triggers all underpin the way risk is perceived and addressed. In an attempt to clarify risk owners and risk appetite, the way accountabilities are set and applied will need to be reviewed, as in the following example.

CASE STUDY

Doing Your Homework

In a national realty company, a great deal of time was spent in defining delegated authority levels at each branch based on head office policies on managing clients and negotiating deals. This exercise was deemed necessary before an effective risk management system could be established.

Controls

Controls are an important equation in setting risk appetite. Controls are set against high levels of inherent risk to reduce this risk down to an acceptable level. The extent to which an operation is controlled depends on an organization's perspective of acceptable risk. The greater the focus on risk taking, to enhance market share, the less the emphasis on fixed controls. Controls nowadays are moving toward being more flexible and organic and entirely responsive to changing risks. *Controls* are defined as follows:

> Any action taken by management, the board, and other parties to manage risk and increase the likelihood that established objectives and goals will be achieved. Management plans, organizes, and directs the performance of sufficient actions to provide reasonable assurance that objectives and goals will be achieved.[35]

Controls respond to risk, and COSO ERM suggest that several matters should be considered when deciding on the application of controls:[36]

- Effects of potential response on risk likelihood and impact—and which response options align with the entity's risk tolerances
- Costs versus benefits of potential responses
- Possible opportunities to achieve entity objectives going beyond dealing with the specific risk

Core Values

Risk appetite is closely aligned to corporate values. When we decide on what is acceptable in the way we work, this requires a value judgment. Acceptability is about appropriateness (i.e., what fits under the circumstances). An organization that has spent a great deal of time and effort to define its core values has a better chance of defining its risk appetite:

> To be most effective, risk management should become part of an organization's culture. It should be embedded into the organization's philosophy, practices and business processes rather than be viewed or practiced as a separate activity. When this is achieved, everyone in the organization becomes involved in the management of risk.[37]

Culture

The next part of the risk appetite model relates to a matter that has already been alluded to—that of culture. Many commentators view governance as a meeting of performance-driven success criteria and conformance-based constraints (i.e., delivering the goods, but in a right and proper manner). This balance is affected by the type of corporate culture in place, ranging from gung ho to stickler for rules employee attitudes:

> Root causes (of risk) can include facets of an organizational culture such as ingrained processes and practices or paradigms that need to change to successfully treat a risk from occurring (and reoccurring). Sources of risk that flow on from attitudes within organization culture, cannot be treated successfully unless changes are made to these facets.[38]

The importance of corporate culture can have a wide-ranging effect on the way risk is perceived and dealt with, as shown in the following example.

CASE STUDY

Working within the Culture

In a listed company, risk management was applied without the use of the terms *risk, control,* or *risk management.* The driver was based around better business, and this focused on achieving better results and more responsive teams that managed their work proactively. A decision was made to apply risk concepts in a way that suited the way people worked and communicated with each other. The main issue was centered around learning and improving, and the risk assessments were applied with this in mind (e.g., much is made of near misses and how they can be avoided in future).

RISK MANAGEMENT FRAMEWORK MODEL: PHASE FOUR

Our model continues in Figure 1.4. Each new aspect of the model is described below.

Figure 1.4 Risk Management Framework Model: Phase Four

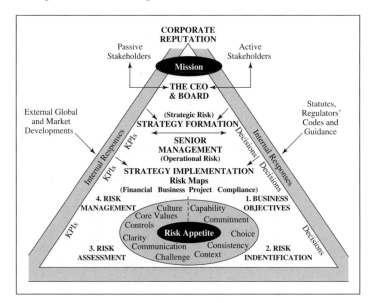

Senior Management

In most organizations, management makes the most impact on whether the corporate objectives will be achieved or not. If senior management does not adopt the risk management concept wholeheartedly, there is little chance that a systematic analysis of risk will be undertaken and applied to steering the business through rocky waters. This point is brought out in the Australian/New Zealand standard:

> The directors and senior executives are ultimately responsible for managing risk in the organization. All personnel are responsible for managing risks in their areas of control. This may be facilitated by:[39]
>
> • Specifying those accountable for the management of particular risks or categories of risk, for implementing treatment strategies and for the maintenance of risk controls;

- Establishing performance measurement and reporting processes and ensuring appropriate levels of recognition, reward, approval and sanction.

Business Objectives

All risk frameworks have the term *objectives* set somewhere in their central components. This is a key point. Risk as a vague concept that floats above an organization is often associated with disasters and accidents (i.e., things that appear out of the blue and are largely uncontrollable). In this sense, risk is something that one suffers in silence and not as we suggest something that can be anticipated and managed. We can view risk as anything that affects our objectives, and in this way encourage people to take charge of their work by viewing many risks as potentially controllable, or at least potentially minimized. The use of ERM in promoting the achievement of objectives has been documented by the IIA:

> ERM can make a major contribution towards helping an organization manage the risks to achieving its objectives. The benefits include:[40]
>
> - Greater likelihood of achieving those objectives
> - Consolidated reporting of disparate risks at board level
> - Improved understanding of the key risks and their wider implications
> - Identification and sharing of cross business risks
> - Greater management focus on the issues that really matter
> - Fewer surprises or crises
> - More focus internally on doing the right things in the right way
> - Increased likelihood of change initiatives being achieved
> - Capability to take on greater risk for greater reward
> - More informed risk-taking and decision-making

Risk Identification

Once the need for effective risk management has been recognized, we come to the task of isolating all possible risks. This is before we have weighed each risk to determine whether it is substantial or not. Risk identification is the process of capturing all those risks that affect the relevant business objectives. This task is included in our model as an important step in promoting better-run organizations. The following short example will help illustrate this point.

CASE STUDY

Being Risk Smart

In one division, the goal was to get a risk-smart attitude into the workforce. Risk concepts were built into team meetings, and people started to think ahead and plan for the consequences of their actions. People were told not to accept any blame for problems that lay elsewhere, but to find out what needed fixing and delegate it to those who were responsible to act. For example, a staff shortage lies with those whose job it is to ensure staffing quotas and absence planning. Most of the problem lay in poor communications between the resource planning team and the front-line managers. A workshop between the two offices was held to isolate the risks, consequences of these risks, and ways forward. This approach is now used whenever an interface-based problem impacts service delivery.

COSO ERM uses the concept of an *event* to drive the risk identification stage of the risk management cycle:

> An event is an incident or occurrence emanating from internal or external sources that affects implementation of strategy or achievement of objectives. Events may have a positive or negative impact, or both.[41]

Risk Assessment

The next part of the model relates to assessing known risks for their potential impact on an organization's ability to achieve its objectives. The most popular approach to risk assessment is to judge the possible impact of the risk if it materializes, and then judge the extent to which the risk is likely to occur. The results are normally plotted on a graph that measures these two axes, so that risks that fall in the top right corner (see Figure 1.5) would have a high impact on the objectives and are also likely to occur unless managed properly, as noted in the Australian/New Zealand standard, which describes the concept of *risk* as:

> The chance of something happening that will have an impact on objectives:[42]
> - A risk is often specified in terms of an event or circumstances that may flow from it.
> - Risk is measured in terms of a combination of the consequences of an event and their likelihood.
> - Risk may have a positive or negative impact.

Risk Management

Risk management comes into the model in suggesting that having assessed our risks, we can then determine what steps to take to deal with anything that causes a concern (i.e., risk that is significant and likely to arise). COSO ERM supports that application of good risk management:

> Recent years have seen heightened concern and focus on risk management, and it became increasingly clear that a need exists for a robust framework to effectively identify, assess, and manage risk.[43]

There are many possible responses to different types and levels of risk, and the options are found in COSO ERM:[44]

- Avoidance
- Reduction
- Sharing
- Acceptance

Figure 1.5 Risk Management Responses

Impact		Likelihood			
	High	*Sharing*	*Reduction*	*Reduction*	*Avoidance*
	Medium2		*Reduction*	*Reduction*	*Reduction*
	Medium1	*Exploit?*	*Acceptance*	*Reduction*	*Reduction*
	Low	*Exploit?*	*Exploit?*		*?????*
		Low	Medium1	Medium2	High

Avoidance and reduction strategies will tend to be associated with high-impact, high-likelihood risks, whereas sharing fits more with high-impact, low-likelihood risks. Acceptance will tend to focus on low-impact, low-likelihood risks—or where the cost of controls is prohibitive. Using the COSO ERM risk-response categories, we can set out the Impact/Likelihood chart and locate the appropriate strategies of Avoidance, Reduction, Sharing, and Acceptance.

One further risk response has been added to the chart in Figure 1.5, located toward the bottom left-hand corner, where both impact and likelihood are low. This is marked as Exploit, where parts of the business are encouraged to do more and be more innovative because their operations are far below the corporate risk appetite.

KPIs

Having used risk management to arrive at an action plan to improve controls or refine the way work is planned and performed, there is a need to consolidate these measures. The model is enriched by adding in the attachment of performance indicators to action plans that result from an assessment of risk. The facts of corporate life mean that any actions that are needed to grow the business must feed into personal or team performance targets to have any real chance of happening, but targets should be set with care:

> Setting realistic targets is sound motivational practice, reducing counter-productive stress as well as the incentive for fraudulent reporting.[45]

COSO ERM goes on to list 12 considerations that an organization may make in determining information requirements to underpin performance, in their guide on application techniques that accompanies the main guidance:[46]

- What are the key performance indicators for the business?
- What key risk indicators provide a top-down perspective of potential risks?
- What performance metrics are required for monitoring?
- What data are required for performance metrics?
- What level of granularity of information is needed?
- How frequently does the information need to be collected?
- What level of accuracy or rigor is needed?

- What are the criteria for data collection?
- Where and how should data be obtained?
- What data/information are present from existing processes?
- How should data repositories be structured?
- What data recovery mechanisms are needed?

Disclosures

The model turns now to the need for formal disclosures from the organization. Transparency relates to the obligations assumed from corporate accountability, and this point is brought out in the Australian/New Zealand standard:

> Sound risk management not only contributes to good governance, it also provides some protection for directors and office holders in the event of adverse outcomes. Provided risks have been managed in accordance with the process set out in the Standard, protection occurs on two levels. Firstly, adverse outcomes may not be as severe as they might otherwise have been. Secondly, those accountable can, in their defence, demonstrate that they have exercised a proper level of diligence.[47]

In the United States, the accountability regime that has emerged in the form of documented certifications over the last few years has been described by the IIA:

> The strength of all financial markets depends on investor confidence. Events involving allegations of misdeeds by corporate executives, independent auditors, and other market participants have undermined that confidence. In response to this threat, the U.S. Congress and a growing number of legislative bodies and regulatory agencies in other countries passed legislation and regulation affecting corporate disclosures and financial reporting. Specifically in the United States of America the Sarbanes-Oxley Act of 2002 (the Sarbanes-Oxley Act) enacted sweeping reform requiring additional disclosures and certifications of financial statements by principal executive and financial officers.[48]

RISK MANAGEMENT FRAMEWORK MODEL: FINAL

Our complete model is presented in Figure 1.6. Each new aspect of the model is described below.

Figure 1.6

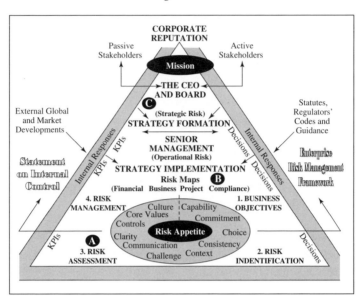

Enterprise Risk Management Framework

One major aspect of the model is the all-consuming ERM framework that sweeps up all of the issues that have appeared so far in the model. ERM has been described as consisting of several activities as follows:[49]

- Articulating and communicating the objectives of the organization
- Determining the risk appetite of the organization
- Establishing an appropriate internal environment, including a risk management framework
- Identifying potential threats to the achievement of the objectives
- Assessing the risk (i.e., the impact and likelihood of the threat occurring)
- Selecting and implementing responses to the risks
- Undertaking control and other response activities
- Communicating information on risks consistently at all levels in the organization
- Centrally monitoring and coordinating the risk management processes and the outcomes and providing assurance on the effectiveness with which risks are managed

Good ERM means that an organization is in a better position to meet its set objectives while also complying with external regulations. It is about strong but sensible business continuity, against all types of problems that result from an uncertain environment. Good risk management is also required by the federal sentencing guidelines along with a system for ensuring compliance and reliable decision making. ERM is a significant business tool that comes into play whenever there is an objective to be met and whenever there is an understanding that there will always be some risk associated with achieving these objectives. Risk is not to be dreaded, but it is also not to be laughed at. There must be a careful balance between these two extremes, as explained in the following:

> If every possible risk that might occur in everyday life—never mind business life—could be recognized, anticipated, assessed and managed then life for all of us would be considerably easier than it is. However, it can't be done; it's an impossible dream. Besides, it's by taking risks that commercial organizations thrive and achieve their objectives. The existence of sufficient entrepreneurs to keep capitalism going year in, year out is testament to the turning of risk to good advantage—at least for most of the time.[50]

The important point to note is that a framework is needed to capture the essence of risk and risk management. A *risk framework* has been described as:

> A set of elements of an organization's management system concerned with managing risk: Management system elements can include strategic planning, decision making, and other strategies, processes and practices for dealing with risk.[51]

The Statement on Internal Control

Our model suggests that the CEO's Statement on Internal Control is related to the ERM process applied by an organization. Meanwhile, COSO ERM starts with a background to internal control:

> Among the outgrowths in the United States is the Sarbanes-Oxley Act of 2002, and similar legislation has been enacted or is being considered in other countries. This law extends the long-standing requirement for public companies to maintain systems of internal control, requiring management to certify and the independent auditor to attest to the effectiveness of those systems. Internal Control—Integrated Framework, which continues to stand the test of time, serves as the broadly accepted standard for satisfying those reporting requirements.[52]

The equation is fairly straightforward. Risks cause an element of uncertainty in meeting objectives. Controls help guard against risks that threaten an organization's ability to achieve its objectives. A good ERM process incorporates a good system of internal control and a mechanism to update controls as and when risks alter in type, impact, or likelihood. Moreover, any examination of a listed company by the Securities and Exchange Commission (SEC) into internal controls will start with the risk management system in operation. The bottom line of our model suggests that it is not possible to establish a sound system of internal control without first establishing an effective ERM process.

Monitoring

The entire risk management process must be kept up to date and vibrant. It must also be reviewed to ensure that it still does the job as intended. This all-important review is described as follows:

> Ongoing review is essential to ensure that the management plan remains relevant. Factors that may affect the likelihood and consequences of an outcome may change, as may factors that affect the suitability or cost of the treatment options. It is therefore necessary to repeat the risk management cycle regularly.[53]

Validation

Another aspect of our first risk management model is that risk activities need to be done in such as way that they can be validated, if necessary. This means there should be good documentation in place. Validation enables the board to set a mandate that designates that an effective risk management process will be put in place and in turn make several firm statements about their risk management policy, including the following lines:[54]

- The processes to be used to manage risk
- Accountabilities for managing particular risks
- Details of the support and expertise available to assist those accountable for managing risks
- A statement on how risk management performance will be measured and reported
- A commitment to the periodic review of the risk management system
- A statement of commitment to the policy by directors and the organization's executive

The use of formal documentation and validation has to be treated with care. The possible impact on employees should be properly managed. Records are essential, but there is a warning about their use:

> Records of communication and consultation will depend on factors such as the scale and the sensitivity of the activity.[55]

Improvement

Risk management must be set within a learning environment for it to be of any use. As such, our model includes the need to provide continuous improvement to the process for capturing real risks in a meaningful way. The Australian/New Zealand standard provides some of the most useful advice on this matter:[56]

> Incidents, accidents and successes provide a useful occasion to monitor and review risks and treatments and to gain insight on how the risk management process can be improved. The intention should be to adopt a systematic process to review causes of successes, failures and near misses to learn useful lessons for the organization. Ideally a systematic analysis process would be used. When successes and failures are analyzed, the questions to be answered are:
>
> * Did we previously identify and analyze the risks involved?
> * Did we identify the actual causes in risk identification?
> * Did we rate and assess risks and controls correctly?
> * Did the controls operate as intended?
> * Were the treatment plans effective?
> * If not, where could improvements be made?
> * Were our monitoring and review processes effective?
> * How could our risk management process in general be improved?
> * Who needs to know about these learnings and how should we disseminate these learnings to ensure that learning was most effective?
> * What do we need to do to ensure that failure events are not repeated but that successes are?

Continual Integration

The final part of the model captures the need to integrate risk management into the actual business systems and work methods. The business responds to risk, and it does this by incorporating threats and opportunities into the way it works:

Management looks to align the organization, people, processes, and infrastructure to facilitate successful strategy implementation and enable the entity to stay within its risk appetite.[57]

SUMMARY

Risk management is now part of mainstream corporate life that touches all aspects of all types of organizations. One way to consider risk management is to go through the following five steps:

1. Consider risk management in its widest format as what most people call enterprise risk management (or enterprise-wide risk management).

2. Align ERM to the governance framework that incorporates the impact of stakeholders and the organization's corporate reputation.

3. Use strategy formation and implementation as the process by which risk is understood and addressed within the executive management of the business.

4. Set the operational risk cycle of business objectives, risk identification, risk assessment, and risk management within the framework set by ERM and the organization's management structure.

5. Superimpose the ERM framework and reporting on internal controls over these matters (1–4 above) and ensure that these two items can be formally documented and reported on to stakeholders.

Note that Appendix A contains checklists that can be used to assess the overall quality of the ERM system and also judge the type of audit approach that may be applied to supporting and reviewing the ERM process.

NOTES

1. Institute of Internal Auditors, UK & Ireland, Position Statement 2004, *The Role of Internal Audit in Enterprise-Wide Risk Management,* Conclusion.
2. Institute of Internal Auditors, definition of *internal auditing.*
3. Institute of Internal Auditors, *www.theiia.org,* October 2004.
4. Institute of Internal Auditors, Glossary of Terms.
5. Institute of Internal Auditors, Glossary of Terms (IIA, UK & Ireland).
6. Committee of Sponsoring Organizations, *Enterprise Risk Management,* September 2004, Forward to the Executive Summary.

7. *Ibid.*, p. 13.

8. Institute of Internal Auditors, Glossary of Terms.

9. Committee of Sponsoring Organizations, *Enterprise Risk Management*, September 2004, Foreword to the Executive Summary.

10. Walmart company, *www.walmart.com*, Letter from the Chairman of the Board, October 2004.

11. Ford company, *www.ford.com*, October 2004.

12. *Ibid.*

13. OECD Principles of Corporate Governance, "Organization for Economic Co-Operation and Development" (2004), p. 50.

14. Australian/New Zealand Standard: Risk Management Guidelines AS/NZS 4360:2004, p. 30.

15. Institute of Internal Auditors, Glossary of Terms.

16. Sharron Watkins, interviewed by Nancy Hala, "If Capitalists Were Angels," *The Internal Auditor* (April 2003): 38–43.

17. Committee of Sponsoring Organizations, *Enterprise Risk Management*, September 2004, Foreword to the Executive Summary, p. 83.

18. Californian Employees' Retirement System, *www.calpers.ca.gov*, October 2004.

19. Committee of Sponsoring Organizations, *Enterprise Risk Management*, September e2004, Foreword to the Executive Summary, p. 85.

20. BASEL Committee on Banking Supervision, Bank for International Settlement, February 2003, Principle 3.

21. Australian/New Zealand Standard: Risk Management Guidelines AS/NZS 4360: 2004, p. 6.

22. *Ibid.*, p. 11.

23. *Ibid.*, Foreword.

24. Committee of Sponsoring Organizations, *Enterprise Risk Management*, September 2004, Foreword to the Executive Summary, pp. 14–15.

25. *Ibid.*, p. 42.

26. *Ibid.*, p. 39.

27. BASEL Committee on Banking Supervision, Bank for International Settlement, February 2003, Principle 1.

28. Committee of Sponsoring Organizations, *Enterprise Risk Management*, September 2004, Executive Summary.

29. Australian/New Zealand Standard: Risk Management Guidelines AS/NZS 4360:2004, p. 8.

30. BASEL Committee on Banking Supervision, Bank for International Settlement, February 2003, Principle 6.

31. Australian/New Zealand Standard: Risk Management Guidelines AS/NZS 4360:2004, p. 86.

32. *Ibid.*, p. 27.

33. *Ibid.*, p. 21.

34. *Ibid.*, p. 23.

35. Institute of Internal Auditors, Glossary of Terms.

36. Committee of Sponsoring Organizations, *Enterprise Risk Management*, September 2004, Foreword to the Executive Summary, p. 56.

37. Australian/New Zealand Standard: Risk Management Guidelines AS/NZS 4360:2004, Foreword.

38. *Ibid.*, p. 74.
39. *Ibid.*, p. 27.
40. Institute of Internal Auditors, UK & Ireland, Position Statement 2004, *The Role of Internal Audit in Enterprise-Wide Risk Management*, Conclusion.
41. Committee of Sponsoring Organizations, *Enterprise Risk Management*, September 2004, Foreword to the Executive Summary.
42. Australian/New Zealand Standard: Risk Management Guidelines AS/NZS 4360:2004, p. 4.
43. Committee of Sponsoring Organizations, *Enterprise Risk Management*, September 2004, Foreword to the Executive Summary.
44. *Ibid.*, p. 55.
45. *Ibid.*, p. 30.
46. *Ibid.*, p. 75.
47. Australian/New Zealand Standard: Risk Management Guidelines AS/NZS 4360:2004, p. 11.
48. Institute of Internal Auditors, Practice Advisory 2120.A1-3.
49. Institute of Internal Auditors, UK & Ireland, Position Statement 2004, *The Role of Internal Audit in Enterprise-Wide Risk Management*, Conclusion.
50. Neil Cowan, *Corporate Governance That Works* (Prentice Hall, Pearson Education South Asia Pte Ltd., 2004), p. 37.
51. Australian/New Zealand Standard: Risk Management Guidelines AS/NZS 4360:2004, p. 5.
52. Committee of Sponsoring Organizations, *Enterprise Risk Management*, September 2004, Foreword to the Executive Summary.
53. Australian/New Zealand Standard: Risk Management Guidelines AS/NZS 4360:2004, p. 22.
54. *Ibid.*, p. 27.
55. *Ibid.* (extracts only), p. 11.
56. *Ibid.*, p. 93.
57. Committee of Sponsoring Organizations, *Enterprise Risk Management*, September 2004, Foreword to the Executive Summary, p. 40.

2

DETERMINING RISK MANAGEMENT MATURITY

Internal auditors should refrain from assessing specific operations for which they were previously responsible. Objectivity is presumed to be impaired if an internal auditor provides assurance services for an activity for which the internal auditor had responsibility within the previous year.

IIA Standard 1130.A1

INTRODUCTION

We need to be clear about the audit role in risk management, and this is not as straightforward as it appears. There are various different interpretations of the audit role. Both internal and external audits have the potential to make a fundamental impact on the success or otherwise on the efforts of an organization to get risk management in place and running. This input is further explained:

Internal auditing is an organizational function, established by top management to monitor the organization's risk management and control processes. By review of the critical control systems and risk management processes, the internal auditor can provide important assistance to organizational management.[1]

In practice, audit roles may include:

- Being a risk champion
- Offering education and guidance
- Providing formal recommendations that promote risk-based controls
- Being a center of research and best practice

- Coordinating risk management efforts across the organization
- Providing objective assurances on the state of risk management
- Regularly disclosing operational risk levels during and after specific audits
- Driving a change program that seeks to tackle resisters and helps drive risk-smart practices
- Facilitating a program of risk workshops throughout the business
- Developing suitable standards and practical tools

Most published guidance makes it clear that internal auditors should not be responsible for risk management, but this is not enough—auditors must be responsible for some type of input into the daunting task of getting good risk management in place. Auditors have an historical association with risk-based activities, and this point has been noted in the past:

> Without question, internal auditors have engaged in risk assessment from the earliest days of the profession. Internal auditors have always asked, "What can go wrong?" The identification of potential errors and/or irregularities is an absolute requirement for determining what control procedures should be in place. After all, would there be a control if there were no risk? How can the auditor determine whether a particular control is an effective control—the right control—in the circumstances unless the risk is identified and evaluated?[2]

We need to return to the formal definition of *internal audit* to start our discussions on the audit role in risk management:

> Internal auditing is an independent, objective assurance and consulting activity designed to add value and improve an organization's operations. It helps an organization accomplish its objectives by bringing a systematic, disciplined approach to evaluate and improve the effectiveness of risk management, control, and governance processes.[3]

The essence is that auditing needs to evaluate and improve the risk management process. Evaluation enables the auditor to give formal assurances to management, and *assurance services* are defined as follows:

> Assurance services involve the internal auditor's objective assessment of evidence to provide an independent opinion or conclusions regarding a process, system or other subject matter. The nature and scope of the assurance engagement are determined by the internal auditor. There are generally three parties involved in assurance services: (1) the person or group

directly involved with the process, system or other subject matter—the process owner, (2) the person or group making the assessment—the internal auditor, and (3) the person or group using the assessment—the user.[4]

In contrast, *consulting services* are described as:

Consulting services are advisory in nature, and are generally performed at the specific request of an engagement client. The nature and scope of the consulting engagement are subject to agreement with the engagement client. Consulting services generally involve two parties: (1) the person or group offering the advice—the internal auditor, and (2) the person or group seeking and receiving the advice—the engagement client. When performing consulting services the internal auditor should maintain objectivity and not assume management responsibility.[5]

The audit role will move between these two dimensions of assuring the board, audit committee, and senior management about the state of risk management and also consulting with business management to help them make suitable improvements. Implicit in this point is that much depends on where the organization stands in terms of developing good risk management, as hinted in the following quote:

Internal audit may provide consulting services that improve an organization's governance, risk management, and control processes. The extent of internal audit's consulting in ERM will depend on the other resources, internal and external, available to the board and on the risk maturity of the organization and it is likely to vary over time. Internal audit's expertise in considering risks, in understanding the connections between risks and governance and in facilitation mean that it is well qualified to act as champion and even project manager for ERM, especially in the early stages of its introduction.[6]

The model applied in this chapter is built on this basic theme of risk maturity.

RISK MANAGEMENT MATURITY MODEL: PHASE ONE

The audit role in risk management depends on what adds the most value in the context of the need to evaluate and make improvements. Much depends on where the organization stands in terms of the extent to which risk, and how risk is addressed, is embedded into the way it works. Our first model starts with the degree to which an organization has implemented risk management in Figure 2.1.

Figure 2.1 Risk Management Maturity Model: Phase One

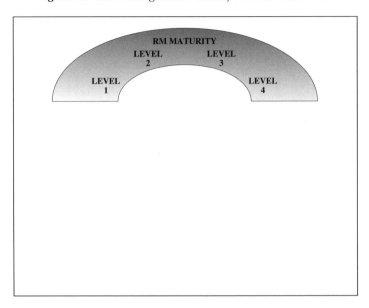

Each organization needs to set a benchmark for where it stands in terms of getting good risk management in place. One way forward is to set various levels of risk maturity and then plot progress through these levels. COSO recognizes that organizations may be at different stages in their risk management maturity:

> When the risk management philosophy is well developed, understood and embraced by its personnel, the entity is positioned to effectively recognize and manage risk. Otherwise, there can be unacceptably uneven application of enterprise risk management across business units, functions, or departments.[7]

In our model we have noted four main levels that are explained later on in the chapter. The importance of the state of risk management is recognized in IIA guidance:

> If an organization has not established a risk management process, the internal auditor should bring this to management's attention along with suggestions for establishing such a process. The internal auditor should seek direction from management and the board as to the audit activity's role in the risk management process. The charters for the audit activity

and audit committee should document the role of each in the risk management process.[8]

The audit role then reflects the degree of risk maturity, and auditors may need to swing into action to kick-start the process. IIA guidance explains how this may happen:

> If requested, internal auditors can play a proactive role in assisting with the initial establishment of a risk management process for the organization. A more proactive role supplements traditional assurance activities with a consultative approach to improving fundamental processes. If such assistance exceeds normal assurance and consulting activities conducted by internal auditors, independence could be impaired. In these situations, internal auditors should comply with the disclosure requirements of the International Standards for the Professional Practice of Internal Auditing (Standards).[9]

The simple fact is that auditors will assume a role that best fits the circumstances, and this has been described as moving between a continuum that ranges among the following:[10]

- No role
- Auditing the risk management process as part of the internal audit plan
- Providing active, continuous support and involvement in the risk management process, such as participation on oversight committees, monitoring activities, and status reporting
- Managing and coordinating the risk management process

There are many ways to assess how far an organization has progressed in establishing risk management. One diagnostic tool has been described by Basil Orsini that contains five levels of progressively mature organizational behavior. The various levels of risk maturity are set with five performance indicators:[11]

- Organizational Culture
- Leadership and Commitment
- Integration with Departmental Management Practices and Systems
- Risk Management Capability
- Reporting and Control

RISK MANAGEMENT MATURITY MODEL: PHASE TWO

Our model continues in Figure 2.2. Each new aspect of the model is described below.

Figure 2.2 Risk Management Maturity Model: Phase Two

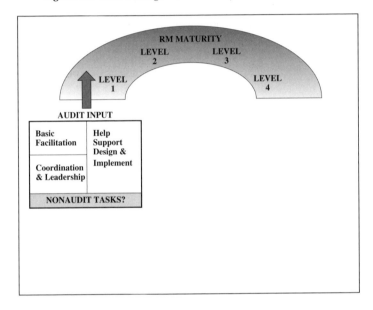

Audit Input

Taking level one (risk immature) from our model, the audit input can be defined in terms of helping to start the risk management process. Although there is much flexibility in establishing an early audit role, it is important that this is part of a negotiated position with the board and audit committee. As such, the audit charter needs to set out this role as a way of defining expectations. The *charter* is the key document for establishing the internal audit role and is defined as follows:

> The charter of the internal audit activity is a formal written document that defines the activity's purpose, authority, and responsibility. The charter should (a) establish the internal audit activity's position within the organization; (b) authorize access to records, personnel, and physical

properties relevant to the performance of engagements; and (c) define the scope of internal audit activities.[12]

As the audit role changes in response to developing risk maturity, the charter will need to be updated to take on board these changes. The concept of *risk maturity* has been explored in professional guidance:

> As the organization's risk maturity increases and risk management becomes more embedded in the operations of the business, internal audit's role in championing ERM may reduce. Similarly, if an organization employs the services of a risk management specialist or function, internal audit is more likely to give value by concentrating on its assurance role, than by undertaking the more consulting activities. However, if internal audit has not yet adopted the risk-based approach represented by the core assurance activities, it is unlikely to be equipped to undertake consulting activities.[13]

Basic Facilitation

Staying with the early stages of risk maturity, our model suggests that the initial internal audit role can be broken down into four main elements. The first relates to basic facilitation. IIA guidance makes clear this facilitating role:

> In summary, internal auditors can facilitate or enable risk management processes, but they should not own or be responsible for the management of the risks identified.[14]

Here internal auditors will help facilitate the growth of risk management on a process level and also engage in specific workshop facilitation exercises. An example illustrates the way facilitated events may be adopted and then refined.

CASE STUDY

Risk Education

One government organization used to undertake dozens of risk workshops each month but now uses short workshops to update the risk profiles as required. Initially, staff received a great deal of training in risk management approaches and tools, but as the organization matured in its use of risk management, this training is now part of new staff orientation programs.

Where the auditor adopts a facilitating role, this changes the audit skills profile. There is a need to ensure that auditors are equipped to deliver this new role. In terms of risk workshops that are used to drive risk management into parts of the business, the auditor may assume a passive or active facilitating role. Passive facilitation is about selling the idea of risk management to the business lines and support services and then letting each team get on with the task of identifying their risks, assessing, and then reviewing the way they are being managed. The team may appoint a workshop leader and decide on how and when they will carry out their program of workshops and assessments. Active facilitation involves a more engaging approach where the auditor may develop a short handbook and lead the teams through a set method for going through the risk management cycle. When embarking on a facilitative role for internal audit, there are several points to note:

- Facilitation is a wide concept that means helping people across the organization come to grips with the risk management concept.
- Team workshops need to be properly programmed and resourced.
- Roles include an organizer, a workshop leader, a recorder, and someone who can explain the risk policy and how the workshops fit into control design and formal disclosures.
- If auditing assumes all or any of these roles, it is good practice to do so in a way that allows work teams to eventually take on these tasks themselves, in due course. Anything less means the teams may not develop properly and take responsibility for their work, which includes managing their risks.
- The facilitated events should have a theme based around drivers such as high energy, good participation, good teamwork, open communications, managerial support, and outcome-based action plans.
- Some type of standard should be in place that ensures workshops are documented and lead to reliable risk registers and internal control disclosure reports.

Facilitation need not revolve around workshops, but it may involve empowering people to understand and deal with risks to their business objectives, as shown in a short example.

CASE STUDY

Taking Control

A most successful initiative was based on getting people to realize that they had some control over many aspects of their work, rather than feeling like a deer trapped in car headlights whenever a problem arose. Teams were urged to deal with high-priority issues on which they could act. High-risk areas that needed input from a different part of the business were referred on, marked as important, and followed through.

Coordination and Leadership

The second role suggested by the model relates to coordination and leadership. Here auditors become *risk champions*. This is a demanding role that has been defined as follows:

> Someone who supports and defends a person or cause. Therefore, a champion of risk management will promote its benefits, educate an organization's management and staff in the actions they need to take to implement it and will encourage them and support them in taking those actions.[15]

The best way to describe this aspect of the audit role, where risk management has not yet matured within an organization, is through a short example.

CASE STUDY

Changing Roles over Time

In one financial services company, the internal auditors started the operational risk management initiative and provided a comprehensive consulting service. This effort was taken over by a risk manager, who designed reporting risk systems along with a risk handbook (that resided on the corporate intranet). Internal audit then assumed an assurance role and commented on the adequacy of operational risk management. As risk management matured in the company, the risk manager left and line management took over the process that had started to become a way of life in the business. Internal auditors then

---

(*continues*)

> ### Changing Roles over Time *(continued)*
>
> developed a quality assurance role, where they examined the standards applied to ensure good risk management and whether these were understood and applied properly in all parts of the organization. Auditors then ran a help line of advice on risk management and internal control, as well as operating a whistleblowers' hotline for staff to report any perceived gaps or abuse of the risk assessment and controls reporting process. The consulting work and assurance work is split in the audit team, and so far they are able to deliver a full range of support, advice, and assurance services to management, the board, and the audit committee.

Driving, leading, championing, and assisting are all laudable aspects of the audit input into good risk management, but with a word of warning that has been clearly highlighted by one author:

> The role of the risk manager is not to manage risk but to ensure that common procedures and practices are adopted throughout the organization, that line managers have responsibility for identifying and managing risk in their own areas and to provide a cohesive overview and reporting line to the Board.[16]

Help, Support, Design, and Implement

Sticking with the less mature organization, the audit role can become proactive at the outset:

> Management are responsible for identifying risk and for the internal control environment. Internal audit reviews the risk assessments and the internal controls in place to ensure they are effective. When risk assessments are not explicit or not documented, the internal auditor may work with management to document them and make them explicit.[17]

Risk management involves people revisiting their internal control after having weighed their risks. The manager is then able to report that they have reviewed their controls, and this report will feed into the formal quarterly disclosures. This process only works when a reliable process is in place that makes sense and is documented. Internal audit can sit back and, under its assurance obligations, may simply report that the state of risk management is poor and in need of further development. Alternatively, auditing could ask what it can do to help stimulate the much-needed movement. This is about helping set up the right structures, policies, channels of communication, and specific processes that underpin good risk management and therefore good business management. In this climate, auditing may embark on many tasks and initiatives that fall short of taking full responsibility:

> A proactive role in developing and managing a risk management process is not the same as an "ownership of risks." In order to avoid an "ownership of risk" role, internal auditors should seek confirmation from management as to its responsibility for identification, mitigation, monitoring, and ownership of risks.[18]

There is a basic view that auditors are essentially auditors and that several core internal audit roles must be kept at the forefront:[19]

- Giving assurances on the risk management process
- Giving assurances that risks are correctly evaluated
- Evaluating risk management processes
- Evaluating the reporting of key risks
- Reviewing the management of key risks

The help, support, design, and implement part of the model suggests that auditing can consider other things where risk management is not really established. Fortunately, some official guidance on this point is given from the IIA on legitimate audit roles (with safeguards):[20]

- Facilitating identification and evaluation of risks
- Coaching management in responding to risks
- Coordinating ERM activities
- Consolidated reporting on risks
- Maintaining and developing the ERM framework
- Championing establishment of the ERM
- Developing risk management strategy for board approval

It is important that there are safeguards over aspects of the audit role that reach out beyond the core tasks, embedded in objective assurance giving. Auditing can perform additional consulting tasks, so long as certain conditions apply:[21]

- It should be clear that management remains responsible for risk management.
- The nature of internal audit's responsibilities should be documented in the audit charter and approved by the Audit Committee.
- Internal audit should not manage any of the risks on behalf of management.
- Internal audit should provide advice, challenge, and support to management's decision making, as opposed to taking on risk management decisions.
- Internal audit cannot also give objective assurance on any part of the ERM framework for which it is responsible. Such assurance should be provided by other suitably qualified parties.
- Any work beyond the assurance activities should be recognized as a consulting engagement, and the implementation standards related to such engagements should be followed.

Nonaudit Tasks

This part of the model ends with the question: nonaudit task? The board members have been presented with a real challenge from the COSO ERM:

> The board of directors provides important oversight to enterprise risk management, and is aware of and concurs with the entity's risk appetite. A number of external parties, such as customers, vendors, business partners, external auditors, regulators, and financial analysts often provide information useful in effecting enterprise risk management, but they are not responsible for the effectiveness of, nor are they a part of, the entity's enterprise risk management.[22]

The board members may well tell internal audit to get something going and feel that they have done their job. The temptation is for the auditors to do just this and find that they have painted themselves into a corner in terms of owning the risk management process and accounting for its progress. The IIA has made clear that this trap should be avoided by issuing suitable guidance on the roles that internal auditors should not undertake:[23]

- Setting the risk appetite
- Imposing risk management processes
- Providing management assurances on risks
- Taking decisions on risk responses
- Implementing risk responses on management's behalf
- Being accountable for risk management

In this way, auditors can define aspects of the risk management process that fall outside of their purview The IIA's code of ethics states that internal auditing services should be performed in accordance with the International Standards for the Professional Practice of Internal Auditing. If there is still a lack of clarity, auditors may turn again to IIA guidance and consider several factors when presented with the opportunity of accepting responsibility for a nonaudit function:[24]

- The IIA's Code of Ethics and standards require the internal audit activity to be independent and internal auditors to be objective in performing their work.
- If possible, internal auditors should avoid accepting responsibility for nonaudit functions or duties that are subject to periodic internal auditing assessments. If this is not possible, then;
- Impairment to independence and objectivity are required to be disclosed to appropriate parties, and the nature of the disclosure depends on the impairment.

RISK MANAGEMENT MATURITY MODEL: PHASE THREE

The next part of the model explores this idea of risk maturity within an organization. We have used four levels to gauge risk maturity, and at each level, the audit role needs to adjust to take on board the changing circumstances. Our model continues in Figure 2.3.

Each new aspect of the model is described below.

Figure 2.3   Risk Management Maturity Model: Phase Three

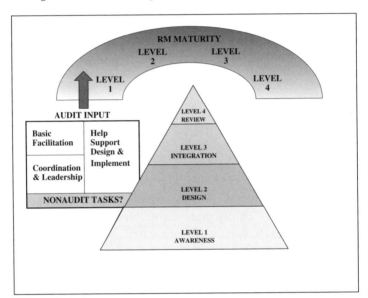

Level One: Awareness

The starting place for risk management is an awareness that some form of system needs to be in place to ensure a methodical approach to dealing with risk. Internal audit is well placed to spread this message to the executives and then throughout the entire business. Professional guidance addresses these early stages and the way that consulting work can help:

> Risk management is a key responsibility of management. To achieve its business objectives, management should ensure that sound risk management processes are in place and functioning. Boards and audit committees have an oversight role to determine that appropriate risk management processes are in place and that these processes are adequate and effective. Internal auditors should assist both management and the

audit committee by examining, evaluating, reporting, and recommending improvements on the adequacy and effectiveness of management's risk processes. Management and the board are responsible for their organization's risk management and control processes. However, internal auditors acting in a consulting role can assist the organization in identifying, evaluating, and implementing risk management methodologies and controls to address those risks.[25]

This evolution of the audit role can best be described through the use of an example.

CASE STUDY

A Step-by-Step Approach

A federal government body used the internal audit team to introduce risk management by breaking the concept down into manageable chunks. A short briefing paper was sent out to all staff saying what risk means and how there needs to be a suitable response. The real benefits of effective risk management were documented, and the importance of all management levels understanding their role and managing their own risks because they were the real experts in their business lines was emphasized. After these ideas were given time to germinate, each manager was visited and the paper discussed, along with an initial view of risks in their work areas. Most managers responded well and took over the tasks of thinking through their objectives, risks, and possible responses. Each person worked at his or her own pace, and without exception, the risk management concepts eventually clicked into place and made sense. Managers were encouraged to take charge and not wait for a senior manager to start things off. The team leaders and middle managers were given permission to talk to their staff and start thinking about their risks and current treatments that could be reported upward (or sideways for some). The main technique was to give people a mandate and a motive to get something going in their section. As the thinking matured, so the process was bolted down into a more systematic methodology. Essentially people were encouraged to proceed in a structured way that worked best for them.

Level Two: Design

Having got the CEO, board, and senior managers to rally around the risk initiative, the next part of the model suggests that an appropriate solution should be prepared. Again, an example will help clarify this point, where auditors start the ball rolling but try to get managers involved and energized.

Risk Management Rollout

One local authority organization used a formal series of pilot programs to launch its risk management program. A project was established by internal audit that involved examining best practices across all local authorities and other types of organization. The aims of the risk management process and milestones that had to be achieved over a set 18-month period were clearly defined. The project's progress was measured, and signs of failure including workshop overload, staff complacency, and important issues left out of the official risk identification process were noted. As the project was rolled out, each manager was asked to present the benefits of formal risk management and share ideas with other divisional managers.

The way risk management is designed, and therefore audited, will vary in different organizations. This is partly the result of the level of maturity but also the type of organization and the way it operates. This point has been highlighted in audit guidance:

> Internal auditors should recognize that there could be significant variations in the techniques used by various organizations for their risk management practices. Risk management processes should be designed for the nature of an organization Depending on the size and complexity of the organization's business activities, risk management processes can be:[26]

- Formal or informal
- Quantitative or subjective
- Embedded in the business units or centralized at a corporate level

Level Three: Integration

Our model describes Level Three as integrating the risk system into the way the business works. More mature organizations have arrived at this stage when risk is seen as it relates to their work and not as a foreign and rather specialist concept. In this sense, risk management becomes just a basic concept that depends on setting the right structures and cultures in place, as explained in the following quote:

> Risk management involves establishing an appropriate infrastructure and culture and applying a logical and systematic method of establishing the context, identifying, analysing, evaluating, treating, monitoring and communicating risks associated with any activity, function or process in a way that will enable organizations to minimize losses and maximize gains.[27]

Integration involves seeing risk management as an holistic approach that is systematically applied to reinforce clear accountabilities and effective decision making. It is about setting good strategy that has been properly thought through. Good governance is about building and maintaining the value of the business through a sound set of values that can be translated into policy and then into performance targets and then into action. That is, a balance exists between sound performance and sensible decision making, based on clear accountabilities and disclosures.

Level Four: Review

The final level of risk maturity sits on top of the integrated business systems that have risk concepts built into them. It relates to the review process. It is one thing to set up risk management and then to build it into the way an organization works. There also needs to be a way of reporting to the outside world how this has been done and whether it is reliable or not. Review, monitoring, and managerial certification can be established when a system is in place, and at this stage the auditors can start to drop off the consulting services and start to revisit their core assurance role. The overall monitoring and review process has been described as consisting of three main elements:[28]

1. Continuous (or at least frequent) monitoring through routinely measuring or checking particular parameters

2. Line management reviews of risk and their treatments (sometimes called control self-assessments)

3. Auditing, using both internal audit and external audit staff. As far as possible, these audits should test systems rather than conditions.

The audit review role is key to successful risk management, and in mature organizations, there would actually be something to review, unlike those that have just started to get risk on the agenda. In terms of discharging this assurance role, audit may have reference to IIA guidance that suggests there are three areas where these assurances may be provided:[29]

- Risk management processes, both their design and how well they are working
- Management of those risks classified as key, including the effectiveness of the controls and other responses to them
- Reliable and appropriate assessment of risks and reporting of risk and control status

To help summarize the issues that we have discussed so far, we can turn to published risk management standards:

> When an organization has a standard risk assessment framework in place, the internal auditor can draw on this. By focusing on the organization's key risks, the internal auditor adds maximum value. When there is no such framework, the internal auditor's work will provide valuable information about the organization's risk to top management.[30]

RISK MANAGEMENT MATURITY MODEL: PHASE FOUR

We started the model by setting a risk-maturing arc that ranged from levels one through four. A mainly consulting role was described for auditors when they worked with Level One organizations. When we get to Level Four, the picture changes, and the model turns into a jigsaw puzzle to set the criteria for assessing audit's role. Our model continues in Figure 2.4.

Each new aspect of the model is described below.

Figure 2.4 Risk Management Maturity Model: Phase Four

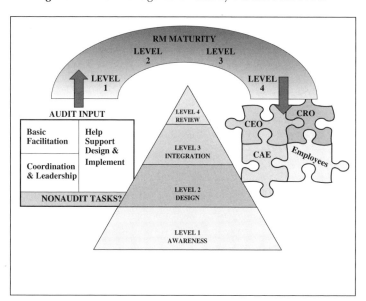

CEO

The CEO and board hold ultimate responsibility for risk management and need to set the overall risk policy. Moreover, the CEO is accountable for monitoring the effects of this policy and reporting back to stakeholders on its impact. We have said before that sound internal control depends on good risk management, and published reports should cover ERM and internal controls. The view that responsibility lies at the top of an organization is reinforced in professional guidance:

> Risk management is a key responsibility of management. To achieve its business objectives, management should ensure that sound risk management processes are in place and functioning. Boards and audit committees have an oversight role to determine that appropriate risk

management processes are in place and that these processes are adequate and effective.[31]

In conjunction with this responsibility, the CEO will need to be kept informed about significant issues that may hurt the organization:

> A chief executive normally would want to be apprised, for example, of serious infractions of policies and procedures. He or she also would want supporting information on matters that could have significant financial impacts or strategic implications or that could affect the entity's reputations.[32]

This dual role of driving and reviewing the way risks are being addressed constitutes an important aspect of the CEO's input into ERM:

> The chief executive's responsibilities include seeing that all components of ERM are in place. The CEO generally fulfills this duty:[33]
>
> - Providing leadership and direction to senior managers
> - Meeting periodically with senior managers responsible for major functional areas...to review their responsibilities, including how they manage risk.

CRO

Many organizations understand the way the auditors need to make some space between themselves and the coordination of the risk management process. This often results in the appointment of a Chief Risk Officer (CRO). Meanwhile, COSO ERM recognizes the role of what they call the risk officer:

> Everyone in an entity has some responsibility for enterprise risk management. The chief executive officer is ultimately responsible and should assume ownership. Other managers support the entity's risk management philosophy, promote compliance with its risk appetite, and manage risks within their sphere of responsibility consistent with risk tolerances. A risk officer, financial officer, internal auditor, and others usually have key support responsibilities.[34]

The development cycle that results in the employment of a CRO can be seen in the following short example.

CASE STUDY

Keeping the Momentum

A large organization employed an army of consultants to kick-start the risk management process. They brought prepackaged software and top consulting skills to the job. The external team also had a wealth of information from other assignments. After a while, the board established a small in-house team to get close to the consultants and absorb some of their skills. This worked well, but the one element that had to be worked on revolved around maintaining the consultants' obvious enthusiasm and their ability to sell the concepts. A chief risk officer was eventually appointed who had these attributes and engaged large numbers of line managers in rolling out risk management across the business.

It is important that someone drives the operational aspects of the risk process. Although we have stated that ownership rests with the CEO, it is not enough just to tell the business management teams to get on with the job. There needs to be a source of advice and expertise that can turn policy into reality. It is also not enough to say that whatever the auditors do in terms of their own risk assessments can be seen as the corporate risk process, as made clear in the following guidance:

> The output from a soundly functioning risk management system, which addresses the full range of business risks, can assist the internal auditor in the internal audit planning process. The risk assessment processes of the internal audit planning process are not, however, sufficient to constitute a proper organizational risk management process.[35]

The CRO needs to coordinate and consolidate the outputs from various risk assessments that arise from disparate parts of the organization:

> The board has overall responsibility for ensuring that risks are managed. In practice, the board will delegate the operation of the risk management framework to the management team, who will be responsible for completing the activities below. There may be a separate function that co-ordinates and project-manages these activities and brings to bear specialist skills and knowledge.[36]

Employees

The next part of the model jigsaw puzzle is about employees (i.e., everyone who is employed, associated, or aligned with an organization). It is here that the risk message is so important. If people within the organization believe in the risk concept, then they will put it to work in everything they do. The board sets the risk policy, the management teams implement this policy, managers employ risk management in their areas of work, and the final aspect is that staff need to understand the risk process and be able and willing to comply with set standards in this respect. Management and the employees' role in ERM have been clearly described:

> Everyone in the organization plays a role in ensuring successful enterprise-wide risk management but the primary responsibility for identifying risks and managing them lies with management.[37]

One organization grasped the importance of getting everyone to rally around the risk concept, and its approach is described in the following example.

CASE STUDY

Risk Management/Change Management Alignment

A useful approach was to align risk management with a change management strategy where some resistance was expected, and strong arguments were compiled to explain the value added. Many managers found it difficult to start identifying their risks and needed a lot of online help before they could take over the process and make it their own. Participants soon found their way and were able to understand their risks and how they can be managed down to an extent. Others rallied around the concept of upside risk, where there are gaps in the current strategy that could be exploited. One useful spin-off was the understanding that traditional controls that do not counter risks and are not required by special rules (e.g., legislation) may be scaled down to speed up the business and make it more efficient.

CAE

Our particular interest is in the way the Chief Audit Executive (CAE) fits into the jigsaw puzzle. Whatever the defined role, it needs to be set clearly within the audit charter and properly negotiated, as described in professional guidance:

> Ultimately, it is the role of executive management and the audit committee to determine the role of internal audit in the risk management

process. Management's view on internal audit's role is likely to be determined by factors such as the culture of the organization, ability of the internal auditing staff, and local conditions and customs of the country.[38]

Having defined the role, it is then necessary to promote a good understanding of the implication throughout the organization. The evolving role of internal audit has often been remarked on by leading figures in the audit world:

> Internal auditors' roles and responsibilities with regard to risk have been a familiar topic of professional discussion in recent years. While internal auditors do not manage risks or make decisions about resource allocations involved in risk management, closer relationships between risk management and internal auditing have been advocated in some quarters. In fact, some observers advocate that the starting place of internal auditing planning should be organization risks, or threats to achievement of business objectives.[39]

Although the assurance role has been held out as a good example of adding value to the organization, the following must be kept in mind as well:

> Internal auditing is an independent, objective assurance and consulting activity. Its core role with regard to ERM is to provide objective assurance to the board on the effectiveness of risk management. Indeed, research has shown that board directors and internal auditors agree that the two most important ways that internal audit provides value to the organization are in providing objective assurance that the major business risks are being managed appropriately and providing assurance that the risk management and internal control framework is operating effectively.[40]

Meanwhile, there will tend to be tensions in the assurance and consulting roles in organizations where risk management is fairly mature. Further IIA guidance explains how consulting services can become proactive:

> Risk management is a key responsibility of management. To achieve its business objectives, management should ensure that sound risk management processes are in place and functioning. Boards and audit committees have an oversight role to determine that appropriate risk management processes are in place and that these processes are adequate and effective. Internal auditors should assist both management and the audit

committee by examining, evaluating, reporting, and recommending improvements on the adequacy and effectiveness of management risk processes. Management and the board are responsible for their organization's risk management and control processes. However, internal auditors acting in a consulting role can assist the organization in identifying, evaluating, and implementing risk management methodologies and controls to address those risks.[41]

Whatever the chosen format, the collective view is that things should not just be left to chance. The audit position should be clarified, documented, and then form the basis for the way audit work is planned and performed. The abundance of professional standards that address this theme create a useful source of advice and support when weighing the pros and cons of particular approaches and styles. In one sense, for less mature organizations, it is easier to define the help and support-based audit role, as risk champions and risk experts. When the organization has developed a way forward, the new audit role is more difficult to explain. It falls back to an assuring and challenging one, where the CAE will hold a view on whether enough is being done and whether what is being done makes sense and stands up to scrutiny. This challenge element is found in risk standards:

> The work of the internal auditor does not reduce the requirement for responsible managers to monitor the risks within their area of responsibilities or the mitigation strategies designed to deal with them. The internal auditor has a duty to challenge the basis of management risk assessments and to evaluate the adequacy and effectiveness of risk treatment strategies.[42]

One point that we will be exploring further is that one cannot help formulate and implement a particular policy and then claim to objectively audit this same policy. Where internal auditors are responsible for establishing and then coordinating the risk management process, their ability to provide effective assurances may be affected. Audit standards address an extreme position where this situation exists:

> Objectivity is presumed to be impaired if an auditor provides assurance services for an activity for which the auditor had responsibility within the previous year. If on occasion management directs internal auditors to perform non-audit work, it should be understood that they are not functioning as internal auditors.[43]

RISK MANAGEMENT MATURITY MODEL: FINAL

We have built our model to illustrate how audit teams may start out singing the risk management song more or less in the dark. As others join in, respective roles and responsibilities become clearer across the organization, and audit can be slotted into the emerging jigsaw puzzle. The final part of the model sets out a new Audit Input box that reflects the journey that has been undertaken through risk maturity levels one, two, three, and four (i.e., from risk-naïve to risk-smart people across the organization). Our complete model is shown in Figure 2.5.

Each aspect of the final model is described below.

Figure 2.5 The Complete Risk Management Maturity Model

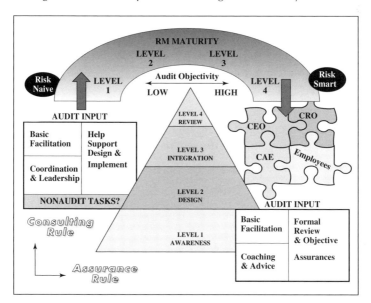

Consulting Role

In a risk-mature organization, the consulting role takes on a new look. Before we go into this, we need to return to the formal definition of *consulting services*:

> Advisory and related client service activities, the nature and scope of which are agreed with the client and which are intended to add value and

improve an organization's governance, risk management, and control processes without the internal auditor assuming management responsibility. Examples include counsel, advice, facilitation and training.[44]

The Australian/New Zealand risk management standard addresses the audit input:

> The internal auditor can also assist the organization by providing advice in the design and improvement of control systems and mitigation strategies. The implementation of controls and strategies remains the responsibility of management.[45]

IIA guidance also makes clear which consulting activities may be undertaken by internal audit in their published guidance:

- Making available to management tools and techniques used by internal audit to analyze risks and controls
- Being a champion for introducing ERM into the organization, leveraging its expertise in risk management and control and its overall knowledge of the organization
- Providing advice, facilitating workshops, coaching the organization on risk and control, and promoting the development of a common language, framework, and understanding by:
  - Acting as the central point for coordinating, monitoring, and reporting on risks
  - Supporting managers as they work to identify the best way to mitigate a risk[46]

In this way auditors may help, assist, cajole, and coordinate but not own the risk management process.

Assurance Role

Assurance, like consulting work, has been formally defined:

> An objective examination of evidence for the purpose of providing an independent assessment on risk management, control, or governance processes for the organization. Examples may include financial, performance, compliance, system security, and due diligence engagements.[47]

A simple example demonstrates the application of audit roles within an organization.

Risk Rewarded

One audit unit was praised as the risk champions. They sold and resold the risk message on an ongoing basis. All audits started with a risk workshop for the management team in question, setting the terms of reference around real emerging risks. The audit work would include a review of soft controls and the way the business area worked together and developed positive values. The audit fieldwork was followed by a further workshop with the management team to consider the findings, controls, compliance issues, financial reporting, and staff value systems with a view to developing ways forward. The auditors had developed a series of one-hour control awareness sessions, which they would present to teams, projects, associates, and managers where appropriate—either on request or when low control awareness was apparent from a recent audit. The entire risk management, audit, and control compliance concept was built around encouraging the right culture, rewarding behaviors, containing threats, managing risk taking, and controlling compliance. Quarterly self-certification resulted from linking risk management to effective systems of internal control.

Audit Input

We have already discussed the basic facilitation role in an earlier part of the model for organizations that had not yet come to grips with risk management. An example is shown as follows.

Facilitation as First Part of Audit

One audit manager uses a combination of CRSA techniques as a gateway into the audit assignment. A questionnaire is sent to the client manager to be completed by the operational work teams, and this is used to help assess the control environment. Interviews are then held to explore apparent weak areas and introduce the audit process. A risk workshop is then facilitated by the audit manager, which involves key staff from the area in question. The feedback from the workshop is used to fine-tune the terms of reference of the audit to focus on high-risk areas and known problems.

When auditing takes a lead in risk management at the outset, some argue that this should be filtered down over time as expertise is accumulated within the organization:

> In practice the Committee recognizes that the audit function at some banks (particularly smaller banks) may have initial responsibility for developing an operational risk management programme. Where this is the case, banks should see that responsibility for day-to-day operational risk management is transferred elsewhere in a timely manner.[48]

Coaching and Advice

A new aspect of the audit consulting role in our model relates to coaching and advice. Auditing may provide support for the established risk management process so long as its role is clearly differentiated from that of others, such as the CRO. An example could be developing a presentation on ERM and how it can be applied to business units as part of a corporate risk policy.

Formal Review and Objective Assurances

The model incorporates the core audit role of providing formal assurances. The overall review process may focus on five key areas described in the following guidance:[49]

- Risks arising from business strategies and activities are identified and prioritized.
- Management and the board have determined the level of risks acceptable to the organization, including the acceptance of risks designed to accomplish the organization's strategic plans.
- Risk mitigation activities are designed and implemented to reduce, or otherwise manage, risk at levels that were determined to be acceptable to management and the board.
- Ongoing monitoring activities are conducted to periodically reassess risk and the effectiveness of controls to manage risk.
- The board and management receive periodic reports of the results of the risk management processes. The corporate governance processes of the organization should provide periodic communication of risks, risk strategies, and controls to stakeholders.

Audit, unlike other parts of the organization, will provide solid evidence to support any reviews of the risk management process. The guidance goes on to explain how this assessment may be undertaken:

> Internal auditors should obtain sufficient evidence to satisfy themselves that the five key objectives of the risk management processes are being met in order to form an opinion on the adequacy of risk management processes.[50]

Audit Objectivity

One issue that needs to be addressed in some detail relates to audit objectivity and the way consulting work needs to be balanced with assurance work. We must first set out what we mean by *audit independence*. IIA standards give some firm direction on this matter:

110.A1   The internal audit activity should be free from interference in determining the scope of internal auditing, performing work, and communicating results

1120   Internal auditors should have an impartial, unbiased attitude and avoid conflicts of interest.

1130   If independence or objectivity is impaired in fact or appearance, the details of the impairment should be disclosed to appropriate parties. The nature of the disclosure will depend upon the impairment.

1130.A1   Internal auditors should refrain from assessing specific operations for which they were previously responsible. Objectivity is presumed to be impaired if an internal auditor provides assurance services for an activity for which the internal auditor had responsibility within the previous year.

1130.A2   Assurance engagements for functions over which the chief audit executive has responsibility should be overseen by a party outside the internal audit activity.

1130.C1   Internal auditors may provide consulting services relating to operations for which they had previous responsibilities.

1130.C2   If internal auditors have potential impairments to independence or objectivity relating to proposed consulting services, disclosure should be made to the engagement client prior to accepting the engagement.[51]

We have already mentioned that some auditing departments may assume the CRO role and be responsible for organizing an effective risk management process. The problem arises when an appointed CRO takes over this role and auditors are then asked to provide formal assurances on the state of risk management and internal controls. The IIA has issued guidance covering situations where auditing reviews areas for which it had some responsibility in the past:

> When operating responsibilities are assigned to the internal audit activity, special attention must be given to ensure objectivity when a subsequent assurance engagement in the related operating area is undertaken. Objectivity is presumed to be impaired when internal auditors audit any activity for which they had authority or responsibility within the past year. These facts should be clearly stated when communicating the results of an audit engagement relating to an area where an auditor had operating responsibilities.[52]

An adequate amount of independence is crucial to the audit function, and this point has often been alluded to:

> The professional internal auditor must have independence to fulfill a professional obligation; render an objective, unbiased, unrestricted opinion; and report matters as they are, rather than as some executives or body would like to see them. Internal auditors must be unfettered by restrictions on their audits—on what examinations they may make and how they may make them. Only then can internal auditors be regarded as auditing professionally.[53]

Risk Naïve

The two final aspects of the model relate to the continuum that moves between two extremes (i.e., naïve and smart employees in terms of their appreciation of risk and ability to respond to high-priority risks). Risk-naïve people have no real understanding of the risks that impact their objectives and are not empowered to review their controls and make important changes. In this environment, auditors may be asked to work with the workforce and build their awareness through training seminars, intranet presentations, and team briefings—all things that auditors can provide under the consulting arm. Where the workforce has matured, the audit role changes to support and advice, and then eventually to formal review, which contrasts with the audit role in a risk-naïve organization, as seen in the following example.

CASE STUDY

ERM Online

A transport company asked its internal auditors to prepare an intranet-based presentation on ERM. This was used to introduce head office staff and depot personnel to the basic concepts of ERM and how it was going to be introduced over the coming year.

Risk Smart

Risk-smart employees are at the other extreme. They are people with the knowledge and the tools to be able to apply risk identification, assessment, and control solutions to a wide range of circumstances and projects, as in the following example.

CASE STUDY

You Have the Power

One company moved away from the formal workshop format and encouraged staff members to review their work areas and undertake their own risk assessments. Any ideas would then be conveyed to the business unit manager for action. This mainly entailed people taking the initiative, when in the past, this had not happened.

We have already suggested that the audit role will change when the workforce is fully conversant with an established risk process. The auditors will want to assess whether what appears to be a sound process and knowledgeable staff are actually reliable and that the board can rely on the certificates and reports from the process. One strategy to address this need has been outlined as follows:

> The key factor in deciding whether consulting services are compatible with the assurance role is to determine whether the internal auditor is assuming any management responsibility. In the case of ERM, internal audit can provide consulting services so long as it has no role in actually managing risks—that is management's responsibility—and so long as

senior management actively endorses and supports ERM. We recommend that, whenever internal audit acts to help the management team to set up or to improve risk management processes, its plan of work should include a clear strategy and timeline for migrating the responsibility for these activities to members of the management team.[54]

The concept of risk and control ownership can cause much confusion. One experienced auditor has described this issue:

> Companies should rethink the way that they evaluate and mitigate risk across the enterprise, and take a holistic and comprehensive approach. In many companies, internal auditing is the only group formally evaluating risk, although more companies are considering hiring a chief risk officer. Internal auditing can assist the audit committee by defining the top risks in the business as well as how and when each risk is being addressed and by which groups. Although the internal audit department can assist management and the audit committee in evaluating risk and controls, management owns internal controls.[55]

One further complication arises from the fact that risk maturity may vary among different parts of the organization. This means the audit approach may need to be multidimensional in response to different contexts for each audit that is undertaken.

SUMMARY

The audit role in risk management varies from organization to organization and in different parts of an organization. It is therefore important that audit teams do not simply fall into one interpretation of this role without assessing the available possibilities. One way to consider the audit role in risk management is to go through the following five steps:

1. Consider the level of risk management maturity within the organization and attempt to plot such progress through set levels, each with defined attributes that can be used as targets.

2. Start the audit role at the existing level of maturity and ensure that good support exists from the audit team in providing help with setting up the structures and approaches at an early stage.

3. As the organization matures, create a jigsaw puzzle of respective roles in the organization's risk management arrangements and ensure that the audit role is clearly established within this format.

4. Develop a greater emphasis on the objective assurance in contrast to facilitation and coaching roles as the organization becomes more confident in the way ERM is developed and embedded within its business systems.

5. Measure progress with ERM in terms of the way the workforce responds to the challenge to build ERM into its working practices and techniques.

Note that Appendix A contains checklists that can be used to assess the overall quality of the ERM system and also judge the type of audit approach that may be applied to supporting and reviewing the ERM process.

NOTES

1. Australian/New Zealand Standard: A Guide to the Use of AS/NVS 4360 Risk Management within the Internal Audit Process—HB 158 2002, p. 3.
2. Lawrence B. Sawyer, Mortimer A. Dittenhofer, and James H. Scheiner, *Sawyer's Internal Auditing,* 5th ed. (Orlando, FL: Institute of Internal Auditors, 2003), p. 121.
3. Institute of Internal Auditors, Introduction to Professional Practices Framework.
4. *Ibid.*
5. *Ibid.*
6. Institute of Internal Auditors, UK & Ireland, Position Statement 2004, *The Role of Internal Audit in Enterprise-Wide Risk Management.*
7. Australian/New Zealand Standard: A Guide to the Use of AS/NVS 4360 Risk Management within the Internal Audit Process—HB 158 2002, Committee of Sponsoring Organizations, *Enterprise Risk Management,* September 2004, p. 28.
8. Institute of Internal Auditors, Practice Advisory 2100-4: *The Internal Auditor's Role in Organizations Without a Risk Management Process.*
9. *Ibid.*
10. Institute of Internal Auditors, Practice Advisory 2100-3.
11. Basil Orsini, "Mature Risk Management," *The Internal Auditor* (August 2002): pp. 66–67.
12. Institute of Internal Auditors, Glossary of Terms.
13. Institute of Internal Auditors, UK & Ireland, Position Statement 2004, *The Role of Internal Audit in Enterprise-Wide Risk Management.*
14. Institute of Internal Auditors, Practice Advisory 2100-4: *The Internal Auditor's Role in Organizations Without a Risk Management Process.*
15. Institute of Internal Auditors UK & Ireland, Glossary.
16. Neil Cowan, *Corporate Governance That Works* (Prentice Hall, Pearson Education South Asia Pte Ltd, 2004), p. 49.
17. Australian/New Zealand Standard: A Guide to the Use of AS/NVS 4360 Risk Management within the Internal Audit Process—HB 158 2002, p. 4.
18. Institute of Internal Auditors, Practice Advisory 2100-4: *The Internal Auditor's Role in Organizations Without a Risk Management Process.*

19. Institute of Internal Auditors, UK & Ireland, Position Statement 2004, *The Role of Internal Audit in Enterprise-Wide Risk Management.*
20. *Ibid.*
21. *Ibid.*
22. Australian/New Zealand Standard: A Guide to the Use of AS/NVS 4360 Risk Management within the Internal Audit Process—HB 158 2002, Committee of Sponsoring Organizations, *Enterprise Risk Management,* September 2004, Executive Summary.
23. Institute of Internal Auditors, UK & Ireland, Position Statement 2004, *The Role of Internal Audit in Enterprise-Wide Risk Management.*
24. Institute of Internal Auditors, Practice Advisory 1130.A1-2.
25. Institute of Internal Auditors, Practice Advisory 2100-4: *The Internal Auditor's Role in Organizations Without a Risk Management Process.*
26. Institute of Internal Auditors, IIA Practice Advisory 2110-1: *Assessing the Adequacy of Risk Management Processes.*
27. Australian/New Zealand Standard: A Guide to the Use of AS/NVS 4360 Risk Management within the Internal Audit Process—HB 158 2002, Foreword.
28. Australian/New Zealand Standard: A Guide to the Use of AS/NVS 4360 Risk Management within the Internal Audit Process—HB 158 2002, p. 89.
29. Institute of Internal Auditors, UK & Ireland, Position Statement 2004, *The Role of Internal Audit in Enterprise-Wide Risk Management.*
30. Australian/New Zealand Standard: A Guide to the Use of AS/NVS 4360 Risk Management within the Internal Audit Process—HB 158 2002, p. 4.
31. Institute of Internal Auditors, Practice Advisory 2100-3.
32. Australian/New Zealand Standard: A Guide to the Use of AS/NVS 4360 Risk Management within the Internal Audit Process—HB 158 2002, Committee of Sponsoring Organizations, *Enterprise Risk Management,* September 2004, p. 81.
33. *Ibid.,* p. 85.
34. *Ibid.,* Executive Summary.
35. Australian/New Zealand Standard: A Guide to the Use of AS/NVS 4360 Risk Management within the Internal Audit Process—HB 158 2002, p. 4.
36. Institute of Internal Auditors, UK & Ireland, Position Statement 2004, *The Role of Internal Audit in Enterprise-Wide Risk Management.*
37. *Ibid.*
38. Institute of Internal Auditors, Practice Advisory 2100-3.
39. Lawrence B. Sawyer, Mortimer A. Dittenhofer, and James H. Scheiner, *Sawyer's Internal Auditing,* 5th ed. (Orlando, FL: Institute of Internal Auditors, 2003), p. 200.
40. Institute of Internal Auditors, UK & Ireland, Position Statement 2004, *The Role of Internal Audit in Enterprise-Wide Risk Management.*
41. Institute of Internal Auditors, IIA Practice Advisory 2110-1: *Assessing the Adequacy of Risk Management Processes.*
42. Australian/New Zealand Standard: A Guide to the Use of AS/NVS 4360 Risk Management within the Internal Audit Process—HB 158 2002, p. 4.
43. Institute of Internal Auditors, Practice Advisory 1130.A1-2.
44. Institute of Internal Auditors, Glossary of Terms.
45. Australian/New Zealand Standard: A Guide to the Use of AS/NVS 4360 Risk Management within the Internal Audit Process—HB 158 2002, p. 4.

46. Institute of Internal Auditors, UK & Ireland, Position Statement 2004, *The Role of Internal Audit in Enterprise-Wide Risk Management.*
47. Institute of Internal Auditors, Glossary of Terms.
48. BASEL Committee on Banking Supervision, Bank for International Settlement, February 2003, Principle 2, paragraph 17.
49. Institute of Internal Auditors, IIA Practice Advisory 2110-1: *Assessing the Adequacy of Risk Management Processes.*
50. *Ibid.*
51. Institute of Internal Auditors, Professional Practices Framework.
52. Institute of Internal Auditors, Practice Advisory 1130.A1-1.
53. Lawrence B. Sawyer, Mortimer A. Dittenhofer, and James H. Scheiner, *Sawyer's Internal Auditing,* 5th ed. (Orlando, FL: Institute of Internal Auditors, 2003), p. 38.
54. Institute of Internal Auditors, UK & Ireland, Position Statement 2004, *The Role of Internal Audit in Enterprise-Wide Risk Management.*
55. Cynthia Cooper, vice president of Internal Audit for MCI (formally known as WorldCom), "One Right Path," *The Internal Auditor* (December 2003): pp. 52–57.

3

ENTERPRISE-WIDE RISK MANAGEMENT

A process to identify, assess, manage, and control potential events or situations, to provide reasonable assurance regarding the achievement of the organization's objectives.

IIA Glossary—Risk Management

INTRODUCTION

The risk community is now using a new term to describe its common ground. This term is what we have referred to so far as *Enterprise Risk Management*, which has been defined as follows:

Enterprise-wide risk management (ERM) is a structured, consistent and continuous process across the whole organization for identifying, assessing, deciding on responses to and reporting on opportunities and threats that affect the achievement of its objectives.[1]

The background to this development is summarized in IIA guidance:

Over the last few years, the importance to strong corporate governance of managing risk has been increasingly acknowledged. Organizations are under pressure to identify all the business risks they face; social, ethical and environmental as well as financial and operational, and to explain how they manage them to an acceptable level. Meanwhile, the use of enterprise-wide risk management frameworks has expanded, as organizations recognize their advantages over less coordinated approaches to risk management.[2]

ERM is a wide concept that has several key features, as it is:[3]

- A process, ongoing and flowing through an entity
- Affected by people at every level of an organization

69

- Applied in a strategy setting
- Applied across the enterprise, at every level and unit, and includes taking an entity-level portfolio view of risk
- Designed to identify potential events that, if they occur, will affect the entity and to manage risk within its risk appetite
- Able to provide reasonable assurance to an entity's management and board of directors
- Geared to achievement of objectives in one or more separate but overlapping categories

We looked at the basic concept of risk management in Chapter 1, and in Chapter 2 we described ERM maturity and the auditor's support and review roles, as well as some of the challenges created by tensions inherent in these roles. This chapter looks in more detail at ERM and how it has emerged as a major new feature of business life.

ENTERPRISE RISK MANAGEMENT MODEL: PHASE ONE

Our first model starts with the fragmented position with risk assessment across the organization in Figure 3.1.

Each aspect of the model is described below.

Figure 3.1 ERM Model: Phase One

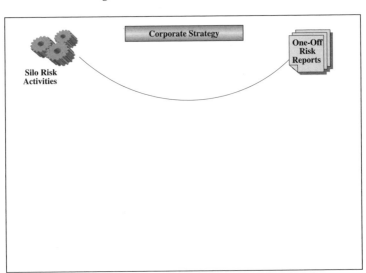

Silo Risk Activities

Risk management is nothing new. Many professionals and specialists have been involved in detailed considerations of risks and use this information to help determine ways forward. The problem has been that these risk activities are disparate and emerge from traditional practices applied by the specialists in question. People from IT security, health and safety, contingency planning, project management, and so on will each have their own approach to using a version of the risk cycle in their work. They will also have their own definitions, terminology, tools, and general attitudes that suit them, but together these do not form an entire collective system. This is what some call silo activities, where each part of the organization works independently from other parts, as seen in the following example.

CASE STUDY

Need for Uniform Approach

One professional body failed to standardize its risk management systems, and each package could not talk to the others. The terminology and formats used by different teams were inconsistent and at times contradictory. These formats developed from a fragmented view of risk management, with pockets of the organization working toward different and incompatible standards. Senior management had no benchmark to assess whether the data and reports were of high quality or not. The net impact of the resulting risk registers was a confusing reporting system that had no overall meaning at higher levels of the organization.

One-Off Risk Reports

The risk-based silo activities get reported up and across the organization, but not in a way that can be read as representing the risk management process. Each report will have its own individual style and level of detail. Unfortunately, the reports cannot be brought together to tell a story. They simply consist of different short stories, with no common theme or collective perspective. This almost parallels the position with individual audit reports, which give one-off fragments of information on specific parts of the business, but it is difficult to put them together in a commentary on the overall risk management process and the underpinning system of internal control. This fragmentation of audit cover into specific detailed audits has been commented on in the past:

Traditionalists defend the status quo on the grounds that the silo approach to audit is necessary to maintain "auditor independence." As long as internal auditors think their job is to decide what constitutes "adequate" control on a fraction of the risk universe, instead of reporting on the quality of the risk assessment process and the reliability of management representations on risk status to the board, true audit independence will not exist.[4]

The need to recognize the interdependencies of risk across the organization is one of the underpinning elements of ERM, and the COSO ERM makes the following observation:

One event can trigger another, and events can occur concurrently. In event identification, management should understand how events relate to one another. By assessing the relationships, one can determine where risk management efforts are best directed.[5]

Corporate Strategy

The starting place for ERM is corporate strategy. In the past, risk has been seen an ethereal concept that consists of dangers that float around the organization, mainly in the form of physical threats. Each threat is countered by building protective bunkers around the business and making contingency plans for anything that crashes through these bunkers. The breakthrough to ERM occurs when we think in terms of strategy. Strategy is driven by an overall mission, while strategic objectives are derived from a corporate strategy. By focusing on strategic issues and factors that affect the heart of the business, we can start to think about holistic risk management as anything that impacts our ability to deliver and grow, rather than seeing risk as only representing physical threats to the business:

In its focus on positive outcomes risk management provides a major contribution to those aspects of corporate governance directed to enhancing organizational performance.[6]

This does not mean that risk reports cannot be made about set parts of the business:

There may, however, be circumstances where the effectiveness of enterprise risk management is to be evaluated separately for a particular business unit.[7]

ENTERPRISE RISK MANAGEMENT MODEL: PHASE TWO

We have so far developed a model that illustrates the old view of disjointed risk management, which needs to be pulled together to make sense to the people at the top of the organization. Our model continues in Figure 3.2.

Each new aspect of the model is described below.

Figure 3.2 ERM Model: Phase Two

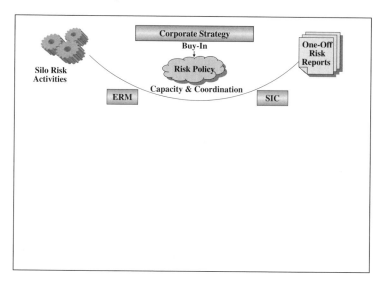

Risk Policy

The main tool for bringing together thinking and decisions on risk and control is found in the form of the risk policy. This document seeks to consolidate all risk-based activities and spread these techniques across the wider business fronts. There is good support for the risk policy:

> Publishing and communicating a policy statement of this type demonstrates the commitment of the organization's executive to risk management. Communication may include:[8]
>
> • Establishing a team, including senior managers, responsible for communicating about managing risk and about the organization's policy; and

- Raising awareness about managing risks and the risk management process throughout the organization.
- Policies should promote good practice, and for banks, this means ensuring that risk is considered in all product and business systems:

Banks should identify and assess the operational risk inherent in all material products, activities, processes and systems. Banks should also ensure that before new products, activities, processes and systems are introduced or undertaken, the operational risk inherent to them is subject to adequate assessment procedures.[9]

Buy-In

Having established strong messages from the top in the form of the risk policy, it is then necessary to spread these messages down into the organization. Words, comments, and gestures have little impact on the way people work if there is no real buy-in from everyone. Much depends on good communications:

Effective internal and external communication is important to ensure that those responsible for implementing risk management, and those with a vested interest, understand the basis on which decisions are made and why particular actions are required.[10]

Good buy-in is about:

- A real belief in the value of risk management that comes straight from the CEO and board
- Efforts to develop a risk policy that fits the organization and accepts the need to develop a growing level of expertise over time
- Clear definition of roles and responsibilities in terms of risk ownership, where to go to for help and advice, and how the arrangements will be reviewed
- All channels of communication employed to spread the points contained in the risk policy
- A well-thought-out program that seeks to implement the matters contained in the risk policy
- A focus on competence, training, awareness, and the use of relevant tools

- An appreciation of the need to set targets for getting risk management in place, perhaps based around defined levels of risk maturity

Capacity and Coordination

Having set a policy to integrate risk into the way people work, it is necessary to recognize the implications of these efforts. People need to be given the resources to take on new challenges, and there needs to be a mechanism for bringing together these efforts in a way that is consistent and methodical. The need to bring different corporate cultures together to reflect the entity's risk management philosophy is commented on by COSO:

> For example, an aggressive selling function may focus its attention to making a sale, without careful attention to regulatory compliance matters, while the contracting unit's personnel focus significant attention on ensuring compliance with all relevant internal and external policies and regulations.[11]

The twist that attaches to ERM is the need to provide a transparent process that may be reported on and reviewed by insiders (internal audit) or even outsiders (external audit). There needs to be a central part of the organization that pulls everything together and acts as a source of expertise and advice. We have discussed the role of internal audit and that of an appointed chief risk officer, and the board will need to determine where it stands on the question of coordination. There are calls for internal audit to take the lead, and our previous chapter explained how this may occur in the early stages of risk maturity:

> Internal auditors are interested in internal control because of the significant role they play in providing assurance to Boards and management that risks are being identified, assessed and controlled. Indeed, internal auditors are often the facilitators of risk practices in organizations because of their special understanding of the relationship between objectives, risks and controls.[12]

ERM Process

After setting a risk policy and getting people to rally around this idea, we can turn to arriving at the actual ERM process. The first consideration is to establish the precise benefits of ERM, which can be listed as follows:[13]

- Greater likelihood of achieving those objectives
- Consolidated reporting of disparate risks at board level
- Improved understanding of the key risks and their wider implications
- Identification and sharing of cross business risks
- Greater management focus on the issues that really matter
- Fewer surprises or crises
- More focus internally on doing the right things in the right way
- Increased likelihood of change initiatives being achieved
- Capability to take on greater risk for greater reward
- More informed risk taking and decision making

Over the years, both the public and private sectors have moved through several key stages in working toward good ERM. Risk-based activities have turned into wider risk management, which has then emerged as ERM, as suggested in Figure 3.3.

Figure 3.3 The Evolution of ERM Concepts

Factor	Risk-Based Activities	Risk Management	ERM
Perspective	Physical threats	All threats	Threats and opportunities
Focus	Specific projects	Specific operations	The entire business and partners
Carried Out by	Specialists	Some managers	Everyone
Level of Detail	Complex analysis	Detailed analysis	General assessments
Timing	One-off	Regular	Continuous
Language	Different terms	Same terms but different perspectives	Common language and perspectives

Figure 3.3 *(continued)*

Factor	Risk-Based Activities	Risk Management	ERM
Selling Points	Stronger controls	Better decision making	Better coordinated decision making and accountability
Reports	Detailed one-off reports	High level but fragmented reports	Integrated accelerated business reporting
Control Focus	Based on security and contingency plans	Based on individual control mechanisms	Based on holistic control frameworks
Tools	Data analysis	CRSA and surveys	Culture change to integrate ERM into working practices
Aim	Lower insurance premiums	Risk identified and managed in risk registers	Objectives achieved in line with set values
Scope	Compliance	Operational	Strategic
Standards	Depends on specialist	Depends on manager	Depends on board's risk policy
Vision	Protect corporate resources	Protect the board and executives	Develop a risk-smart workforce and enhance the corporate reputation
Drivers	External threats	CEO and CRO	Stakeholders, CEO, and CRO

The ERM framework focuses on decision making, accountability, and a clear sense of corporate direction, which is summed up as follows:

Risk management involves managing to achieve an appropriate balance between realizing opportunities for gains while minimizing losses. It is an integral part of good management practice and an essential element of good corporate governance. It is an iterative process consisting of steps that, when undertaken in sequence, enable continuous improvement in decision-making and facilitate continuous improvement in performance.[14]

The COSO ERM framework consists of eight components and four categories of objectives that run across the entire organization, which is illustrated as four different dimensions in Figure 3.4.

Figure 3.4 COSO ERM Objectives and Components

Components	Objectives	Organizational Dimensions
Internal Environment	Strategic	ENTITY LEVEL
Objective Setting		
Event Identification	Operations	DIVISION
Risk Assessment		
Risk Response	Reporting	BUSINESS UNIT
Control Activities		SUBSIDIARY
Information and Communication	Compliance	
Monitoring		

Statement on Internal Control

On the other side of ERM is the statement on internal control (SIC). This is an important equation. Companies listed on the NYSE and NASDAQ, as well as most government and not-for-profit organizations, are required to report on their internal controls. Listed companies focus on internal control over financial reporting but are also concerned with compliance issues and the overall arrangements to deliver and grow. The key issue is summed up as follows:

> Risk management contributes to good corporate governance by providing reasonable assurance to boards and senior managers that the organizational objectives will be achieved within a tolerable degree of residual risk.[15]

The crucial link between risk and control is explored in COSO ERM:

> This Enterprise Risk Management—Integrated Framework expands on internal control, providing a more robust and extensive focus on the broader subject of enterprise risk management. While it is not intended to and does not replace the internal control framework, but rather incorporates the internal control framework within it, companies may decide to look to

this enterprise risk management framework both to satisfy their internal control needs and to move toward a fuller risk management process.[16]

Only through reviewing risks can we determine whether controls make sense and work, and only through a sound ERM process can we develop a good internal control framework. The hope is that published statements on internal control provide some comfort to users of the annual report about the integrity of the organization. One major company describes its system of internal control as follows:

> We maintain a system of internal controls designed to provide reasonable assurances of the reliability of the financial statements, as well as safeguard assets from unauthorized use of disposition. Formal policies and procedures, including an active Ethics and Business Conduct Program, support the internal controls, and are designed to ensure employees adhere to the highest standards of personal and professional integrity. We have established a vigorous internal audit program that independently evaluates the adequacy and effectiveness of these internal controls.[17]

ENTERPRISE RISK MANAGEMENT MODEL: PHASE THREE

Our model continues in Figure 3.5. Each new aspect of the model is described below.

Figure 3.5 ERM Model: Phase Three

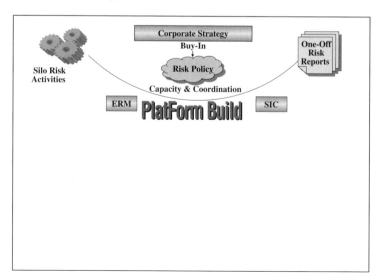

Platform Phase

We have suggested in our model that a good risk policy that supports ERM and enables the organization to report on its internal control system is needed to replace the more traditional fragmented risk reporting. We turn now to the platform that is required to get to this position. Before we address the detailed aspects of this platform, we can draw on the COSO ERM to set out some of the key considerations that should be made to make ERM work:[18]

- *Aligning risk appetite and strategy.* Management considers the entity's risk appetite in evaluating strategic alternatives, setting related objectives, and developing mechanisms to manage related risks.

- *Enhancing risk-response decisions.* Enterprise risk management provides the rigor to identify and select among alternative risk responses: risk avoidance, reduction, sharing, and acceptance.

- *Reducing operational surprises and losses.* Entities gain enhanced capability to identify potential events and establish responses, reducing surprises and associated costs or losses.

- *Identifying and managing multiple and cross-enterprise risks.* Every enterprise faces a myriad of risks affecting different parts of the organization, and enterprise risk management facilitates an effective response to the interrelated impacts and integrated responses to multiple risks.

- *Seizing opportunities.* By considering a full range of potential events, management is positioned to identify and proactively realize opportunities.

- *Improving deployment of capital.* Obtaining robust risk information allows management to effectively assess overall capital needs and enhance capital allocation.

ENTERPRISE RISK MANAGEMENT MODEL: PHASE FOUR

We now get into some level of detail and consider what holds up our ERM platform. Our model continues in Figure 3.6.

Each new aspect of the model is described below.

Figure 3.6 ERM Model: Phase Four

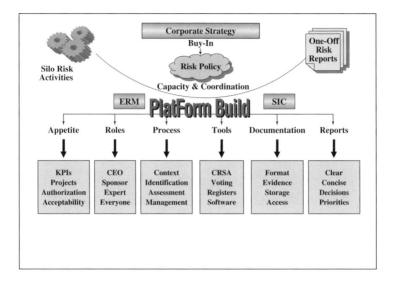

Appetite

We have already noted that risk appetite is such an important topic that it has its own chapter (Chapter 4). Here we simply need to confirm that the board needs to set the risk appetite for the organization, which is described by COSO as a critical challenge:

> Among the most critical challenges for managements is determining how much risk the entity is prepared to and does accept as it strives to create value. This report will better enable them to meet this challenge.[19]

Risk appetites mean different things to different people, and we have developed a model that focuses on:

- Criticality of objectives
- Risk category
- Whether upside or downside risk
- Authorization levels
- Control monitoring levels
- Risk triggers

These items are discussed in more detail in Chapter 4. Knowing the risk exposure across the entire business is important because the board may send messages on areas they need to tighten up and, conversely, areas where there is scope to do much more:

> In cases where the portfolio view shows risks significantly less than the entity's risk appetite, management may decide to motivate individual business units managers to accept a greater risk in targeted areas, striving to enhance the entity's overall growth and returns.[20]

Roles

ERM is based on giving people responsibility for examining and dealing with risk in their work areas. It is also about defining how people fit into the equation from the boardroom right through to the broom room. The CRO, financial controller, audit committee, disclosures committee, risk managers' forum, company lawyers, trainers and HR people, and everyone else has a part to play. Moreover, the auditors will also have a crucial role that should complement what goes on elsewhere. Some of the key roles include the following:

- *CEO.* This person owns the ERM and is entirely responsible for the way it is developed, implemented, and employed.
- *Sponsor.* The sponsor is a board-level (or sub-board-level) person who has to ensure that ERM works. The tasks include reporting back to the CEO and board on the way ERM has matured across the organization and the extent to which it has been integrated into the business systems and processes.
- *Experts.* The CRO and CAE are included in our definition of experts. These people, along with specialist project, insurance, and safety personnel who would have a background in risk management, may be part of a forum that sets standards, provides advice, and coordinates the ERM effort across the business.
- *Everyone.* This includes all employees, associates, consultants, partners, and persons who have a working relationship with the organization. This collective group should possess good knowledge of ERM and be able to apply the tools and techniques to ensure that the risk policy is fully adopted in their areas of responsibility. They

are also charged with bringing to the attention of senior management any flaws, inconsistencies, and problems associated with the way ERM is developed and used.

An example of this point follows.

CASE STUDY

Risk Management Command and Control

A military support organization had, as one would have guessed, a command and control attitude toward implementing new processes. Heads of service were told to get risk management in place and appointed facilitators, who employed a mechanical format for presenting what it is all about and what would happen if people did not carry out the required tasks. Each risk event was fully documented and reported upward through the line.

Process

ERM is a process that runs across the organization:

> Enterprise risk management is not static, but rather a continuous or iterative interplay of actions that permeate an entity. These actions are pervasive and inherent in the way management runs the business.[21]

Another part of the ERM platform relates to how this process fits into the business, as seen in the following example.

CASE STUDY

Risk Surveys

One retail company's risk management framework relies heavily on surveys carried out at local stores that target high-risk areas relating to compliance, pricing, health and safety, performance, and stock movement that need to be addressed. Red risks are accelerated upward until they are fully dealt with.

Each of the following main parts of the process are equally important:

- *Context.* The ERM process starts with a context, which is all of those things that are needed to support a quality process. Contextual issues includes staff awareness, training, an ERM procedures handbook, intranet presentations, a commitment to good risk management, and a structured program for enabling ERM to occur.

- *Identification.* Each organization must put a sound method in place to ensure that all internal and external risks that affect objectives can be identified. Some help is available where there is an agreed-upon framework for classifying risk that suits the business. It is also helped by a sustained effort to scan industry intelligence and global developments that have the potential to adversely or favorably affect the organization.

- *Assessment.* The assessment stage is an important part of the risk cycle, and there needs to be in place a systematic way of working through the impact of risks and the probability that they might materialize. This may involve an adopted scoring system that enables this assessment to occur.

- *Management.* Each business manager, work team, and project manager needs to understand the measures that may be put in place to address unacceptable levels of risk (i.e., the possible risk management arrangements that may be employed depending on the nature and impacts of the risks in question).

Tools

An assortment of tools are available to support the ERM platform, and each one should be assessed to determine whether it can add value to the debate, such as in the following example.

CASE STUDY

Voting Technology

One organization made great use of voting technology to isolate gaps in the way people saw their work and their business. The process developed into an assessment of trust and ethics as a measure of the control environment and staff morale. The process made it clear that there were major differences in the

---

(continues)

Voting Technology *(continued)*

risk appetite of senior managers and what people at the front line would tolerate. The voting patterns also made clear a lack of faith across the organization in the overall corporate direction and strategic objectives. The final outcome was a view that improper practices were happening and that many safeguards were either ignored or poorly designed.

Some of the available tools include the following:

- *CRSA.* Control Risk Self-Assessment (CRSA) is a well-known technique for getting people together to discuss their objectives, risks, and ways that residual risk may be mitigated if necessary. CRSA can be employed to processes, products, projects, people, and procedures. It is driven by the desire to get those most responsible for an aspect of the business to work through better ways of managing this business. In this way we can encourage and empower our workforce to make the right things happen. See Chapter 5 for more details.

- *Voting.* Voting technology is a flexible tool for getting people to understand complex and sensitive issues and build on areas where there may be some concern or divergence of views. It is possible to assess the control environment in a business area by asking people to express their views on the way controls are perceived and employed by voting on several set propositions. Voting can be used to ask staff whether they have confidence in their management; it can be used to ask them whether they are aware of wrongdoings that have not been properly reported; and it can be used to ask them to vote on various risks to assess their range of impact (e.g., low, medium, or high) and the probability that these risks will arise without suitable controls in place.

- *Registers.* Another useful ERM tool is risk registers. These documents capture the results of risk identification, assessment, and mitigation in a way that flows naturally from the risk cycle. CRSA workshops may result in reliable risk registers, or business managers may compile registers through their own reviews and knowledge. Registers can be reported upward and also sideways, because work teams need to be aware of the different priorities of internal customers.

- *Software.* There is an abundance of risk software normally associated with database systems that can be used to capture and report on key risks. These packages can be adopted and adapted across the business to support the way ERM is introduced. The systems can be integrated with business planning processes and lead to risk-based plans and strategies that incorporate relevant and ongoing risk assessments.

Documentation

One interesting feature of ERM is that it is a business initiative that also supports the interests of stakeholders and regulators. If an organization simply focuses on risk to its business, it can get lost in a search for weapons to attack competitors or armor to protect its resources. This situation can become murky as people simply look for material that supports what they want to do and hide anything that makes them look bad. ERM is based on the principles of growth, performance, and accountability, and as such, all efforts should be suitably documented:

> Decisions concerning the extent of documentation may involve costs and benefits and should take into account the reasons for documenting the process. Thus, a process that is of low consequence may be documented only by a diary note or a brief record on file. On the other hand a redesign of a major client service delivery operation might require a detailed explanation of the process for audit and review. There is a range between these extremes, and prudent practical judgement is needed to decide the level of documentation in particular circumstances.[22]

Some of the considerations regarding the appropriate level of documentation include the following:

- *Format.* The way risk assessments and action plans are documented should fit a format that works well for the organization, particularly regarding the way risk registers are used.
- *Evidence.* One issue that affects ERM is the reliability of control reviews and action plans that arrive from risk assessments. Although auditors work to exacting evidential standards, nonauditors do not have such a disciplined approach. For example, any risk assessments that comment on the adequacy of controls to guard against specific risks may accept that the control in question is adequate, but this view presupposes that the control is being applied as intended.

Managers will tend not to gather sound evidence concerning control compliance and should be taught how to deal with this potential problem.

- *Storage.* Another aspect of documentation relates to the retention of records, documents, and material that supports the ERM activities. The simple response is to say that all such records should fall in line with the corporate document retention policy for material that may be of interest to auditors and others.

- *Access.* The final point on documentation is about access rules. When people get together to isolate risk and develop appropriate responses, they will generate a lot of data and notes. Some of the matters discussed may relate to sensitive issues about the way the team works and whether targets will be achieved. There may also be talk of rule infringement and other mistakes that have been made. It is good practice to decide exactly who will have access to this information and make sure this issue is clarified to all those engaged in the exercises.

Most agree that ERM need not become just another bureaucratic burden for corporate bodies:

> In some circumstances, an appropriate level and standard of documentation may be needed to satisfy an independent audit. Whatever the reasons for documenting the process, risk management need not impose another layer of paperwork if a sensible approach is taken. Subject to legislative requirements, decisions and processes involving risk management should be documented to the extent appropriate to the circumstances.[23]

Reports

Outputs from ERM include a risk-smart workforce that is better able to understand and deal with anything that affects its work objectives. Another output is good reports that indicate how ERM is being applied and what actions are needed to address emerging problems or opportunities. It has been argued that risk management information systems may possess certain capabilities:[24]

- Record details of risks, controls, and priorities and show any changes in them
- Record risk treatments and associated resource requirements

- Record details of incidents and loss events and the lessons learned
- Track accountability for risks, controls, and treatments
- Track progress and record the completion of risk treatment actions
- Allow progress against the risk management plan to be measured
- Trigger monitoring and assurance activity

Each main part of the process is equally important, and reports should meet defined standards, including the following:

- *Clear.* Reports should be clear and indicate what objectives are being considered and how risks were identified and assessed. They should specify the risk owner, action plans, and significant outstanding issues.

- *Concise.* Moreover, risk reports should be short and to the point. The whole point to ERM is to focus attention on high-risk areas and concentrate action to address high levels of unmitigated risk. It defeats the objective to hide important findings within a mass of data analysis that results in substantial amounts of paperwork (or detailed spreadsheets).

- *Decisions.* Reports should support decisions about mitigating unacceptable risk and exploiting areas where potential returns look attractive. A fundamental aspect of ERM is that it is used to support sound decision making and underpins corporate transparency. This theme should run throughout all ERM activities.

- *Priorities.* The final point regarding risk reports is that they should focus on priorities (i.e., what is important in terms of the strategic agenda). One way to do this is to accelerate Red Risks from operational risk registers so that big items get reported upward and end up on the board risk register.

ENTERPRISE RISK MANAGEMENT MODEL: FINAL

We have defined the need for ERM and established the platform that supports efforts to distribute risk management around all parts of the organization. There are a few more additions to our model to finish painting the picture. Our complete model is in Figure 3.7.

Each new aspect of the final model is described below.

Figure 3.7 The Complete ERM Model

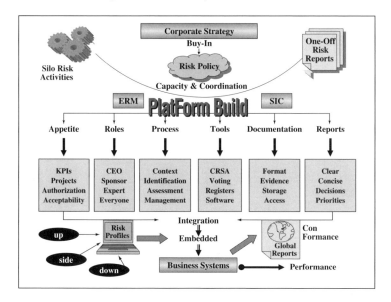

Integration

The next feature of the model relates to the need to integrate ERM with the rest of the business. This means adding ERM into the way managers set and deliver their performance targets and the way they address the risk of noncompliance with important legal or regulatory provisions. It is about adding the concept of dealing with uncertainty into the way people work so that we can arrive at the final stage of ERM being actually embedded into the business:

> The underlying premise of enterprise risk management is that every entity exists to provide value for its stakeholders. All entities face uncertainty, and the challenge for management is to determine how much uncertainty to accept as it strives to grow stakeholder value.[25]

Embedded

We have so far referred to items such as risk activities and risk reporting to describe how ERM may be established. The whole point of ERM is that it sits inside the business and not on top of it (i.e., it needs to be integrated within business systems to make any real sense). Instead of talking about risk activities and risk reporting, a good organization will talk about business activities and reports, and implicit within these tools will be an assessment of uncertainty and suitable responses, such as in the following example.

CASE STUDY

Embedded Risk Management Philosophy

One organization defined risk management as a facilitated process and spent much time developing a team of first-class facilitators and risk management champions. The team passed on this skill to divisional managers and team leaders and encouraged each part of the business to develop its own way of delivering the standard risk cycle. This organization is coming close to making the basics of risk management a way of life for most employees. The way people isolate and respond to risk in their workplace is part of their performance appraisal system and part of the competencies that are looked for in recruitment and staff training. Managers are given a clear role in embedding good risk management arrangements.

COSO ERM discusses the problem of trying to impose risk management on top of an organization:

> Building in enterprise risk management has important implications for cost containment, especially in the highly competitive marketplace many companies face. Adding new procedures separate from existing ones adds costs. By focusing on existing operations and their contribution to effective ERM and integrating risk management into basic operating activities, an enterprise can avoid unnecessary procedures and costs.[26]

Risk Profiles

Our model suggests that the organization needs to see itself as essentially a mechanism for responding to external and internal risks in a way that increases its chances of delivering its goals. In many ways, ERM is like human skin—the largest human organ, which responds to external and internal stimuli in a way that best suits the needs of the individual. When it's hot, the skin sweats to keep cool. When the sun shines, the skin absorbs valuable ultraviolet light, but only to the extent that does not produce harm. Harmful rays cause discomfort, and this encourages the individual to move out of direct sunlight. When the skin gets cut, it forms a protective cover and starts the healing process. It can deal with most risks, but really big ones can be fatal.

Each organization needs to map the way it sees risk and captures risk to allow a considered response to threats and opportunities. This starts with categories and the way risks will be reported throughout the organization.

Up, Side, and Down

One important consideration is about the way risks will be assessed. This goes to the heart of business culture because it is based on the way people relate to each other at work, in the following ways:

- *Down.* Many organizations start the ERM process with an assessment of boardroom risk (i.e., the high-level strategic risk that gets in the way of their overall corporate objectives). The priorities and resultant messages are then sent downward through the organization to create a reference point for everyone to rally around. This is good practice, but if it is not balanced out, it can reinforce a command-led organization where direction is sent down but there is no time to listen to the concerns of the troops on the front lines.

- *Up.* The contrasting approach is to ask teams and managers to get together to identify and assess their risks and then pass the results upward for action or to endorse proposed action. This approach is useful, but it can mean that no central messages on risk holds the ERM process together. It can also result in a lack of direction from the top, where a series of fragmented commentaries come from disparate parts of the business.

- *Side.* An enlightened organization is one in which many people within the business are able to view themselves as a series of internal customers, giving and receiving internal services. The results of various risk assessments may then be passed sideways around the business to reflect the way work processes flow through an organization.

It takes a well-planned combination of upward, downward, and sideways communication that takes on board risk assessments to get ERM to work properly.

Business Systems

We have said that ERM is about getting the risk concept into and inside of the business systems. This is important because planning systems, human resource management, communication networks, performance management arrangements, and the way people input into business projects together form the basis for ongoing decision making. Our model creates a large box for these and other business systems to sweep up the ERM activities before they get reported. In this scenario, risk assessment fits into the business and becomes part of everyday work:

> Although the term "risk assessment" sometimes has been used in conjunction with a one-time activity, in the context of enterprise risk management the risk assessment component is a continuous and iterative interplay of actions that take place throughout the entity.[27]

Conformance

We are coming to the end of this model, and one issue that sits on the radar is conformance (i.e., a process for acknowledging and responding to all those obligations to adhere to a raft of rules, regulations, laws, and procedures that constrain the organization—in the best interests of society). It is good practice to build conformance issues into risk assessments so that people get used to saying, "Let's get a result, but in the right and proper way," rather than simply saying, "Let's get a result—period." An example of this point follows.

CASE STUDY

Adding Value

In one company, the selling feature for risk management was "You have to do it!" To this was added an aside along the lines, "so let's make it real useful." A key focus on risk assessments was whether controls were being adhered to and whether they could be improved on at all. Meanwhile, a subsidiary project was launched that encouraged staff to review and redesign their written procedures. Internal control was seen as a combination of the control framework (including risk management work) and good operational procedures and financial reporting systems.

Performance

Proponents of ERM do it a disservice if they focus on scare tactics on the basis that we "have to do it." This approach is dangerous. If senior people are forced into doing something with no real business case, they will tend to do the bare minimum, and they will tend to have little interest in the topic at hand, beyond ensuring that a box can be checked to say that it has been done. Where ERM is seen as an important way of growing the business and sold as such, there is much more scope for progress. The people at the top will set measures for ERM based on better performance and a better organization, and this is what will be aimed at rather than just a check in a box. ERM tackles the vexing question of uncertainty, which by its nature cannot be entirely resolved, but uncertainty can be better understood and aspects that can be controlled can be addressed, whereas aspects that cannot be controlled can be responded to, in the best way possible:

> Uncertainty presents both risk and opportunity, with the potential to erode or enhance value. Enterprise risk management enables management to effectively deal with uncertainty and associated risk and opportunity, enhancing the capacity to build value.[28]

Global Reports

The final part of the model is the reports that result from a business process that incorporates ERM. These reports help with managing the organization. They help ensure conformance with all relevant matters and performance in line with (or exceeding) stakeholder expectations. Moreover, tailored versions of these reports go out to the public to tell them about the organization and how it is faring. Following the direction set by COSO ERM, it is possible for the organization to report across its business lines, along several key responsibilities covering strategic, operations, reporting, and compliance issues. We can turn once more to COSO ERM's three dimensions for a useful framework that can be used to structure reports:[29]

Entity Objectives:

- Strategic
- Operations
- Reporting
- Compliance

ERM Components:

- Objective setting
- Internal environment
- Event identification
- Risk assessment
- Risk response
- Control activities
- Information and communication
- Monitoring

Entity Units:

- Subsidiary
- Business unit
- Division
- Entity-level

These components derive from an holistic way of managing risk and a formal framework for assessing internal controls. They also derive from an ERM process that fits all of those matters that have appeared on our model. The framework means that management is in charge of its risks and can give assurances on the extent to which any excessive residual risk exists. What is missing from our ERM model is the audit role, which is dealt with elsewhere. The audit role is to tell the organization whether the ERM process it is relying on is in fact reliable. It will also give a view on the level of risk that the organization is exposed to and whether this fits with the stated policies and published reports. In the final analysis, management is responsible for these risks, and auditing can only point them out in formal audit reports:

> Management's responsibility is to make decisions on the appropriate action to be taken regarding significant engagement observations and recommendations. Senior management may decide to assume the risk of not correcting the reported condition because of cost or other considerations. The board should be informed of senior management's decisions on all significant observations and recommendations.[30]

Organizations need to tell their stakeholders about the risks they face and how they are being addressed. This principle is expounded by the Organisation for Economic Co-operation and Development (OECD) in their corporate governance principles:

Users of financial information and market participants need information on reasonably foreseeable material risks that may include: risks that are specific to the industry or the geographical areas in which the company operates; dependence on commodities; financial market risks including interest rate or currency risk; risk related to derivatives and off-balance sheet transactions; and risks related to environmental liabilities.[31]

SUMMARY

Enterprise risk management places risk firmly onto the corporate agenda. The ERM challenge is to draw together all aspects of an organization in an integrated manner. One way to consider an integrated ERM is to go through the following five steps:

1. Assess the various pockets of risk-based activities across the organization and isolate their language, techniques, and approaches to work.
2. Draw the risk activities together through a well-considered risk policy that is driven by the need to bring risk management into all parts of the organization.
3. Build a firm platform for ERM using the key factors covering risk appetite, roles, processes, tools, documentation, and reports.
4. Ensure that risk is captured throughout the business and that it is aligned to the communication systems that move upward, downward, and across all parts of the organization.
5. Incorporate ERM into the business systems so that the global reports published within and outside of the organization address risks to performance as well as compliance issues.

Note that Appendix A contains checklists that can be used to assess the overall quality of the ERM system and also judge the type of audit approach that may be applied to supporting and reviewing the ERM process.

NOTES

1. Institute of Internal Auditors, UK & Ireland, Position Statement 2004, *The Role of Internal Audit in Enterprise-Wide Risk Management*.
2. *Ibid.*

3. Committee of Sponsoring Organizations, *Enterprise Risk Management*, September 2004, Executive Summary.
4. Tim Leech, "Getting to Grips with ERM," *Internal Audit & Business Risk* (August 2002): p. 11.
5. Committee of Sponsoring Organizations, *Enterprise Risk Management*, September 2004, p. 45.
6. Australian/New Zealand Standard: Risk Management Guidelines AS/NZS 4360:2004, p. 11.
7. Committee of Sponsoring Organizations, *Enterprise Risk Management*, September 2004, p. 25.
8. Australian/New Zealand Standard: Risk Management Guidelines AS/NZS 4360: 2004, p. 27.
9. BASEL Committee on Banking Supervision, Bank for International Settlement, February 2003, Principle 4.
10. Australian/New Zealand Standard: Risk Management Guidelines AS/NZS 4360:2004, p. 11.
11. Committee of Sponsoring Organizations, *Enterprise Risk Management*, September 2004, p. 28.
12. Neil Cowan, *Corporate Governance That Works* (Prentice Hall, Pearson Education South Asia Pte Ltd, 2004), p. 41.
13. Institute of Internal Auditors, UK & Ireland, Position Statement 2004, *The Role of Internal Audit in Enterprise-Wide Risk Management*.
14. Australian/New Zealand Standard: Risk Management Guidelines AS/NZS 4360: 2004, Foreword.
15. *Ibid.*, p. 11.
16. Committee of Sponsoring Organizations, *Enterprise Risk Management*, September 2004, Foreword to the Executive Summary.
17. Kellogg Company: Management's Responsibility for Financial Statements, Annual Report 2002/2003, signed January 28, 2004.
18. Committee of Sponsoring Organizations, *Enterprise Risk Management*, September 2004, Executive Summary.
19. *Ibid.*, Foreword to the Executive Summary.
20. *Ibid.*, p. 60.
21. *Ibid.*, p. 17.
22. Australian/New Zealand Standard: Risk Management Guidelines AS/NZS 4360: 2004, p. 96.
23. *Ibid.*, p. 96.
24. *Ibid.*, p. 28.
25. Committee of Sponsoring Organizations, *Enterprise Risk Management*, September 2004, Executive Summary.
26. *Ibid.*, p. 18.
27. *Ibid.*, p. 49.
28. *Ibid.*, Executive Summary.
29. *Ibid.*, Executive Summary.
30. Institute of Internal Auditors, Practice Advisory 2060-1.
31. "Organisation for Economic Co-Operation and Development," *OECD Principles of Corporate Governance*, 2004, p. 53.

4

RISK APPETITE

When the chief audit executive believes that senior management has accepted a level of residual risk that *may be* unacceptable to the organization, the chief audit executive should discuss the matter with senior management.

IIA Standard 2600

INTRODUCTION

The topic of risk appetites goes to the heart of the relationship between the board, management, and the internal auditor. The board sets a so-called risk appetite, which management subscribes to by installing suitable controls to contain risk. Meanwhile, the internal auditor will furnish objective reports on the system of internal control. These audit reports will review the extent to which residual risk, after taking account of controls, is acceptable, and that in turn means whether this risk falls in line with the defined risk appetite. This dependency cycle is extremely important and hinges on respective perceptions of risk appetite. Bearing this in mind, Sawyer has already set the challenge for the internal auditor:

> Every entity is subject to its own inherent risks and the internal auditor should catalogue them for use in risk assessment. The internal auditor's position as part of the organization offers an opportunity to observe inherent risks over an extended time period. The internal auditor should be aware of the differing inherent risks present in different parts of the organization.[1]

The challenge, then, for the audit world is simple: To help get ERM in place and working well:

> The internal audit activity should assist the organization by identifying and evaluating significant exposures to risk and contributing to the improvement of risk management and control systems.[2]

RISK APPETITE MODEL: PHASE ONE

We use this chapter to draw a model that captures some of the key considerations concerning risk appetite. Our first model starts with a matrix for assessing the factors that should be addressed in determining risk appetite in Figure 4.1.

Each aspect of the model is described below.

Figure 4.1 Risk Appetite Model: Phase One

Business Area...................... Risk Owner.......................... Date........				
NARRATIVE		**HIGH**	**MEDIUM 2**	**MEDIUM 1**	**LOW**
Set Objectives and Criticality Level	1	Basic Support	Operationally Significant	Strategically Significant	Strategically Crucial

Business Area

Each part of the business needs to adhere to a defined perspective of risk appetite. The adopted risk map will break down parts of the organization in a way that reflects the types of internal and external risk that have a potential effect on the ability to perform and deliver. Once again, we need to define certain terms in talking about risk and controls in a business area. *Risk* is defined as:

> The possibility of an event occurring that will have an impact on the achievement of objectives. Risk is measured in terms of impact and likelihood.[3]

While a *control* is seen as:

> Any action taken by management, the board, and other parties to manage risk and increase the likelihood that established objectives and goals will be achieved. Management plans, organizes, and directs the performance of sufficient actions to provide reasonable assurance that objectives and goals will be achieved.[4]

Inherent risk after taking account of controls gives residual risk, and these *residual risks* are defined as:

> The risk remaining after management takes action to reduce the impact and likelihood of an adverse event, including control activities in responding to a risk.[5]

The acceptability or otherwise of residual risk depends on the risk appetite in the area in question. *Risk appetite* is defined as:

> The level of risk that is acceptable to the board or management. This may be set in relation to the organization as a whole, for different groups of risks or at an individual risk level.[6]

Risk Owner

Each risk should have a principal risk owner, and this is the person who is most responsible for delivering the objectives affected by the risk in question. When defining risk appetite, we need to consider who is required to make decisions in respect of these risks and then work through the way tolerances are set and observed, as in this example.

CASE STUDY

The Blame Game

One organization experienced real resistance to the risk management process, mainly because it started with refining responsibilities and accountabilities. The root cause was found to be a blame culture, which meant people spent most of their time avoiding responsibility for anything or working out an escape route when a venture they were involved in had some chance of failing.

The risk owner must report upward to senior executives regarding the state of controls that guard against risk and whether the net risk is acceptable or not. These reports, in turn, feed into the boardroom so that board members can take a view of risk across the organization:

> One of the key requirements of the board or its equivalent is to gain assurance that risk management processes are working effectively and that key risks are being managed to an acceptable level.[7]

Low, Medium, High

The next part of the model suggests that each business area will need to work out whether its risk appetite is low, medium, or high—or, in other words, whether inherent risk needs to be contained, monitored, or exploited in conjunction with the associated low, medium, and high designations. The model allows each manager to work through a set of criteria to assess the degree to which defined risks can be tolerated—or, whether there needs to be close intervention to address and keep a tight rein on the business area in question. The low, medium1, medium2, and high levels of risk tolerance create a framework for deciding the extent of controls that should be in place to constitute *adequate control*, which is defined as being:

> Present if management has planned and organized (designed) in a manner that provides reasonable assurance that the organization's risks have been managed effectively and that the organization's goals and objectives will be achieved efficiently and economically.[8]

The concept of adequate control depends in part on the experiences of an organization and its workforce, and this point is made by COSO:

> A company that has been successfully accepting significant risks is likely to have a different outlook on enterprise risk management than one that has faced harsh economic or regulatory consequences as a result of venturing into dangerous territory.[9]

The model can be used to help an organization agree on a position on risk and help communicate this position both within the business area and to internal customers and ultimately to stakeholders. Note that effective communication has been seen as a key consideration in ERM:

Within an organization, good communication is essential in developing a "culture" where the positive and negative dimensions of risk are recognized and valued. Communication about risk helps an organization to establish its attitude towards risk.[10]

Set Objectives and Criticality Level

Now that we have described the framework for assessing risk appetites, we can turn to the first criteria to assess using this framework. This relates to the objectives and criticality levels. The more important the objective, the greater the need to manage risk to these objectives and, therefore, there is a lower tolerance toward such risks. The link between objectives and risk appetites has been described as follows:

Enterprise risk management is a process, effected by an entity's board of directors, management and other personnel, applied in strategy setting and across the enterprise, designed to identify potential events that may affect the entity, and manage risk to be within its risk appetite, to provide reasonable assurance regarding the achievement of entity objectives.[11]

Criticality is a further consideration, and if we have key objectives that address critical parts of the business, we will be concerned about the robustness of controls and whether they work properly, but not all objectives have the same level of criticality:

Although objectives provide the measurable targets toward which the entity moves in conducting its activities, they have differing degrees of importance and priority.[12]

Criticality can be summed up as the extent to which decisions need to be precise and sound. People tend to make decisions about acceptability of risk based on a range of factors, including the following:[13]

- The degree of personal control that can be exercised over the activity
- The potential for an event to result in catastrophic consequences
- The nature of the potential consequences
- The distribution of the risks and benefits amongst those potentially affected

- The degree to which exposure to the risk is voluntary
- The degree of familiarity with or understanding of the activity

Controls seek to mitigate risks to achieving objectives, and even with the best intentions, there can never be a cast-iron guarantee that things will always work out as planned. This idea of reasonableness is firmly built into risk management and sets the raison d'être for setting some form of risk appetite. In this sense, reasonableness is a widely discussed concept, and it sits firmly within the definition of risk management:

> A process to identify, assess, manage, and control potential events or situations, to provide reasonable assurance regarding the achievement of the organization's objectives.[14]

In terms of classifying objectives, the model suggests four descriptions:

- *High-risk tolerance: Basic support.* These objectives are subsidiary supporting ones that simply contribute to the core objectives. An example would be to supply suitable statistical data for annual central returns.
- *Medium2 risk tolerance: Operationally significant.* These objectives are more significant and relate to, say, retaining a few extra backups of information systems.
- *Medium1 risk tolerance: Strategically significant.* These objectives are slightly more important and, using our examples, may consist of reporting monthly account details to customers.
- *Low-risk tolerance: Strategically critical.* Business-critical objectives are much more strategic and could relate to, say, maintaining an online service for new and existing customers.

RISK APPETITE MODEL: PHASE TWO

We have established a framework for assessing risk appetite and argued that the defined tolerance depends on the importance of the relevant objectives. The next item is designed to tighten up the criteria by bringing in the wide variety in types of risk that impact each business area in an organization. Our model continues in Figure 4.2

Each new aspect of the model is described below.

Figure 4.2 Risk Appetite Model: Phase Two

Business Area...................... Risk Owner.......................... Date........				
NARRATIVE	**HIGH**	**MEDIUM 2**	**MEDIUM 1**	**LOW**
Set Objectives and Criticality Level	1 Basic Support	Operationally Significant	Strategically Significant	Strategically Crucial
Assign Risks to Appropriate Categories	2 Other	Operational	Financial & Compliance	Reputational

Assign Risk to Appropriate Category

Just as we have different levels of business objectives, we also have different types of risk that affect these objectives. When deciding on risk appetite, much consideration should be given to classifying the type of risks in question, and COSO ERM is built around set risk categories:

> This categorization of entity objectives allows a focus on separate aspects of enterprise risk management. These distinct but overlapping categories—a particular objective can fall into more than one category—address different entity needs and may be the direct responsibility of different executives. This categorization also allows distinctions between what can be expected from each category of objectives.[15]

When thinking about what level of risk we would be prepared to tolerate, we need to address the nature of these risks. Executives need to avoid inflating results, encouraging a poor ethical climate, developing an autocratic power base, allowing suspicious financial transactions, and infringing on governance codes, in addition to avoiding losses and poor performance. Some organizations set risk categories along lines that reflect business priorities, such as the following:

- Strategic
- Operational
- External threats
- Financial systems
- Human resources
- Business processes
- Information systems
- Partners and associates
- Corporate values
- Market share

They then attempt to set tolerance levels for each of these risk categories. Other organizations simply have unwritten rules about which types of risk are important and which are not, as hinted at by one author:

> Gut rules the measurement. Ask passengers in an airplane during turbulent flying conditions whether each of them has an equal degree of anxiety. Most people know well that flying in an airplane is far safer than driving in an automobile, but some passengers will keep the flight attendants busy while others will snooze happily regardless of the weather. And that's the good thing. If everyone valued every risk in precisely the same way, many risk opportunities would be passed up.[16]

The Sarbanes-Oxley Act has brought with it a whole new raft of risks, which could result in jail terms and large fines for companies that do not work hard enough to ensure they meet the provisions and resulting regulations. Sarbanes-Oxley means management should consider the risks relating to the following:

- Documenting a project to implement the provisions
- Identifying weaknesses in internal control over financial reporting
- Developing sound quarterly disclosure arrangements
- Ensuring that the financial reporting system is sound and reliable

In fact, the auditor may go further and add several fundamental components to the governance and risk management debate to take on board a much wider vision of risk:

The internal audit activity should evaluate risk exposures relating to the organization's governance, operations, and information systems regarding the:[17]

- Reliability and integrity of financial and operational information.
- Effectiveness and efficiency of operations.
- Safeguarding of assets.
- Compliance with laws, regulations, and contracts.

In terms of assigning risks to categories, the model suggests four descriptions:

- *High tolerance: Other.* Risks that do not fit into the remaining categories may be placed into this other category. Less significant risks such as staff taking too many absence days from work can be assigned to this group.
- *Medium2 tolerance: Operational.* Matters that impact the business operation fit here because they affect the day-to-day running of the business. Risks such as a breakdown in processing systems may well fit here because they will interfere with the smooth running of the business.
- *Medium1 tolerance: Financial and compliance.* This category is given higher importance and therefore less tolerance as it relates to important disclosures to stakeholders. The risk of significant breach of procedure would be included here.
- *Low tolerance: Reputational.* Anything that makes the business look bad or gets in the way of making the business look more attractive is of the highest significance and fits into this category (i.e., it cannot be tolerated and all reasonable steps should be taken to mitigate the effects). The risk of a class of major lawsuits that would undermine public confidence in the organization may appear in this grouping.

RISK APPETITE MODEL: PHASE THREE

The next aspect of risk appetite we need to address relates to the idea of threats and opportunities, or what some call downside and upside risks. Our model continues in Figure 4.3.

Each new aspect of the model is described below.

Figure 4.3 Risk Appetite Model: Phase Three

NARRATIVE		HIGH	MEDIUM 2	MEDIUM 1	LOW
Business Area....................... Risk Owner.......................... Date........					
Set Objectives and Criticality Level	1	Basic Support	Operationally Significant	Strategically Significant	Strategically Crucial
Assign Risks to Appropriate Categories	2	Other	Operational	Financial & Compliance	Reputational
Determine Upside/Downside Position	3	Business Opportunity	Operational Threats	Strategic Threats	Strategic Crisis

Determine Upside/Downside Positions

We need to return to our definition of *risk* before we can launch into its two main components:

> The possibility of an event occurring that will have an impact on the achievement of objectives. Risk is measured in terms of impact and likelihood. [18]

So if risks are big and likely to materialize, they become significant in the sense that they drive our control design. In most organizations, risks are things that can trip us up and hold us back. They are things that may attack us and lead to lost resources, but they are also things that make us too scared to reach out and grow, and so lead to fewer prospects. Being too brave, however, is just as bad as being too scared:

> Although the concept of risk is often interpreted in terms of hazards or negative impacts, this Standard is concerned with risk as exposure to the consequences of uncertainty, or potential deviations from what is planned or expected. The process described here applies to the management of both potential gains and potential losses. [19]

A good football team has a good offense and a good defense. The players shut down opposing action and probe openings, to avoid giving points to the opposition and also avoid missing points that are there for the taking. Risk consists of perceived threats that are not shut down and perceived opportunities that are not fully grasped. It is about minimizing failures by attacking known problems that allow this to happen while maximizing competitive advantage, again by attacking anything that stops this from happening. Some organizations use threats to the industry, such as higher oil prices, to drive strategic growth by, say, being more fuel efficient than others. COSO recognize these two dimensions of risk:

> Events can have negative impact, positive impact, or both. Events with a negative impact represent risks, which can prevent value creation or erode existing value. Events with positive impact may offset negative impacts or represent opportunities. Opportunities are the possibility that an event will occur and positively affect the achievement of objectives, supporting value creation or preservation. Management channels opportunities back to its strategy or objective-setting processes, formulating plans to seize the opportunities.[20]

In terms of determining upside/downside positions, the model suggests four descriptions:

- *High tolerance: Business opportunities.* The level of risk that may be tolerated may be fairly high in areas where we would want to encourage creativity and some experimentation, even with much uncertainty, so long as this does not drive the risk into any of the other three groups. For example, several new business projects may be set up to probe an emerging overseas market, and even though there is little information or certainty that these will prove profitable, it may be worth throwing this resource at an immature market to keep one step ahead of the opposition, which is stuck in the safety zone of mature markets.

- *Medium2 tolerance: Operational threats.* These threats should be tackled to ensure continuity and success. If left alone, they could well become strategic threats. It is necessary to deal with threats to the business as a priority, and even if there is a policy of exploring new opportunities, the current business machine must be kept going. We would not want to divert operational people to new overseas projects and risk losing ground in our current local markets.

- *Medium1 tolerance: Strategic threats.* These threats must be addressed with more force because they could lead to a crisis. Before we can turn to new market opportunities, we need to bolt down significant problems that mean we lose control of the direction of the business. A poorly focused board and hesitant CEO will always pose problems if not addressed.

- *Low tolerance: Strategic crisis.* This is where the organization is in danger of coming to a halt. Organizations that are continually in crisis mode find it difficult to grow in any meaningful way because, as suggested by the model, they need to tackle the downside risks before they can get into the upside challenges. Most crisis situations arise from a failure to handle operational and strategic threats that escalate out of control.

RISK APPETITE MODEL: PHASE FOUR

Risk appetite should drive the risk management system because it sets the corporate tone for determining where we concentrate our efforts. Our model continues in Figure 4.4

Each new aspect of the model is described below.

Figure 4.4 Risk Appetite Model: Phase Four

Business Area...................... Risk Owner.......................... Date........					
NARRATIVE		**HIGH**	**MEDIUM 2**	**MEDIUM 1**	**LOW**
Set Objectives and Criticality Level	1	Basic Support	Operationally Significant	Strategically Significant	Strategically Crucial
Assign Risks to Appropriate Categories	2	Other	Operational	Financial & Compliance	Reputational
Determine Upside/Downside Position	3	Business Opportunity	Operational Threats	Strategic Threats	Strategic Crisis
Determine Authorization Levels	4	Team Level	Business Management	Executive Management	Board Level

Determine Authorization Levels

Most organizations are structured along the lines of a defined set of authorization levels. This means that the CEO and board have powers to set policy and a strategic direction that is interpreted and driven throughout the organization by senior executives and then business managers. Authorizations relate to authority levels, and this will be set and devolved across the organization in a way that reflects the way delegations are defined and devolved. The formula will affect both the structure and the culture in place and the way risk is assessed and addressed:

> The concept of inherent risk is one that should be of particular concern to the internal auditor. The nature of the business or activities of the organization and the style of management create an atmosphere that has a great impact on the entity's inherent risks.[21]

High-risk areas need to receive greater attention from senior management than less significant ones. This is a good indicator of risk appetite, in that risk-taking organizations will allow much scope for junior people to make decisions and go with them, whereas those organizations that work with a lower risk tolerance will ensure that most decision making is made by a small head office management team. Organizations that allow their staff members to release their energies may make more mistakes but learn faster to adapt and improve. This is why a high-risk tolerance, as defined by the authorization levels, can actually become less risky by being able to learn fast and flex the workforce in response to changing circumstances:

> We all consider risk implicitly in our decision making and thinking. However, by discussing each step with other interested parties it becomes a conscious and formal discipline. It provides a mechanism to help ensure that the lessons of the past are taken into account.[22]

Organizations that have authorization levels too loosely aligned to fixed responsibility levels may become chaotic, whereas those that are too tight may become slow and cumbersome. However, authorization levels aligned to the need to make quick delegated decisions concerning new staff teaming arrangements should not be the same as those relating to the more serious treatment of major financial transactions. We can assess risk appetite by working out how much of what affects the business area hits the top executive's radar. In terms of authorization levels, the model suggests four descriptions:

- *High tolerance: Team level.* These are basic day-to-day decisions for which authority lies with front-line staff (e.g., changes to shift arrangements to provide cover over a peak period).

- *Medium2 tolerance: Business management.* These decisions rest with the line management and provide for sound and continuing operations (e.g., this may relate to recruitment of new team members over the year).

- *Medium1 tolerance: Executive management.* More significant issues get decided on by the senior executive team because they affect the direction and market share of the entire business (e.g., a downsizing exercise in which two stateside offices are merged into one).

- *Low tolerance: Board level.* Things that hit the hearts and minds of stakeholders will have to be dealt with by the board (e.g., bad press concerning alleged financial shenanigans that hit the corporate image).

RISK APPETITE MODEL: FINAL

There are a few more items to add to the model to make it a rounded business tool to judge the risk appetite in the business area in question (i.e., two more lines that relate to the extent to which management needs to monitor what goes on and intervene when required). Our complete model is in Figure 4.5.

Each new aspect of the final model is described below.

Figure 4.5 The Complete Risk Appetite Model

Business Area...................... Risk Owner......................... Date........				
NARRATIVE	**HIGH**	**MEDIUM 2**	**MEDIUM 1**	**LOW**
Set Objectives and Criticality Level	1	Basic Support	Operationally Significant	Strategically Significant	Strategically Crucial
Assign Risks to Appropriate Categories	2	Other	Operational	Financial & Compliance	Reputational
Determine Upside/Downside Position	3	Business Opportunity	Operational Threats	Strategic Threats	Strategic Crisis
Determine Authorization Levels	4	Team Level	Business Management	Executive Management	Board Level
Determine Control Monitoring Levels	5	Basic Procedures (Supervisor)	Monthly Review (Manager)	Ongoing Monitoring (Manager)	Ongoing Monitoring (Executives)
Set Risk Trigger Levels	6	Managed Risk Taking	Marginal Risk Taking	Marginally Cautious	Risk Averse

Determine Control Monitoring

Levels

Our first criterion is about setting levels at which controls are monitored. Low levels of monitoring mean we have a high tolerance for risk and vice versa for high levels of monitoring. We will ask staff members to document their rough notes for areas where there may be some exposure where something may be challenged or go wrong. This is not required in business areas where there is little scope for external challenge, and so there is a higher tolerance for risks related to this type of activity. Before deciding which areas a staff member needs to check with a colleague before signing an account off, we will need to set a tolerance and judge whether more or less monitoring is needed. This is the essence of risk management, where the extent to which control monitoring is derived from the level of tolerance to the defined risks. Moreover, control is about getting the executives to set a direction that is fleshed out to guide the way work is performed and services delivered:

> Control activities usually involve two elements: a policy establishing what should be done and procedures to effect the policy.[23]

In terms of classifying levels of control monitoring, the model suggests four descriptions:

- *High tolerance: Supervisor's basic procedures.* High-risk tolerance is evidenced by a level of control monitoring that is mainly based at team leader and supervisory levels. For example, the work outputs for the business area may be determined by junior management, and little monitoring is done outside that level.
- *Medium2 tolerance: Manager's ongoing reviews.* There is slightly less tolerance for matters that get reviewed as part of an ongoing management system. Here we argue that there needs to be a constant flow of information to ensure that things are bolted down properly. For example, ongoing reports on the quality statistics from a business line may be built into an information system because there is concern that any potential problems may lead to unmitigated risk and poor products.
- *Medium1 tolerance: Manager's monthly reviews.* We shift into higher levels of monitoring where there are, say, monthly reports

that receive managerial attention. These may be specific to the business area and have to be examined and signed off on periodically. For example, customer complaints may be reported each month for one office because there needs to be a tight rein on the operation.

- *Low tolerance: Executive monitoring.* The lowest level of risk tolerance relates to business areas where top management is involved in control monitoring. For example, executive management may ask for progress reports on compliance with corporate procedure in a vulnerable safety-driven business unit where it is essential that everything is done properly.

Set Risk Trigger Levels

The final criterion is the all-important triggers that are set for the business unit. Areas where there is a high level of tolerance will need little or no triggers to ensure they are in control. Conversely, an organization will want a whole raft of triggers where there is little appetite for problems to break out in a more significant part of the business. Triggers involve the quantification of tolerance where any activity that reaches a set trigger point gets stopped and reported upward or is actioned and then reported upward for attention and action:

> Operating within risk tolerances provides management greater assurance that the entity remains within its risk appetite, which, in turn, provides a higher degree of comfort that the entity will achieve its objectives.[24]

An assessment of appetite can be made from the way these triggers have been set and the way they are dealt with once set. The link between objectives, tolerances, and variation is described by COSO:

> Risk tolerances relate to the entity's objectives. Risk tolerance is the acceptable level of variation relative to achievement of a specific objective, and often is best measured in the same units used to measure the related objectives.[25]

In terms of trigger levels, the model suggests four descriptions:

- *High tolerance: Risk taking.* Where there are no real triggers set for the business area, there is little ongoing intervention, and much can be achieved without constraints. For example, a project team may be set up to go away and report back in six months, with no real reports back during this time period.

- *Medium2 tolerance: Marginally risk taking.* The next level involves some degree of intervention. The project in our example may include a small number of exception reports, which are generated during the six-month period so that management can see how the project is progressing.

- *Medium1 tolerance: Marginally cautious.* We provide less tolerance when a greater range and number of triggers is established. In the project, a series of, say, 10 key indicators may be designed that get reported back to management because there is some need to ensure less scope for failure.

- *Low tolerance: Risk averse.* We arrive at the most risk-averse position where an abundance of triggers is set for most aspects of the business, and any variation jumps out at management for quick action. An important project may have to provide a weekly update on progress, variations from plan, under- or overspending changes from plan, user satisfaction, and many other triggers that make for a watertight review mechanism.

It is less about developing one risk criterion and more about having a range of criteria that together define where one stands in terms of tolerances across the organization. Risk does not follow a standard pattern of behavior, as made clear in the following guidance:

Setting evaluation criteria from historical risk estimates introduces the problems that:[26]

- A risk may need to be treated in one set of circumstances, but not another.

- A risk may have been "accepted" in the past but may not be "acceptable" now using current methods of analysis and taking into account society's current level of tolerance.

- Background risks are different in different situations (e.g., different countries), raising the question of whether evaluation criteria should be tailored to the situation and not globally applied.

As a result of problems like these, political or economical judgements may be used in addition to available risk data.

As mentioned at the start of the chapter, the concept of risk appetite has several implications for the internal auditor:

1. Internal audit will need to work out what level of risk the management team is working with, before it can perform competent audit work:

   Before controls can be evaluated, management should determine the level of risk they want to take in the area to be reviewed. Internal auditors should identify what that level of risk is. This should be identified in terms of reducing the potential impact of the key threats to the achievement of the major objectives for the area under review.[27]

2. Controls that are evaluated by internal audit will have to be done so in conjunction with the level of risk that the control is meant to work toward:

   Once the risk level is determined, the controls currently in place can be assessed to determine how successful they are expected to be in reducing the risk to the desired level.[28]

3. But there is help at hand. The auditors can also work with managers to get them to understand the way risk is managed down to an acceptable level:

   If management has not identified the key risks and the level of risk they want to take, the internal audit may be able to help them through the facilitation of risk identification workshops or other techniques used by the organization.[29]

4. The auditors should accelerate any concerns they have with the perceived level of risk tolerance through the management chain:

   When the chief audit executive believes that senior management has accepted a level of residual risk that may be unacceptable to the organization, the chief audit executive should discuss the matter with senior management. If the decision regarding residual risk is not resolved, the chief audit executive and senior management should report the matter to the board for resolution.[30]

SUMMARY

Risk appetite is something that top management struggles with in terms of how to formalize what in many ways is a vague concept. One way to consider an organization's risk appetite is to go through the following five steps:

1. Develop a model, which seeks to capture the essential features of risk appetite for each business area in the organization in terms of fixed categories of low, medium, and high impact/likelihood risks. Two categories of medium can be used to avoid the practice of placing everything in one medium category.

2. Using this model, define the factors that can be used to benchmark the level of risk that is deemed acceptable to the business.

3. For each of the factors from the model, define what may be viewed as low, medium, or high levels of risk tolerance in terms of what can be tolerated and what needs to be much more tightly controlled.

4. Go through each part of the business and determine where risk tolerances, using the models and set scales, are deemed low, medium, or high.

5. Provide strong corporate messages about levels of risk tolerance to managers in each part of the organization, and ensure that they are able to use this information to drive the way risks are assessed and managed. For example, significant areas where there is the potential for financial misreporting may be seen as having a low risk tolerance and therefore be subject to tight risk triggers at both corporate and local levels.

Note that Appendix A contains checklists that can be used to assess the overall quality of the ERM system and also judge the type of audit approach that may be applied to supporting and reviewing the ERM process.

NOTES

1. Lawrence B. Sawyer, Mortimer A. Dittenhofer, and James H. Scheiner, *Sawyer's Internal Auditing,* 5th ed. (Orlando, FL: Institute of Internal Auditors, 2003), p. 129.
2. Institute of Internal Auditors Standard 2110.
3. Institute of Internal Auditors, Glossary of Terms.
4. *Ibid.*
5. Institute of Internal Auditors, UK & Ireland, Glossary.
6. *Ibid.*
7. Institute of Internal Auditors, UK & Ireland, Position Statement 2004.
8. Institute of Internal Auditors, Glossary of Terms.
9. Committee of Sponsoring Organizations, *Enterprise Risk Management*, September 2004, p. 28.

10. Australian/New Zealand Standard: Risk Management Guidelines AS/NZS 436: 2004, p. 21.
11. Committee of Sponsoring Organizations, *Enterprise Risk Management*, September 2004, Executive Summary.
12. *Ibid.*, p. 39.
13. Australian/New Zealand Standard: Risk Management Guidelines AS/NZS 436: 2004, p. 23.
14. Institute of Internal Auditors, Glossary of Terms.
15. Committee of Sponsoring Organizations, *Enterprise Risk Management*, September 2004, Executive Summary.
16. Peter L. Bernstein, *Against the Gods: The Remarkable Story of Risk* (Hoboken, NJ: John Wiley & Sons, 1996), p. 105.
17. Institute of Internal Auditors, Standard 2110.A2.
18. Institute of Internal Auditors, Glossary of Terms.
19. Australian/New Zealand Standard: Risk Management Guidelines AS/NZS 436: 2004, Foreword.
20. Committee of Sponsoring Organizations, *Enterprise Risk Management*, September 2004, Executive Summary.
21. Lawrence B. Sawyer, Mortimer A. Dittenhofer, and James H. Scheiner, *Sawyer's Internal Auditing,* 5th ed. (Orlando, FL: Institute of Internal Auditors, 2003), p. 128.
22. Australian/New Zealand Standard: Risk Management Guidelines AS/NZS 436: 2004, p. 22.
23. Committee of Sponsoring Organizations, *Enterprise Risk Management*, September 2004, p. 64.
24. *Ibid.*, p. 40.
25. *Ibid.*, p. 20.
26. Australian/New Zealand Standard: Risk Management Guidelines AS/NZS 436: 2004, p. 67.
27. Institute of Internal Auditors, Practice Advisory 2120.A4-1.
28. *Ibid.*
29. *Ibid.*
30. Institute of Internal Auditors Standard 2600.

5

CONTROL RISK
SELF-ASSESSMENT

> Based on the results of the risk assessment, the internal audit activity
> should evaluate the adequacy and effectiveness of controls encompass-
> ing the organization's governance, operations, and information systems.
>
> IIA Standard 2120.A1

INTRODUCTION

Control risk self-assessment (CRSA) is a powerful tool that may be used
to support ERM. It is about getting managers and the work team to self-
assess their risk and controls, typically in workshops or facilitated meetings. ERM is the big picture, while CRSA is one of the tools that can be
used to promote good ERM. Figure 5.1 illustrates this point.

The point is that CRSA is not ERM; it is just part of it. Just because
the auditor feels there is a sound CRSA program in place, this does not
mean there is bound to be a good ERM process as a result. Having said
this, CRSA, with its emphasis on people and how they work, has been
given good press by many important people:

> In the years since it first started, CSA has spread rapidly across the world
> and now appears in a number of guises such as RSA, QSA, etc. It is
> being practiced in industry, government, health, education and interna-
> tional multilateral bodies, and not-for-profit agencies. In all these sectors
> it has been well received by thousands of clients who see it as a breath
> of fresh air. Why? Perhaps it is because we are now asking them about
> issues in their world—the real world—and recognizing their expertise.
> Perhaps, also, because we are beginning to understand that people, not
> procedures are the root cause of organizational success.[1]

Figure 5.1 ERM/CRSA Comparison

ERM	CRSA
Board room initiative	Management tool
Covers all risks	Covers specific risks
Driven by risk policy	Driven by desire for improved operations
Mainly risk concepts for entire enterprise	Mainly workshops on risk and controls
Based on corporate risk reporting system	Based on local risk registers
Runs across the organization	Runs in specific parts of the business
ERM supported by CRSA	CRSA driven by ERM
Review overall system of controls	Review specific controls
Coordinated by the board	Coordinated by risk champion

Auditors have a vested interest in CRSA because if this works well, it means the audit process can attach itself to the initiative and support it as being a shortcut to doing extensive audit testing and analysis:

> Internal audit's investment in some CSA programs is fairly significant. It may sponsor, design, implement, and, in effect, own the process, conducting the training, supplying the facilitators, scribes and reporters, and orchestrating the participation of management and work teams. In other CSA programs, internal audit's involvement is minimal, serving as interested party and consultant of the whole process and as ultimate verifier of the evaluations produced by the teams. In most programs, internal audit's investment in the organization's CSA efforts is somewhere between the two extremes described above.[2]

CONTROL RISK SELF-ASSESSMENT MODEL: PHASE ONE

CRSA does not just happen. It must be carefully planned and launched if it is to have any chance of success. Our first model starts with the launch of the CRSA program in Figure 5.2.

Each new aspect of the model is described below.

Figure 5.2 CSRA Model: Phase One

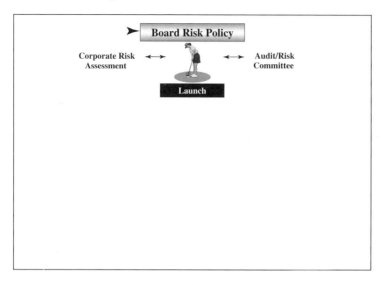

Board Risk Policy

The board should design a corporate risk policy that sets out exactly what CRSA is about and how it will be applied across the organization. A good starting place in defining CRSA is the IIA's professional guidance:

> A methodology encompassing self-assessment surveys and facilitated workshops called CSA is a useful and efficient approach for managers and internal auditors to collaborate in assessing and evaluating control procedures.[3]

Corporate Risk Assessment

Some organizations set up a program of CRSA events and just let people get on with it. This then results in pockets of data and detailed reports that are difficult to pull together in any meaningful way. It is better to develop common themes and then encourage the CRSA program to feed from and back into these themes. In support of this perspective, it is a good idea to develop a high-level corporate risk assessment that seeks to identify the board's top 10 or 12 risks. This will give the necessary direction to the subsequent risk assessments done in various parts of the business. For example, if the board feels that financial impropriety and employee fraud are major concerns, this factor can be built into the CRSA events, and people can be asked to comment on the risk of abuse and irregularity as they develop their operational risk profiles. If, however, the board is concerned about safety issues, then again, this theme can be used to drive the direction of the CRSA program. Where the board chooses to focus on better corporate social responsibility as the way forward, it will want to see this theme driven through the various business units within the organization. In this way, each business unit will be asked to deal with risks to promoting good social responsibility. One final example may be that employee competence and succession planning are major corporate concerns, and this issue can be incorporated into any workshops that are being developed throughout the business. The link between corporate priorities and operational decision making is important and means that people are equipped to take responsibility for their work:

> The outcomes that may be derived from self-assessment methodologies are:[4]
>
> - People in business units become trained and experienced in assessing risks and associating control processes with managing those risks and improving the chances of achieving business objectives.
> - Informal, soft controls are more easily identified and evaluated.
> - People are motivated to take "ownership" of the control processes in their units and corrective actions taken by the work teams are often more effective and timely
> - The entire objectives-risks-controls infrastructure of an organization is subject to greater monitoring and continuous improvement.

Audit/Risk Committee

The next part of the model relates to the role of the audit/risk committee. The importance of the audit committee has been duly recognized:

> The Audit Committee is an ideal vehicle for reviewing the company's risk management process since it is an oversight committee, has no day-to-day operational responsibilities and, in principle, should be made up of non-executive directors. Additionally, must haves for the 21st century Audit Committee are independent directors and at least one member with financial acumen. Indeed, the complexity of much of the current approaches to financial management makes a degree of financial knowledge virtually mandatory for a majority of Audit Committee members.[5]

Audit committee members will need to be made aware of deficiencies in the risk management process that fall within their purview and will need to establish a clear criteria for such reports:

> Parties to whom deficiencies are to be communicated sometimes provide specific directives regarding what should be reported. A board of directors or audit committee, for example, may ask management or internal or external auditors to communicate only those deficiencies meeting a specified threshold or seriousness or importance.[6]

Companies that are quoted on the New York Stock Exchange are now required to ensure that their audit committees discuss policies with respect to risk assessment and risk management.

Launch

The final part of our first model consists of steps to ensure that CRSA is properly launched. A word of warning has been issued on the dangers of a poorly conceived CRSA program:

> CSA is both simple and amazingly complex. It is simple because it involves a group of people with a common purpose and shared experience coming together to identify opportunities for improvement. However, any process involving people is complex and affected by recent and historical events beyond the knowledge of the facilitator. Consequently there are many pitfalls to trap the unwary and inexperienced.[7]

There are many different ways that CRSA may be designed and implemented:

> The wide variety of approaches used for CSA processes in organizations reflects the differences in industry, geography, structure, organizational culture, degree of employee empowerment, dominant management style, and the manner of formulating strategies and policies.[8]

Some larger organizations use small pilot programs in, say, one or two parts of the organization to test the way that the main program may be launched, whereas others go for the big bang approach. The following case study example illustrates how one approach to CRSA was employed.

CASE STUDY

The Risk Management Imperative

A large construction company prepared a detailed risk management hand-book that covered every aspect of getting risk identified, managed, and reported—particularly in relation to project management. The risk manage-ment process was seen as the implementation of set procedures that were employed throughout the company. Meanwhile, staff members attended extensive training programs based around the handbook. Risk management was seen as a must-do process rather than a may-do concept.`

CONTROL RISK SELF-ASSESSMENT MODEL: PHASE TWO

So far we have dealt with those components that should be in place before the CRSA program can be launched. Now we deal with the issues that have to be resolved to get to a clear methodology that can be used to ensure that there is a systematic approach to operational risk management. Our model continues in Figure 5.3.

Each new aspect of the model is described below.

Figure 5.3 CSRA Model: Phase Two

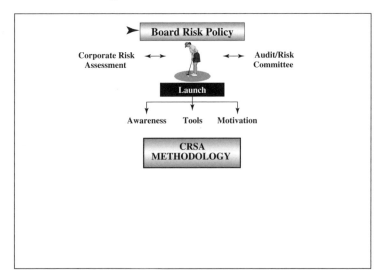

Awareness

Many CRSA initiatives fail because people turn up at risk workshops, spend a few hours discussing their risks and what to do about the bigger ones, and then get back to their day jobs. If asked about the experience, many will say it was useful, but there is little real understanding of the potential for CRSA to make a difference and how it fits into the wider ERM and governance arrangements. In fact, some employees will not really understand the risk cycle and how this can be applied to everyday work. Staff awareness of the importance of the CRSA process is demonstrated in the following example.

CASE STUDY

Using an Online Resource

In a financial services company, the corporate intranet is used as the main risk management resource. Online presentations, audio messages, case studies, and policy statements were considered by employees in a structured manner and then on an as-required basis. An attractive illustration using a non-work-related example was used to convey basic elements of risk management that included context setting, buy-in, risk identification, assessment, and management for a group of friends planning an overseas holiday. The resource was complemented by a telephone help line.

Tools

CRSA is about getting people to understand their risks and to review their controls, and to apply useful tools and techniques to the task. Many CRSA practitioners believe there are three main approaches to CRSA: questionnaires, workshops, and management reviews:

> The three primary forms of CSA programs are facilitated team workshops, surveys, and management-produced analysis. Organizations often combine more than one approach.[9]

Workshops are dealt with later on in this chapter. In terms of the use of questionnaires, the Practice Advisory goes on to say:

> The survey form of CSA utilizes a questionnaire that tends to ask mostly simple Yes-No or Have-Have Not questions that are carefully written to be understood by the target recipients. Surveys are often used if the

desired respondents are too numerous or widely dispersed to participate in a workshop. They are also preferred if the culture in the organization may hinder open, candid discussions in workshop settings or if management desires to minimize the time spent and costs incurred in gathering the information.[10]

Management-produced analysis is described in the following way:

> The form of self-assessment called management-produced analysis covers most other approaches by management groups to produce information about selected business processes, risk management activities, and control procedures.[11]

Another CRSA tool relates to control models that can be used to focus the discussions:

> All self-assessment programs are based on managers and members of the work teams possessing an understanding of risks and controls concepts and using those concepts in communications. For training sessions, to facilitate the orderly flow of workshop discussions and as a check on the completeness of the overall process, organizations often use a control framework such as the COSO and COCO models.[12]

Motivation

Many CRSA programs fail because people do not have a real interest in them or do not believe that risk management tools will help them in their work. The model includes motivation among the workforce, because much hinges on the way people use or fail to use the concept. An example illustrates the importance of generating energy and buy-in from everyone.

CASE STUDY

Importance of a Dynamic Leader

In one risk workshop, the leader was pompous and boring. He insisted on defining the historical roots of the word *risk* and providing detailed explanations of the view that "what we do not know we do not know" poses a real threat. The event dragged on for several hours and was not well received at all. The workshop leader had a deep knowledge of risk and risk management techniques but did not possess any zest or ability to empathize with the delegates. The term *workshop* thereafter held much dread for those employees.

Where this buy-in is achieved, CRSA can make a big difference:

A consultative team approach is useful to help define the context appropriately, to help ensure risks are identified effectively, for bringing different areas of expertise together in analysing risks, for ensuring different views are appropriately considered in evaluating risks and for appropriate change management during risk treatment. Involvement also allows the "ownership" of risk by managers and the engagement of stakeholders. It allows them to appreciate the benefits of particular controls and the need to endorse and support a treatment plan.[13]

CRSA Methodology

Another key issue relates to the need to install a defined approach to CRSA. If workshops are being applied, this must be done to some form of standard in order to be of any real use. Some organizations rely on the expertise and presence of the facilitator to drive the way CRSA is run and applied. When the facilitator leaves or gets bored, the entire program falls over. It is much better to establish a clear way of performing CRSA events and make sure the organization applies this format or to set out some formal principles and ensure that CRSA workshops, although different for each section, fall within the confines of these principles.

CONTROL RISK SELF-ASSESSMENT MODEL: PHASE THREE

We need to enrich our model on CRSA by adding in several more considerations (i.e., the control culture and the way CRSA may be applied across the organization). Our model continues in Figure 5.4.

Each new aspect of the model is described below.

Control Culture

Control cultures or control environments have an important affect on the CRSA process because the state of control culture affects the way CRSA is applied. Good cultures can use CRSA to pinpoint those difficult-to-

Figure 5.4 CSRA Model: Phase Three

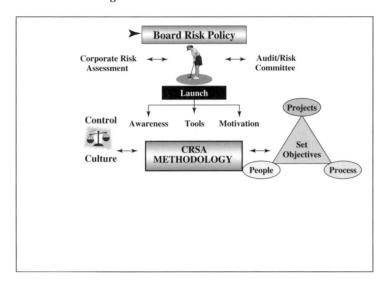

grasp risks that need to be assessed and addressed. In this context, CRSA is simply seen as a set of tools that consolidate the level of expertise people have in managing operational risk. Poor cultures will have a lower starting place and may use CRSA to simply develop a better awareness of risk and the way controls can be applied to improve the chances of success. The control environment is described as:

> The attitude and actions of the board and management regarding the significance of control within the organization. The control environment provides the discipline and structure for the achievement of the primary objectives of the system of internal control. The control environment includes the following elements:[14]

- Integrity and ethical values
- Management's philosophy and operating style
- Organizational structure
- Assignment of authority and responsibility
- Human resource policies and practices
- Competence of personnel

See the case study below:

CASE STUDY

Communicating to Key Stakeholders

One organization failed to get its key managers and associates into risk awareness seminars so that they were able to work at a basic level of competence in risk management and reporting. This meant that many who did not attend became defensive and actually hid things from the auditors because they felt exposed, not understanding that people can only do as much as they are able to in the circumstances and cannot be perfect. As a result, many senior people did not use the expertise of the audit staff to help them perform but put up barriers instead. Audit was seen as the enemy because of this lack of understanding of the entire audit, risk, and control processes.

Set Objectives

We have already alluded to the importance of objectives in risk management, and this is also true for CRSA. COSO explains its definition of risk management in more detail:

> It captures key concepts fundamental to how companies and other organizations manage risk, providing a basis for application across organizations, industries, and sectors. It focuses directly on achievement of objectives established by a particular entity and provides a basis for defining enterprise risk management effectiveness.[15]

Working with teams and groups of employees to get them to understand and manage risk starts with the way they set and perceive their objectives. This focus on what people are trying to achieve means that surveys and workshops as well as management reviews can contribute to what is important to people at work, which contrasts with a perception of risk as an obscure concept that relates to a vague mix of fate and possible external attacks. The objective-driven approach is useful in driving CRSA to its full potential. This fine balance between objectives, risk, and controls has been described in a Practice Advisory:

> Facilitated team workshops gather information from work teams representing different levels in the business unit or function. The format of the workshop may be based on objectives, risks, controls, or processes.[16]

The next part of our model covers the three P's: projects, processes, and people. It is possible to break down the type of CRSA workshop into these three basic categories for ease of use.

Projects

CRSA can be applied to promote the use of risk assessment in the various projects that run across a typical organization. There is a head start in most project management systems in that they tend to have a risk assessment aspect built into the way they are set up and run. The problem is that many such systems see risk assessment as a one-off exercise that is carried out at the start and results in a standing document that records all big risks and risk strategies. CRSA asks that the concept of risk identification and assessment is built into the way team members work and appears at all stages of the work. It also means that risk assessment becomes inclusive rather than a distant desk-based exercise completed by the project manager.

Process

The other way CRSA can be used is to apply it to processes that run across the organization. The way staff members are recruited, the way quality is checked, the way IT systems are made secure, the way new products are developed, and the way statutory disclosure information is provided all result from processes that have objectives, risks, and controls. It is possible to get key players or representative people together to review the way risks to process objectives are currently being managed.

People

The final big category for CRSA work is about people. CRSA is such a flexible tool that it can be applied to soft controls such as the way people communicate or the extent to which staff members trust their managers to give good advice and direction. CRSA can be used to tackle poor team-working practices in a way that defines this problem as a risk to achieving team goals, so that ways forward may be sought and agreed. Some workshops include the line manager, whereas others see it as a chance for the team to engage in open debate without the manager being present all the time. See the following example.

CASE STUDY

Defining Management's Role

One production company decides whether the business unit manager should attend the team's risk workshops by applying a criteria based on net value added from any attendance. The manager's role is clearly defined and may involve attending at the start, at the end, or for the entire workshop. The aim is to encourage full involvement from all participants while not undermining management's line responsibilities.

The focus on the group and what can be achieved when people work well together is important:

> In the typical CSA facilitated workshop, a report will be largely created during the deliberations. A group consensus will be recorded for the various segments of the discussions, and the group will review the proposed final report before the end of the final session. Some programs will use anonymous voting techniques to ensure the free flow of information and viewpoints during the workshops and to aid in negotiating differences between viewpoints and interest groups.[17]

Some teams have all the right skills and are equipped with dynamic techniques but just cannot perform well. Many of them are victims of silent risks:

> Silent risks—so called because they creep up unseen and unannounced—are the most dangerous risks simply because of their nature. They have not been recognized in the process of identifying, assessing and managing risks so that, if they do occur, and there is the luxury of time to attempt to manage them, they may result in unconsidered and inappropriate defensive measures, i.e., "gut reactions." Hopefully the occurrence of a silent risk does not result in a catastrophe and can become a learning opportunity.[18]

CONTROL RISK SELF-ASSESSMENT MODEL: PHASE FOUR

We need to add a few more items onto our model to get it right and put in some more detail, particularly when the workshop approach is being used. Our model continues in Figure 5.5.

Each new aspect of the model is described below.

Figure 5.5 CSRA Model: Phase Four

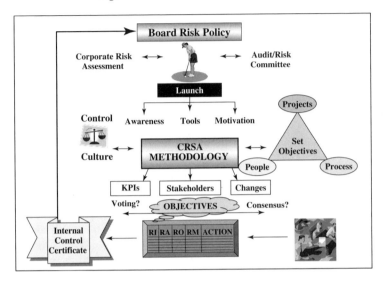

KPIs

Having established the team objectives (or project/process objectives), it is good to set a context before attendees start brainstorming risks. The first of the contextual matters are the key performance indicators (KPIs) that the team is working toward. Discussion, debate, and commentary that does not take into account those matters that the team will be judged on may become vague and unreal if not linked to work drivers. The way targets are set and assessed needs to be discussed by the team to ensure that no risks arise from a poorly conceived set of KPIs. Also, when the action plans start to come together as a result of the workshop, these plans need to be attached to the way teamwork is planned and assessed. People tend to respond to issues that fall onto the KPI radar screen. Anything outside of this may get lost or simply forgotten.

Stakeholders

The next point that needs to be aired in team workshops is the position, expectation, and involvement of internal and external stakeholders. Corporate governance is about planning to meet stakeholder expectation, and risk management is about achieving these plans to deliver the goods.

CRSA must therefore fit into the equation in order for it to make an impact. Teams, projects, and people who run corporate and operational processes must appreciate what stakeholders want, and they must understand the way any tensions may be managed. Some time should be spent on this topic to widen the framework within which risks can be captured and then analyzed:

> Stakeholders are likely to make judgments about risk based on their perceptions. These can vary due to differences in values, needs, assumptions, concepts and concerns as they relate to the risks or the issues under discussion. Since the views of stakeholders can have a significant impact on the decisions made, it is important that their perceptions of risk be identified and recorded and integrated into the decision making process.[19]

The Australian/New Zealand risk standard quoted previously goes on to discuss where stakeholders fit in:

> Involving others, or at least looking at things from another point of view, is an essential and crucial ingredient of an effective approach to risk management. Engagement with stakeholders makes risk management explicit and more soundly based, and adds value to an organization. It is particularly important where stakeholders may:[20]
> - Impact on the effectiveness of the proposed risk treatments
> - Be affected in risk incidents
> - Add value in the assessment of risk
> - Incur additional costs
> - Be constrained by future risk controls

Change

The final topic that makes up the contextual framework is change. The change programs, strategic plans, and proposals to merge, downsize, upsize, or realign parts of the business are all part of the workforce agenda. These issues will be uppermost in the minds of most staff members, who are affected to a greater or lesser extent. If the risk workshop does not acknowledge some of the big changes that have occurred, are now happening, or are simply being proposed, then we may well miss an opportunity to talk about real risks and not just standard items relating to procedure and documentation.

RI, RA, RO, RM, Action

The next item on the model is what some call the *risk cycle*. The CRSA workshop should involve taking people through the standard stages of risk identification (RI), risk assessment (RA), defining the risk owner (RO), and risk management (RM) in a way that can be documented to fall into a risk register. Action is then agreed on that results from this risk management cycle to ensure that any residual risk is properly contained and that key controls are checked for functionality. This risk cycle can be used to form a professional methodology for getting risk management in place and covering all key aspects of dealing with upside and downside risk, and this approach complies with risk standards:

> To develop a comprehensive list of risks a systematic process should be used that starts with the statement of context. To demonstrate that risks have been identified effectively it is useful to step through the process, project or activity in a structured way using the key elements defined while establishing the context. This can help provide confidence that the process of identification is complete and major issues have not been missed.[21]

A good facilitator can get a CRSA group to score risks and suggest ways of handling high-profile risks that have a potential to affect our ability to achieve objectives and are likely to arise if not contained. A standard risk register may contain details such as the following:

- Reference
- Risk description
- Category
- Risk owner
- Adequacy of current mitigation
- Impact of residual risk
- Likelihood
- Recent change in risk profile
- Action plan
- Review date

The Picture

The picture on the right of the model is about effective facilitation, which is important in the CRSA process. Many CRSA programs win or lose by the quality of facilitation that is applied to ensure the program meets its goals. The main criticism of CRSA workshops is that they start out okay but then drag on as people get bogged down in fine detail and personality clashes. The following basic principles for using facilitated workshops should be applied to CRSA events:

- Make sure the workshop has a clear aim based around empowering people to make their controls work properly.

- Encourage attendance by making clear what participants will achieve from the time spent. One approach is to use building blocks to start with basic concepts that are developed into a workable system. People do not mind getting into detail as long as they can see how it fits into the big picture.

- Make sure there is a simple way of capturing all relevant information, agreements, and comments that come from the event. The risk register is a good way of recording information that comes from taking the group through the risk cycle of identification, assessment, and actions to help manage unacceptable levels of residual risk.

- Maintain a challenge element where people are encouraged to move out of their comfort zones. Where we can get rid of redundant controls, then this should be set as a challenging task. When identifying risks, the group can start with the basics and then work toward those that are not so well defined. Tell the group members that they are feeding into formal reports on systems of internal control and that their work may be reviewed by external review agencies.

- Focus on the climate and develop ways of encouraging positive and open communications. Much depends on good listening skills, and people can practice this skill. A small number of domineering participants may try to take over the event, and this tendency needs to be carefully managed. When a facilitator poses a question and looks toward someone, he or she will tend to answer, whereas when this question is posed and the facilitator turns away from a domineering person, others will tend to respond.

- People feel more comfortable when they have a clear picture of the day and what is coming next at each juncture. Well-structured workshops take the group through the risk cycle in a sensible manner. If the cycle is put up at the start, the facilitator can plot the group's progress and make links between each part.

- Make sure the facilitation is set within the confines of the risk policy so that the facilitator can make short presentations on the risk policy and how the CRSA events fit in with the wider ERM concept. A facilitator who has no knowledge of risk management will struggle.

- Make sure it is clear that facilitation is not just about driving people toward a particular goal; it is about equipping people to want to and be able to get to this goal. Some facilitators develop a group agreement that is prepared and adopted by the members.

- Make sure the right people are taken on board and attend the event. Many workshop leaders make contact with the group members before the event with a view toward getting them to understand the risk management process and how to address any concerns people may have.

- Understand and tell people what falls within the scope of the workshop and what is outside its terms of reference. For example, the event will not be about preparing plans to be used to negotiate a pay raise for the team. It can be used to ensure that the team is efficient, and this point can be of use to the team, but workshops are not about taking sides and playing local politics.

- Good workshops are well paced. If they move too quickly, people get left behind, whereas if they move too slowly, they get bored. A good facilitator will be constantly checking the pace and encourage the group to alter it where necessary.

- Some groups move through stages when they get together for a specific task. People start off by feeling their way around the power bases and work out where they fit in. After some tensions are experienced, they get into a positive working mode and then slow down as energy levels decrease and people want to move on to new pastures. The facilitator can gauge these stages and deal with tensions, exploit positives, and develop new challenges when energies are declining.

- Brainstorming is a useful technique, and the group may be broken into smaller groups where there are different objectives to address. People may be encouraged to produce volume rather than quality and agree that they will allow all new thinking, without making judgments.

- For quiet groups, it is possible to quote what was said in a previous workshop and use this as a framework for developing some discussion. The group members may be asked to talk about their experiences on a particular matter when this would help stimulate discussion. The facilitator can draw out quiet groups by having a presence and driving them on. For more dynamic groups, the facilitator can withdraw a little (e.g., by sitting down and avoiding eye contact) and allow the high energy levels to drive the group on.

- When people make suggestions, capture this information, but also ask the group to develop a criterion for assessing whether the suggestion should be taken forward or not. This is an interesting point. Good facilitators concentrate on the process for achieving the workshop aims, but the actual content that is agreed on belongs to the group and not the facilitator. There are no fixed rules for CRSA workshops, and if a complex issue needs to be explained, a specialist may be brought in to make a short presentation to the group. If the group is being too cozy and using corporate sound bites that sound false, the facilitator can stop them and ask for a reality check. So long as the workshop aims are achieved and people's self-esteem is protected, many different techniques can be applied.

- The main aim of CRSA is to empower people to become engaged in the risk and control agenda and equip them to move forward and report on their efforts. If this point is kept at the forefront of everyone's minds, a great deal can be achieved.

Internal Control Certificate

The final part of this stage of the model is the task of reporting upward on the state of controls. This is really important. It is one thing getting people together to chew the fat and talk about what helps them succeed and what gets in the way, but it is essential to do this in conjunction with the formal control disclosure requirements that affect almost all types of organizations:

> Internal control is an integral part of enterprise risk management. This enterprise risk management framework encompasses internal control, forming a more robust conceptualization and tool for management.[22]

Good CRSA usually means good reviews of internal control and hopefully leads to workable control arrangements. As managers use CRSA to help them give their verdict on internal control, so can auditors review the way this development is contributing to better controls:

> Although providing staff support for the CSA program as facilitator and specialist, the internal audit activity often finds that it may reduce the effort spent in gathering information about control procedures and eliminate some testing.[23]

Meanwhile, the audit role can have a fundamental impact on the degree to which management's reports on internal control are perceived:

Internal auditors should compare processes for complying with Section 302 of the Sarbanes-Oxley Act (quarterly financial reporting and disclosures) to procedures developed to comply with Section 404 concerning management's annual assessment and public report on internal controls....In organizations where management conducts its own assessment of controls as the basis for an opinion, internal auditors should evaluate management assessment and supporting documentation.[24]

CONTROL RISK SELF-ASSESSMENT MODEL: FINAL

There are just a few more extras that float above our CRSA model to help paint a final picture of how CRSA might come together in an organization. Our complete model is shown in Figure 5.6.

Each new aspect of the final model is described below.

Figure 5.6 The Complete CSRA Model

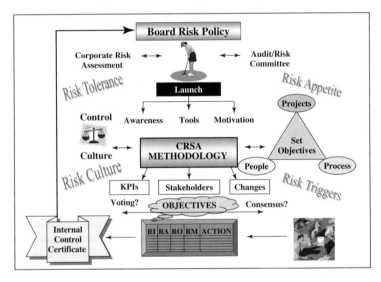

Risk Appetite

We return to the topic of risk appetites. It is not enough to embark on high-level discussions on corporate risk appetite and assume that the workforce will understand this concept. A clear direction should be conveyed to staff so they understand that CRSA is about getting risk exposures to fall within the overall appetite of the board. People should understand that different elements of their job attract different risk appetites. For example, one framework that could be used to help determine tolerance levels includes the following aspects:

- Entrepreneurial aspects—high risk appetite
- Financial reporting—low risk appetite
- Quality issues—low risk appetite
- Change programs—medium risk appetite
- Insurability—areas where there are good insurance arrangements, medium risk appetite

In this way, CRSA can be used to focus on the extent to which residual risk is interfering with the ability of a business to achieve and prosper:

A CSA program augments the traditional role of internal audit activity by assisting management in fulfilling its responsibilities to establish and maintain risk management and control processes and to evaluate the adequacy of that system. Through a CSA program, the internal audit activity and the business units and functions collaborate to produce better information about how well the control processes are working and how significant the residual risks are.[25]

Risk Tolerance

An overall risk appetite needs to be translated into risk tolerance for different parts of the business, which is an important consideration for the internal auditor:

An important contextual issue for the internal auditor is the risk tolerance of the organization as a whole. This is an intrinsic part of the corporate culture and will often be specifically addressed by an organization as a part of its risk management framework. In the event that the organization's top management has determined a risk tolerance level the internal auditor should use this. In the absence of corporate determination, internal auditors should use their own judgment after consultation with management. The risk tolerance level may vary between different parts of an organization.[26]

In setting risk tolerance, managers, team members, and associates need to consider the following:

- Set criticality levels
- Past experience of problems and successes
- The level of certainty that they have in achieving targets
- The adequacy of controls that are in place
- Whether there is a need for more resources to tackle priority areas to reduce criticalities
- The nature and type of risks that are present—whether external, operational, or financial
- The way decisions are made
- The way new projects and new products are established
- Whether decisions made can be readily reversed or not
- Exposure to legal action

Also, see Chapter 4 on risk appetite. Even where assurances have been given on parts of the business where risk is being effectively managed, this does not mean that there is no room for failure, as suggested by COSO:

> In other words, even effective enterprise risk management can experience a failure. Reasonable assurance is not absolute assurance.[27]

Risk Culture

We have already mentioned control culture, which is mainly about the extent to which people behave in terms of ethical standards. Risk culture comes into play in CRSA work because the backdrop may be that staff are risk naïve or risk smart—or a combination of these features. CRSA events for risk-naïve staff involve extensive training and formal workshops to get people to understand the issues involved in working with risk. Risk-smart cultures, however, may mean the use of short one-hour meetings to update risk profiles in light of new developments.

Risk Triggers

The final element for our model is risk triggers. After all the CRSA activity, whether consisting of formal workshops, short surveys, or management checks on controls, there needs to be in place a mechanism that triggers intervention whenever a risk breaks and needs to be addressed. An example may help illustrate this point:

CASE STUDY

CRSA and Business Planning

In one business, risk management was seen as part of business planning and built into the way plans were developed, implemented, and reviewed. Progress was monitored via the performance management system, and again, key risk triggers were defined where information got reported upward outside of the local office.

One major trigger that is relevant to the auditor is the accelerated reporting of audit findings where the level of risk involved warrants further attention at a more senior level:

> The CAE should consider whether it is appropriate to inform the board regarding previously reported, significant observations and recommendations in those instances when senior management and the board assumed the risk of not correcting the reported condition. This may be particularly necessary when there have been organization, board, senior management, or other changes.[28]

SUMMARY

Control risk self-assessment is a dynamic business tool that can be used to promote a sound ERM process and that should be considered for use in all organizations. One way to consider a CRSA process is to go through the following five steps:

1. Develop a clear policy on the use of CRSA that fits firmly inside the wider ERM policy.
2. Launch the CRSA program in a way that focuses on awareness, appropriate tools, and ways that people can be motivated to understand and use the tools.
3. Assess the control culture in place across the organization and ways that CRSA may be used to help develop a risk-smart workforce.
4. Use the concept of corporate risk appetite to help people determine their risk tolerance in projects, processes, and the way people work.
5. Use risk registers to focus the CRSA process around the risk cycle and the need to develop documentation that feeds into better business and internal control certificates.

Note that Appendix A contains checklists that can be used to assess the overall quality of the ERM system and also judge the type of audit approach that may be applied to supporting and reviewing the ERM process.

NOTES

1. Lawrence B. Sawyer, Mortimer A. Dittenhofer, and James H. Scheiner, *Sawyer's Internal Auditing*, 5th ed. (Orlando, FL: Institute of Internal Auditors, 2003), p. 431.
2. Institute of Internal Auditors, Practice Advisory 2120.A1-2.
3. *Ibid.*
4. *Ibid.*, extracts only.
5. Neil Cowan, *Corporate Governance That Works* (Prentice Hall, Pearson Education, South Asia PteLtd, 2004), p. 111.
6. Committee of Sponsoring Organizations, *Enterprise Risk Management*, September 2004, p. 81.
7. Lawrence B. Sawyer, Mortimer A. Dittenhofer, and James H. Scheiner, *Sawyer's Internal Auditing,* 5th ed. (Orlando, FL: Institute of Internal Auditors, 2003), p. 430.
8. Institute of Internal Auditors , Practice Advisory 2120.A1-2.
9. *Ibid.*
10. *Ibid.*
11. *Ibid.*
12. *Ibid.*
13. Australian/New Zealand Standard: Risk Management AS/NZS 4360:2004, p. 11.
14. Institute of Internal Auditors, Glossary of Terms.
15. Committee of Sponsoring Organizations, *Enterprise Risk Management*, September 2004, Executive Summary.
16. Institute of Internal Auditors, Practice Advisory 2120.A1-2.
17. *Ibid.*
18. Neil Cowan, *Corporate Governance That Works* (Prentice Hall, Pearson Education, South Asia PteLtd, 2004), p. 40.
19. Australian/New Zealand Standard: Risk Management AS/NZS 4360:2004, p. 11.
20. *Ibid.*, p. 21.
21. *Ibid.*, p. 39.
22. Committee of Sponsoring Organizations, *Enterprise Risk Management*, September 2004, Executive Summary.
23. Institute of Internal Auditors, Practice Advisory 2120.A1-2.
24. Institute of Internal Auditors, Practice Advisory 2120.A1-3.
25. Institute of Internal Auditors, Practice Advisory 2120.A1-2.
26. Australian/New Zealand Standard: A Guide to the Use of AS/NVS 4360 Risk Management within the Internal Audit Process, p. 4.
27. Committee of Sponsoring Organizations, *Enterprise Risk Management*, September 2004, p. 207.
28. Institute of Internal Auditors, Practice Advisory 2060-1.

6

DEVELOPING AN AUDIT APPROACH

Internal auditors should identify, analyze, evaluate, and record sufficient information to achieve the engagement's objectives.

IIA Standard 2300

INTRODUCTION

We have used various models to describe risk management and the emerging ERM frameworks that are starting to appear across all types of organizations. We have also considered topics such as risk appetite and the risk cycle. We now turn to the all-important matter of auditing the risk management process, or at least determining approaches to this task. The nature of audit work is clearly spelled out in auditing standards:

The internal audit activity should evaluate and contribute to the improvement of risk management, control, and governance processes using a systematic and disciplined approach.[1]

In defining how auditors add value to their organizations, we can turn to experienced practitioners for advice. One author argues that internal auditing adds value to the risk management environment by performing the following functions:[2]

- Reviewing risk management processes and internal control systems across the organization

- Identifying business risks and assessing internal controls designed to mitigate those risks in terms of reliability, integrity, compliance, protection, efficiency, and effectiveness

- Educating the organization with respect to the development and use of cost-efficient risk management processes, and the promotion of best practices through internal auditing's role as a change agent

This focus on risk runs throughout and across all aspects of audit work and is nothing new. Strategic reviews, overall assessments of risk management, and detailed assessment of particular aspects of the ERM framework are all valid audit tasks. Individual audit engagements should also take relevant risk factors on board:

> Internal auditors should conduct a preliminary assessment of the risks relevant to the activity under review. Engagement objectives should reflect the results of this assessment.[3]

Professional audit guidance has outlined what are considered the core internal audit roles, which include the following:[4]

- Giving assurances on the risk management process
- Giving assurances that risks are correctly evaluated
- Evaluating risk management processes
- Evaluating the reporting of key risks
- Reviewing the management of key risks

Consulting, facilitation, and ongoing advice may be superimposed over these basic roles to provide a comprehensive assurance and consulting service to management and the board. Internal auditors may offer an assortment of services, for example:

- Support and advice in helping to establish a sound risk management process
- Ongoing review of the risk management framework to report on the extent to which it is reliable
- Reviews of aspects of the risk management process as a contribution to sustaining and improving its quality and impact
- Recommendations that help resolve shortcomings in the ERM framework or that help fix problems in specific parts of the business where risks are running out of control
- An annual review of progress made in establishing good risk management at strategic and operational levels

The results of this audit work should be reported to the organization on at least an annual basis:

> The report of the CAE on the state of the organization's risk management and control processes in the quest for the organization's objectives, and it should refer to major work performed by internal audit and to other important sources of information that were used to formulate the overall assurance judgment.[5]

A further perspective on the audit role is neatly summed up in professional audit guidance:

> The purposes of evaluating the adequacy of the organization's existing risk management, control, and governance processes is to provide:[6]
>
> 1. reasonable assurance that these processes are functioning as intended and will enable the organization's objectives and goals to be met, and
> 2. recommendations for improving the organization's operations, in terms of both efficient and effective performance. Senior management and the board might also provide general direction as to the scope of work and the activities to be audited.

The final references we will make before developing our model relates to the scope of audit coverage. Auditors support all significant activity that grows the business and helps it deliver its stated mission. However, other important considerations underpin the way organizations work, which are also promoted by the audit function. These other considerations are summed up in the universal scope of audit work:

> Based on the results of the risk assessment, the internal audit activity should evaluate the adequacy and effectiveness of controls encompassing the organization's governance, operations, and information systems. This should include:[7]
>
> - Reliability and integrity of financial and operational information
> - Effectiveness and efficiency of operations
> - Safeguarding of assets
> - Compliance with laws, regulations, and contracts

The transition that auditing has made over the years has been remarkable. Moreover, the way that auditing has developed to reflect the growing interest in risk management has been described in terms of going through four main stages:[8]

1. Control-based auditing
2. Process-based auditing

3. Risk-based auditing

4. Risk management–based auditing

Risk management–based auditing is described in the following manner:

> Risk management–based auditing embodies many of the characteristics of risk-based auditing, with an expanded focus on key business objectives, management's tolerance to risk, key risk measurements or performance indicators, and risk management capabilities. Additionally, while risk-based auditing primarily focuses on mitigating risks to an acceptable level, risk management–based auditing considers optimizing key risks where necessary to achieve business objectives. In fact, risk management–based auditing is a key part of a successful ERM program.[9]

AUDIT APPROACH MODEL: PHASE ONE

We have set out how audit work fits into the risk management framework, and we can now start building the audit approach model, which can be used as a benchmark for developing an appropriate audit approach. Our first phase starts with several high-level considerations in Figure 6.1.

Each new aspect of the model is described below.

Figure 6.1 Audit Approach Model: Phase One

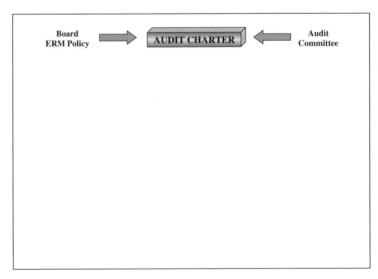

Board ERM Policy

The board has some influence over the way audit work is planned:

> The internal audit activity's plan of engagements should be based on a risk assessment, undertaken at least annually. The input of senior management and the board should be considered in this process.[10]

Listed companies must comply with an abundance of Securities and Exchange Commission (SEC) regulations, including the now-famous Section 404, which requires a formal statement of management's responsibilities for establishing and maintaining adequate internal control over financial reporting for the company and management's assessment of the effectiveness of the company's internal controls over financial reporting as of the end of the company's most recent fiscal year. Although the SEC rules do not cover ERM and business controls, they do address the need to safeguard assets as a primary objective of internal accounting control. Moreover, management needs to identify the control framework used to assess the effectiveness of internal control. Management must disclose "material weaknesses" in internal control over financial reporting and maintain suitable evidential material to support this assessment. Quarterly disclosures are required regarding the evaluation of internal control over financial reporting, but these are not as extensive as the annual disclosure. The quarterly reports mainly focus on disclosing significant changes in internal controls. ERM supports the control review and reporting process by ensuring that control design is driven by systematically formulated risk assessments across all parts of the business. The ERM policy allows the board to explain how this process works and defines respective roles and responsibilities for all key players. Auditors cannot just sit back and make up a role that suits them. Their role is driven by the board ERM policy, along with professional auditing standards and guidance. One document that can be used as a framework for developing respective roles is detailed:[11]

- Executive management is the owner of the control environment and financial information, including the notes accompanying the financial statements and the accompanying disclosures in the financial report.
- The external auditor assures the financial report user that the reported information fairly presents the financial condition and result of operations of the organization in accordance with generally accepted accounting principles.

- The internal auditor performs procedures to provide a level of assurance to senior management and the audit or other committee of the governing board, that controls surrounding the processes supporting the development of financial report are effective.

Although the board has clear responsibilities for establishing good systems of risk management and internal control, the following is also true:

> One of the tasks of a board of directors is to establish and maintain the organization risk management and control processes. Senior management's role is to oversee the establishment, administration, and assessment of that system of risk management and control processes. The purpose of that multifaceted system of control processes is to support people of the organization in the management of risks and the achievement of the established and communicated objectives of the enterprise. More specifically, those control processes are expected to ensure, among other things, that the following conditions exist:[12]
>
> - Financial and operational information is reliable and possesses integrity.
> - Operations are performed efficiently and achieve effective results.
> - Assets are safeguarded.
> - Actions and decisions of the organization are in compliance with laws, regulations, and contracts.

To add to these demands, the Organisation for Economic Co-operation and Development (OECD) has set an important challenge for boards in their principles of corporate governance, in terms of managing risk. They argue that one of the main responsibilities for the board includes:

> Reviewing and guiding corporate strategy, major plans of action, risk policy, annual budgets and business plans; setting performance objectives; monitoring implementation of corporate performance; and overseeing major capital expenditure, acquisitions and divestitures.[13]

Audit Committee

The next factor that feeds into the Audit Charter box on our model is the position of the audit committee. Many audit departments have a tentative reporting line to the CEO or CFO but in reality report to the audit committee, and the audit committee needs to be satisfied that the audit role is properly defined and leads to a successful audit process. The starting place is to work out what the audit committee is responsible for and then build the audit charter from aspects that relate to the internal audit cover. The audit committee refers to:

> The governance body that is charged with oversight of the organization's audit and control functions. Although these fiduciary duties are often delegated to an audit committee of the board of directors, the information in this Practice Advisory is also intended to apply to other oversight groups with equivalent authority and responsibility, such as trustees, legislative bodies, owners of an owner-managed entity, internal control committees, or full boards of directors.[14]

In understanding what internal auditing can do for the audit committee, it is advisable to get an example straight from the horse's mouth, in this case an audit committee chair:

> A key element of our risk assessment and review was the internal audit report we received at each meeting. As we had participated in the formulation of the internal audit plan, these reports gave us a sense of assurance that key control risks were being monitored. But still, there are always the worries: What have we missed? Did we focus on the right issues?[15]

The audit committee will want to know whether:

- ERM is being developed and implemented in the organization.
- The ERM process is working well and provides a sound platform for reporting on internal controls.
- The risk management process is challenging and helps drive the business toward its stated goals.
- Significant new developments, projects, and systems have all been risk-assessed so that there is a reasonable chance they will be successful.
- The business is being managed in conjunction with the corporate risk appetite, and employees are risk-smart in the way they make decisions and plan progress.
- The internal audit process is reliable and has a key influence over the way ERM is developed and reviewed.
- The external audit process fulfills its statutory responsibilities and contributes to good financial controls as well as attesting to the CEO/CFO's statement on internal control.

- Fraud and compliance issues are understood and well managed by the business.
- The financial accounts and applied accounting policies make sense.
- Whether there is any need to commission special investigations that fall in line with the aforementioned matters.

Three areas of activities are key to an effective relationship between the audit committee and the internal audit function:[16]

- Assisting the audit committee to ensure that its charter, activities, and processes are appropriate to fulfill its responsibilities
- Ensuring that the charter, role, and activities of internal audit are clearly understood and responsive to the needs of the audit committee and the board
- Maintaining open and effective communications with the audit committee and the chairperson

Audit Charter

We turn now to the audit charter. That is the document that captures the position of internal auditing within the context of the ERM policy and the needs of the high-level audit committee. Moreover, auditing must fit into what is best for the organization in question, in order for it to have any real impact:

> Internal auditing evolved to satisfy management needs, and the most effective audit staffs keep management and organizational objectives at the forefront of their own planning and activities. Audit goals are aligned with those of management, so that internal auditors position themselves to produce the highest possible value in areas that management regard as the most crucial to organizational success.[17]

In terms of internal auditing's input into areas that are of concern to the audit committee, the CAE may consider certain topics in supporting the organization's governance process and the oversight responsibilities of the governing body and the audit committee to ensure the reliability and integrity of financial reports. In terms of ERM, the audit charter will need to make clear that audit assurance work covers the overall management process (i.e., all business systems, processes, operations, functions, and activities):

The comprehensive scope of work of internal auditing should provide reasonable assurance that the:[18]

- Risk management system is effective.
- System of internal control is adequate, effective, and efficient.
- Governance process is effective by establishing and preserving values, setting goals, monitoring activities and performance, and defining the measures of accountability.

Added to this is the consulting role that is in fact aligned to the aforementioned assurance role:

Internal auditors should be observant of the effectiveness of risk management and control processes during formal consulting engagements. Substantial risk exposures or material control weaknesses should be brought to the attention of management. In some situations the auditor's concerns should also be communicated to executive management, the audit committee, and/or the board of directors. Auditors should use professional judgment (a) to determine the significance of exposures or weaknesses and the actions taken or contemplated to mitigate or correct these exposures or weaknesses and (b) to ascertain the expectations of executive management, the audit committee, and board in having these matters reported.[19]

The audit charter is a brief document, but building on this platform, the auditor should be able to provide a full range of important services, including:

- Advising the audit committee on the way it is discharging its areas of responsibility
- Assisting the board in setting up its published disclosures infrastructure and ensuring that the audit input in these disclosures is well organized
- Encouraging dialogue with key stakeholders so that, wherever possible, their concerns are built into the risk management process
- Helping management establish a reliable risk management process and effective internal controls
- Promoting compliance with legal and regulatory requirements
- Providing assurance and consultancy services that fit in with the other tasks

The audit charter sets out how the role and responsibilities of internal auditing and the mission will be delivered and to what standards. Moreover, the board should be kept informed about the way audit work is defined and delivered:

> The chief audit executive should report periodically to the board and senior management on the internal audit activity's purpose, authority, responsibility, and performance relative to its plan. Reporting should also include significant risk exposures and control issues, corporate governance issues, and other matters needed or requested by the board and senior management.[20]

AUDIT APPROACH MODEL: PHASE TWO

Having put in place a sensible and agreed-upon audit charter, the next issue to address is how the assurance and consulting services will be delivered to help improve the risk management process. Note that the audit role with respect to ERM is discussed in Chapter 2. We start with the consulting aspects of the audit role, and our model continues in Figure 6.2.

Each new aspect of the model is described below.

Figure 6.2 Audit Approach Model: Phase Two

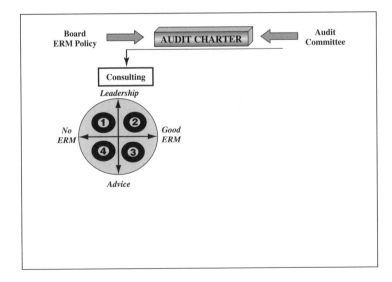

Consulting

The consulting model used in this model has two axes. One relates to a state in which there is no real ERM process in place, and the other extreme is where ERM is well developed. Auditing will provide some degree of consulting services that range from leading the ERM process to simply giving advice. The dynamic nature of the client-agent relationship has been commented on by one author:

> The dynamics of principal-agent theory apply to the relationship between internal auditors and their clients. When examined in the light of auditing's traditional role, the board can be identified as the principal, management as the agent, and the internal auditor as the board's trusted, independent, and neutral monitor.... During consulting work we do not vote on management's proposed actions. Instead, we identify available alternatives, as well as the pros and cons for each alternative. In addition, we do not "partner" with management, but rather listen to management's views, provide advice, and seek solutions that are in the best interests of the organization.[21]

Leadership

In this scenario, auditors may provide a leading role in ERM and act as risk champions in the sense that they provide a source of expertise and guidance that can be shared across the organization. Some audit teams perform a coordinating role where they help set up the infrastructure and ensure that all parts of the business are brought together around the common themes of performance and compliance. This is much more relevant when an organization has not yet been able to start building an ERM framework. See the following example.

CASE STUDY

Working with the Board

One audit committee asked its CAE to undertake extensive research into the use of ERM and to provide advice to the board on how it might develop and apply an ERM framework within the organization.

Advice

The provision of ongoing and ad hoc advice has always been part of the audit role. Here we simply argue that this is now a formal aspect of the consulting services and contrasts with a leadership role. In this case, instead of driving the ERM process, auditors simply provide advice as and when appropriate. This advice may include suggesting pointers as to how the ERM process may be developed, including the appointment of a risk champion or a CRO. There is an overriding requirement to report any significant issues that impact the risk management, control, and governance agenda:

> During consulting engagements, risk management, control, and governance issues may be identified. Whenever these issues are significant to the organization, they should be communicated to senior management and the board.[22]

No ERM

The audit roles of leadership and/or basic advice should be set within the degree to which the organization has been able to make progress with its arrangements for developing ERM. Whatever the format, auditing is about adding value, which is described as follows:

> Value is provided by improving opportunities to achieve organizational objectives, identifying operational improvement, and/or reducing risk exposure through both assurance and consulting services.[23]

Where there is no real ERM in place, the leadership role may well emerge as auditors seek to get this deficiency on the corporate agenda and send out a constant stream of messages to promote better awareness and generate a reaction from top management, on the basis that risk management supports good internal controls. Where there are gaps, these gaps need to be fixed before we can make much progress. Auditing standards accept that this is where the auditors can be asked to roll up their sleeves and work alongside their colleagues to make progress:

> Adequate criteria are needed to evaluate controls. Internal auditors should ascertain the extent to which management has established adequate criteria to determine whether objectives and goals have been accomplished. If adequate, internal auditors should use such criteria in

their evaluation. If inadequate, internal auditors should work with management to develop appropriate evaluation criteria.[24]

If, however, there is a strong and unjustified resistance to making good progress, this point must be conveyed to executive management and the board. In general, audit consulting work cannot be placed over and above core assurance work:

> A primary internal audit value is to provide assurance to senior management and audit committee directors. Consulting engagements cannot be rendered in a manner that masks information that in the chief audit executive's (CAE) judgment should be presented to senior executives and board members. All consulting is to be understood in that context.[25]

Good ERM

Where ERM is firmly in place, however, there may well be a scaled-down version of audit consulting services applied to the risk and control arena, consisting, say, of providing occasional advice on request. Value is seen as what is best depending on what will help the business most:

> The value proposition of the internal audit activity is realized within every organization that employs internal auditors in a manner that suits the culture and resources of that organization. That value proposition is captured in the definition of internal auditing and includes assurance and consulting activities designed to add value to the organization by bringing a systematic, disciplined approach to the areas of governance, risk, and control.[26]

The four dimensions in our model relate to drivers that are available to the CAE when deciding where to position the audit consulting services. Note that point two relates to a situation where internal auditing has assumed a CRO role.

AUDIT APPROACH MODEL: PHASE THREE

We have described where consulting work fits into the model, and now it is the turn of audit assurances services. Our model continues in Figure 6.3.

Each new aspect of the model is described below.

Figure 6.3 Audit Approach Model: Phase Three

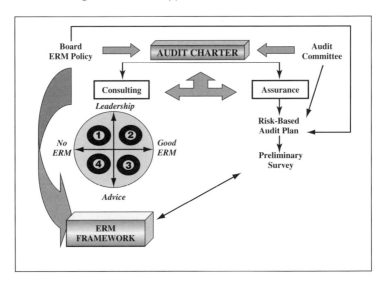

Assurances

ERM is a serious business. It means an organization can explain how it develops its risk appetite and open up a constructive dialogue with its stakeholders. It also means that people throughout the organization understand their risks and set clear tolerances within their controls and the overall risk management strategy that is needed to address significant risks. The board, managers, associates, and employees generally are encouraged to discuss their concerns and proposals in a structured way that makes sense and can be documented and reviewed. It is essential that the board and audit committee have access to objective assurances about what is working well and what needs improving in its ERM arrangements. This means audit's assurance role becomes very important in terms of helping the board direct the pace and direction of the business. Assurance work is driven by the board's ERM policy and derives from the formal audit charter that reinforces internal auditing's mission and future vision. Section 404 of the Sarbanes-Oxley Act requires certificates on internal control from management, and this means managers must do their own testing before they can be sure their internal controls are sound. However, internal auditing can point to aspects of control that need improving or aspects that are reliable. There is also a crossover in audit work in that the internal audit findings can be used by external auditors to enable them to reduce their testing, although the external auditor's findings must be based mainly on their own work. The primary role of internal auditing is located in the need to provide a clear position on where the business stands on the ERM:

> The primary role of the internal audit activity will continue to include the validation of the evaluation process by performing tests and the expression of its professional judgment on the adequacy and effectiveness of the whole risk management and control systems.[27]

In terms of corporate disclosures, the signing officer relies on a good ERM process that fully recognizes the risk of incorrect disclosure. The signing officer has a major burden to bear in that the company has to certify that, for the fiscal year in question, it has been able to:

- Establish and maintain systems of internal control over financial reporting
- Make sure all material information is known to the signing officer
- Put in place a method for evaluating the organization's systems of internal control
- Present the control evaluation in the annual published report
- Discuss disclosure requirements with the audit committee and the external and internal auditors
- Uncover and disclose any significant control weaknesses
- Disclose any significant fraud that impact on the internal controls
- Ensure that employees certify that they are not aware of any significant deficiencies in internal control

The CAE will want to form a view on each of these requirements and be prepared to report this opinion to the board.

Risk-Based Audit Plans

Our model continues with audit plans to provide the assurance and consulting services to the organization. There is an important link shown on the model between the board ERM and the risk-based plans. The next book in the Auditing New Horizons series tackles risk-based auditing in some detail and develops various toolkits to help users get to grips with this topic. The starting place for risk-based plans is what some call the audit universe (i.e., a list of all those aspects of the organization that can be translated into auditable areas and form the basis of individual audit assignments). The audit universe needs to sit alongside the organization:

> The audit universe can include components from the organization's strategic plan. By incorporating components of the organization's strategic plan, the audit universe will consider and reflect the overall business objectives. Strategic plans also likely reflect the organization's attitude toward risk and the degree of difficulty to achieving planned objectives. The audit universe will normally be influenced by the results of the risk management process. The organization's strategic plan should have been created considering the environment in which the organization operates. These same environmental factors would likely impact the audit universe and assessment of relative risk.[28]

Audit plans must be carefully thought through, and the impact of the risk management process can be seen in the way standards are set covering the way auditors should plan their work:

> The CAE should develop a proposed audit plan normally for the coming year that ensures sufficient evidence will be obtained to evaluate the effectiveness of the risk management and control processes. The plan should call for audit engagements or other procedures to gather relevant information about all major operating units and business functions. It should include a review of the major risk management processes operating across the organization and a selection of the key risks identified from those processes. The audit plan should also give special consideration to those operations most affected by recent or expected changes.[29]

What we can say at this juncture is that the ERM activity that results in a corporate risk register can be used to drive the audit plans, so long as the ERM process is in place and is reliable. It is necessary to explore this link further. The audit plan is not simply a reproduction of the corporate risk register, and likewise, the corporate risk register cannot simply be extracted from the audit risk assessment carried out by the internal auditor, as explained in the Australian/New Zealand risk management standard:

> The output from a soundly functioning risk management system, which addresses the full range of business risk, can assist the internal auditor in the internal audit planning process. The risk assessment processes of the internal audit planning process are not, however, sufficient to constitute a proper organizational risk management process.[30]

Risk-based plans are useful in that they reinforce the concept that planning cannot be done in a vacuum. There is little or no point in a CAE sitting in the confines of the audit offices and drawing up a detailed audit plan for the coming year. Objectives drive a business. They determine what goes on at work as each part of the business strives to meet its set objectives. The overarching glue comes from high-level strategic goals. This basic equation also applies to the audit department:

> The chief audit executive should establish risk-based plans to determine the priorities of the internal audit activity, consistent with the organization's goals.[31]

In our model, risk-based plans are heavily influenced by the needs of the audit committee, the board's ERM policy, and the audit charter that has been put in place to underpin assurance and consulting work. It is also driven by the need to come to grips with ERM:

> The internal audit activity should monitor and evaluate the effectiveness of the organization's risk management system.[32]

Another reason why the CAE should not plan the audit work in isolation is to avoid duplication. Audit plans need to be smoothly aligned with other reviews that impact the risk management arrangements:

> In determining the proposed audit plan, the CAE should consider relevant work that will be performed by others. To minimize duplication and inefficiencies, the work planned or recently completed by management in its assessments of the risk management process, controls, and quality improvement processes as well as the work planned by the external auditors should be considered in determining the expected coverage of the audit plan for the coming year.[33]

The front-line assurance work that finds its way into audit plans is complemented by consulting projects that may also get programmed into the work plans:

> The chief audit executive should consider accepting proposed consulting engagements based on the engagement's potential to improve management of risks, add value, and improve the organization's operations. Those engagements that have been accepted should be included in the plan.[34]

Risk-based plans may include a wider vision of the organization than might appear at first sight. For example, the auditor may argue that the risk that management, associates, partners, and employees may be involved in fraud and abuse should be included on any corporate risk register. Many feel that ethics is so important that it should be included in the planned audit coverage:

> The internal audit activity should evaluate the design, implementation, and effectiveness of the organization's ethics-related objectives, programs, and activities.[35]

A major consideration for risk-based plans is to ask what they are meant to deliver. This simple question requires one to work backward from a view of the final audit product:

> If the scope of the proposed audit plan is insufficient to enable the expression of assurance about the organization's risk management and control processes, the CAE should inform senior management and the board of the expected deficiency, its causes, and the probable consequences.[36]

In organizations where ERM is not at all developed, it is difficult to use the corporate risk register to drive the audit plans. Internal auditing will focus on getting ERM up and running, but will also have to develop a planning model that can be used to support the annual audit plan:

> A variety of risk models exist to assist the chief audit executive in prioritizing potential audit subject areas. Most risk models utilize risk factors to establish the priority of engagements such as: financial impact; asset liquidity; management competence; quality of internal controls; degree of change or stability; time of last audit engagement; complexity; employee; and government relations; etc.
>
> In conducting audit engagements, methods and techniques for testing and validating exposures should be reflective of the risk materiality and likelihood of occurrence. [37]

One final point relates to the need to flex plans to keep them aligned with the direction of the organization. As risks change, so should the audit plans alter and adapt to these changes:

> Changes in management direction, objectives, emphasis, and focus should be reflected in updates to the audit universe and related audit plan. It is advisable to assess the audit universe on at least an annual

basis to reflect the most current strategies and direction of the organization. In some situations, audit plans may need to be updated frequently
(e.g., quarterly) in response to changes in the organization's environment of management activities.[38]

Preliminary Survey

The next feature of our model is the preliminary survey. This is an attempt
to perform some background work so that audits from the risk-based
annual plan can be properly structured and planned. The model shows a
clear link between the preliminary survey and the ERM framework. This
means that the audit topic should be assessed against the policies and procedures for managing risk that derive from the way it fits into the overall
ERM process. A good starting place is to assess whether the audit area has
a connection with the overall direction of the organization, as judged
through the way its objectives have been set up:

> Internal auditors should ascertain the extent to which operating and pro-
> gram goals and objectives have been established and conform to those
> of the organization.[39]

Business risk management depends on good objective setting. The
auditor needs to make sure the operational objectives for the area under
review pass this test before we can start to think about the way risks
have been identified and assessed. The preliminary survey will ask several
key questions:

- How are objectives set, and are these objectives aligned to
  corporate objectives?
- What is the level of risk awareness among managers and staff,
  and have staff expressed any concerns about the way risk is being
  dealt with?
- Are there clearly defined roles and responsibilities and assigned
  risk owners for each aspect of the business?
- Is there a good understanding of risk appetite and the acceptability
  levels for residual risks after controls have come into play?
- Is there good communication between staff and open discussion on
  issues that affect the way objectives are being delivered?
- How are risks identified and assessed, and is this flexible enough
  to take on board changes and new developments?

- Is there a reliable process in place to ensure that all new risks can be captured and placed into the risk management process?

- How are material risks addressed in terms of mitigation and contingencies?

- How reliable is the current risk register, and what kind of documentation is applied and retained to support the risk management process?

- Is there a quality assurance process operated by the line manager that comments on whether risks are being addressed systematically and reliably?

- Is there good compliance with key controls, and have contingency arrangements been tested?

- Is there a good use of technology that helps the business analyze risk and capture comments, data, and decisions made on keeping risk to acceptable levels?

- Are near misses recorded and used to update the risk register?

- Has there been any attempt to benchmark the risk management arrangements against the corporate risk policy and what goes on elsewhere in the organization or in other similar functions of other organizations?

- Do controls do what they are supposed to do, and are they properly understood by staff?

- Are controls documented wherever this is reasonable?

- Is there an acceptable method for reporting to senior management substantial risk, control failure, and the way risk management is being performed and updated?

ERM Framework

The final part of this stage of the model covers the ERM framework that is applied by the organization. This is a crucial point. The main change in audit approaches over the years is that they have moved from a focus on compliance with procedures to a focus on the way risks are managed to support a strategic internal control framework. This shift places the ERM framework inside the audit methodology, which affects the way audit work is planned, performed, and reported. The preliminary survey then changes to use the ERM process to prompt several considerations regarding the way audit's assurance and consulting activity can assist the business in several key tasks:

- Working toward a meaningful business *mission*
- Developing a future *vision* of what the business needs to grow toward
- Having a good understanding of all major *threats* to achieving the mission
- Being able to capture all major *opportunities* that drive the business closer to its vision
- Having a clear *strategy* to move the business from its current position to where it needs to be, bearing in mind threats and opportunities
- Being able to *demonstrate* how the business works and how each part fits into the corporate whole that is reported back to stakeholders

This move to make risk management work distinguishes the successful from the unsuccessful organization. Audit has a lot to offer so long as respective roles are properly understood and applied:

> Managers, not internal auditors, make operating decisions. But internal auditors can supply or validate the data on which those decisions are made. Also, they can evaluate the effect of decisions made and point out risks that were not anticipated.[40]

The ERM framework informs the preliminary survey that the auditor undertakes before developing firm audit engagement plans, but, at the same time, the audit work will help determine whether ERM is really reaching the front line. There are three main considerations regarding assurances that the auditor should have in mind when putting an audit assignment plan together:[41]

- Risk management processes, both their design and how well they are working
- Management of those risks classified as key, including the effectiveness of the controls and other responses to them
- Reliable and appropriate assessment of risks and reporting of risk and control status

AUDIT APPROACH MODEL:
PHASE FOUR

We add two important components to our model to make the preliminary survey stage much more dynamic. Our model continues in Figure 6.4. Each new aspect of the model is described below.

Figure 6.4 Audit Approach Model: Phase Four

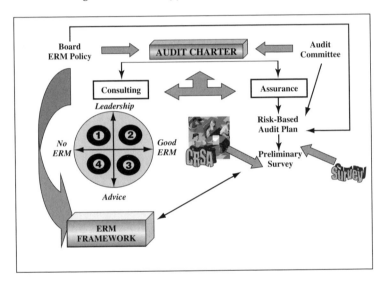

CRSA

CRSA has been mentioned earlier in the book as a management tool for getting employees to review their risks and controls. Internal auditors may also use CRSA to progress the audit process in two ways. The first is to rely on any CRSA events that have recently been employed by the staff from the area that is being reviewed. This information will represent management's attempt to isolate key risks and check that the current controls are satisfactory. If this process is sound and well documented, the auditors may well be able to use the outputs to drive the terms of reference for the pending audit.

CASE STUDY

Risk-Based Plans

The work team in an area that was scheduled to be audited had performed a recent CRSA, which suggested that safety risks were paramount and that a key control was special checks by a team member who had been sent to a training course and appointed as safety advisor. In recognition of this fact, the terms of reference for the audit included checking that the assessment of safety risk was carried out to high standards and that the new safety role had in fact adequately mitigated this risk.

The other way in which CRSA may be used in the preliminary survey is to introduce the following procedure when starting a new audit:

- Use the outline terms of reference as a basis for opening discussions with the line manager for the audit in question.
- Ask the line manager about any other concerns that may be incorporated into the draft terms.
- Get key people from the area under review together in a facilitated workshop to work through the standard stages of their objectives, risk identification, and risk assessment—in the light of their set objectives.
- Use the outputs from this audit-driven CRSA workshop to develop and finalize the terms of reference for the audit.

In this way the planned audit may be entirely focused on the real risks in the area in question. These two approaches move audit from backroom checkers who turn up with preconceived ideas of what is important to a forward-looking function that immerses the audit process in the real issues, concerns, and perceptions of the business area in question. But remember, auditing cannot simply take what management says is important and plan around this. There is also a need to consider a wider range of risks:

The internal auditor should consider the probability of significant errors, irregularities, noncompliance, and other exposures when developing the engagement objectives.[42]

Surveys

The second model entry relates to surveys or questionnaires that can be sent out to people in the area under review before the audit is started. The idea is to gather relevant information about the state of control and the level of control awareness and to use these findings to help focus the planned audit. One big issue that is starting to appear on the governance radar is the type of control culture that is in place across the organization. Surveys, followed up with a few interviews, can be used to judge the state of control awareness, and trends can be plotted over a period to judge whether the position is improving or not. The audit work can then be concentrated in areas where there are poor control cultures. Poor cultures contain people who have little understanding of risk and no appreciation of the importance of good controls and ensuring that these controls are adhered to. Good cultures are the opposite, and the auditor may need to do much less detailed work where managers and staff have a good handle on the way their risks are identified and managed. Good staff also know about governance, accountability, and public disclosures. The impact of corporate culture is recognized in auditing standards:

> Management plans, organizes, and directs the performance of sufficient actions to provide reasonable assurance that objectives and goals will be achieved. Management periodically reviews its objectives and goals and modifies its processes to accommodate changes in internal and external conditions. Management also establishes and maintains an organizational culture, including an ethical climate that understands risk exposures and implements effective risk strategies for managing them.[43]

Some argue that well-controlled parts of an organization may be audited on an exception basis, when it is clear that problems need resolving rather than be subject to regular periodic audits:

> As enterprise-wide systems proliferate and entities move toward a continuous audit approach consistent with their evaluation of risk, the auditor's traditional field work will change, especially for high risk areas. The field work will not be in a discrete time period but will be a continuous one in which reports will be issued as exception reports for ongoing auditors and summary reports at the end of specific periods. In addition, field work may be performed at central audit locations rather than at specific regional or plant sites.[44]

CRSA workshops and control awareness surveys are all techniques that are well known to auditors and that can be applied to audit work.

These techniques can also be used by management as they struggle with the need to get their systems right. This blurring of roles regarding who should use what technique does not present a problem, as is made clear in professional guidance:

> Senior management is charged with overseeing the establishment, administration, and evaluation of the processes of risk management and control. Operating managers' responsibilities include assessment of the risks and controls in their units. Internal and external auditors provide varying degrees of assurance about the state of effectiveness of the risk management and control processes of the organization. Both managers and auditors have an interest in using techniques and tools that sharpen the focus and expand the efforts to assess risk management and control processes that are in place and to identify ways to improve their effectiveness.[45]

AUDIT APPROACH MODEL: FINAL

A few more matters have to be placed onto our model to ensure that it covers the audit approach for reviewing the risk management process. These final items drill down a little further into the audit process without going into too much detail. Our complete model is in Figure 6.5.

Each new aspect of the model is described below.

Figure 6.5 The Complete Audit Approach Model

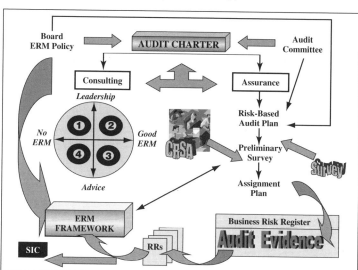

Assignment Plan

Having worked out exactly what the state of play is with risk management in the area under review, it is possible to write a firm audit engagement plan. The plan sets out exactly what will be done and who will do what:

> Internal auditors should develop and record a plan for each engagement, including the scope, objectives, timing and resource allocations.[46]

There is much to consider when setting the audit engagement plan and, as discussed earlier, much of this material may be gathered working with and alongside the client:[47]

- The objectives of the activity being reviewed and the means by which the activity controls its performance
- The significant risks to the activity; its objectives, resources, and operations; and the means by which the potential impact of risk is kept to an acceptable level
- The adequacy and effectiveness of the activity's risk management and control systems compared to a relevant control framework or model
- The opportunities for making significant improvements to the activity's risk management and control systems

The engagement planning process also involves assigning the right resources to the assurance work or consulting project. We have argued that the ERM context sets new challenges for the auditor, and a checklist approach may not capture the dynamic nature of reviewing changing risk profiles and how these risks are being managed. The new context calls for a new set of skills from the auditor. There is little point in setting up an audit-facilitated CRSA event to feed into engagement objectives setting if the audit team is not equipped to lead such complex facilitations:

> Internal auditors should determine appropriate resources to achieve engagement objectives. Staffing should be based on an evaluation of the nature and complexity of each engagement, time constraints, and available resources.[48]

The assignment plan should address several considerations for the area under review:

- Final audit objectives, scope, and methodology for the work
- Corporate perspective of risk aspects of the operation and risk appetites

- Risks that have been identified as high impact and/or high likelihood
- Associates and partners whose risk profiles affect the business area
- The type of work in question, be it assurance or consulting based
- Legal and disclosure requirements for the area in question
- List of key people, contacts, and locations
- Internal control procedures currently in place
- Financial aspects, budgets, and spending plans
- Clearance on ways that the audit will be performed, including interviews, data interrogation, document analysis, and interim reporting arrangements
- Assignment of audit staff to the audit
- Outline program of work for each auditor
- Any issues to be followed up from the previous audit
- Work of other review teams and consultants
- How the work will be supervised and reviewed
- Any issues regarding sensitive data, copying, storage, and security considerations
- Background to any reported staff abuse or allegations
- Any restrictions on audit coverage as a result of time, resources, timing, or practicalities
- State of the control environment among managers and staff in the work area
- Any concerns brought up during briefings with the audit team
- Time budgets for each audit team member and time charging arrangements
- Initial assessment of problem areas in the business systems
- Any requests for additional work
- Changes in management and information systems in the business area

A lot of these items will be incorporated into work programs developed for the audit:

Internal auditors should develop work programs that achieve the engagement objectives. These work programs should be recorded.[49]

Business Risk Register

One crucial aspect of auditing the risk management process is the role of the risk register. This document becomes a focal point for the entire audit process. First, we need to put the risk register into perspective, as evident in our model. The risk register captures the risk cycle of identification, assessment, and management—that should be compiled by any good business manager. This could be through reviews by the manager and management team, or risk workshops by teams reporting up to the manager, or through an assessment of intelligence and trend analysis. Whatever the format, each organization that has a mature approach to risk management will want to ensure that business managers assess their risks and record the results in their risk register. In impoverished organizations, this will not happen and risks will be managed in a hit-or-miss fashion and certainly will not be recorded in a systematic manner. In this case, the auditor will want to assess internal controls by performing the following basic tasks:

- Identify the business objectives for the area in question
- Work out who is responsible for each objective (these people become the risk owners)
- Identify risks to the achievement of these objectives in terms of threats or missed opportunities
- Assess these risks for their potential impact on the objectives and the likelihood that they will arise if no controls are in place
- Judge the effectiveness of the existing controls in terms of mitigating risk to the accepted tolerances
- Find out whether key controls (that guard against material risks) actually work in practice and whether there is any evidence to this effect
- Probe areas where controls are poor or what would be sound control is diminished through noncompliance, and gather evidence of actual problems
- Form an overall opinion of areas where controls are weak (i.e., unmitigated risk is excessive), and determine why this is the case
- Formulate appropriate recommendations to address weak controls, and strengthen the overall risk management arrangements in place
- Communicate the findings and recommendations to those who are most able to effect the necessary changes

- Document the previous tasks and follow up the work after a defined time period

This final task involves compiling what will in fact look a lot like a risk register:

> Internal auditors should record relevant information to support the conclusions and engagement results.[50]

As such, the risk register can be compiled by a good manager, formulated by an auditor, or alternatively developed through the combined efforts of the auditor and the manager (and perhaps staff as well). The risk register in the model relates to the aggregation of risk registers across the organization in a way that recognizes links and associations between different parts of the business. For example, operational areas that have risks relating to the competence of workers may have their risks cross-linked to the Human Resources team to demonstrate the sharing of resultant action plans to deal with this issue. Moreover, a low-level risk register may well feed into higher-level strategic ones where a risk is accelerated upward because it covers more than one part of the business and actually belongs to the executive team.

Audit Evidence

The final component of our audit approach model is about evidence that must meet certain standards in order to be of any use:

> Information should be sufficient, competent, relevant, and useful to provide a sound basis for engagement observations and recommendations. Sufficient information is factual, adequate, and convincing so that a prudent, informed person would reach the same conclusions as the auditor. Competent information is reliable and the best attainable through the use of appropriate engagement techniques. Relevant information supports engagement observations and recommendations and is consistent with the objectives for the engagement. Useful information helps the organization meet its goals.[51]

Evidence sits within the risk register in the sense that it determines whether the information recorded about risks in each part of the organization can be verified or at least supported by good evidence. One risk management standard asks that the risk process be reviewed and several general questions addressed and answered as a result of this review:[52]

- What is the reliability of the information?
- How confident are we that the list of risks is comprehensive?
- Is there a need for additional research into specific risks?
- Are the objectives and scope covered adequately?
- Have the right people been involved in the risk identification process?

In addition, the auditor will wish to make three key considerations in reaching an evaluation of the overall effectiveness of the organization's risk management and control processes:[53]

- Were significant discrepancies or weaknesses discovered from the audit work performed and other assessment information gathered?
- If so, were corrections or improvements made after the discoveries?
- Do the discoveries and their consequences lead to the conclusion that a pervasive condition exists, resulting in an unacceptable level of business risk?

Herein lies the problem. Auditors may gather lots of evidence on the state of risk management and internal control in their travels throughout the organization, but can they as a result form an opinion on the overall state of risk management? This question parallels the ERM equation that suggests that organizations with pockets of good risk management practice spread across its business areas cannot necessarily gather these positives into an overall ERM framework. What is needed is a defined framework and then risk activities conducted in reference to this framework. Much the same goes for the auditor, who needs to obtain evidence on the general state of ERM. This complex task has been described as a challenge:

> The challenge for internal audit is to evaluate the effectiveness of the organization system of risk management and controls based on the aggregation of many individual assessments. Those assessments are largely gained from internal audit engagements, management's self-assessments, and external auditor's work. As the engagements progress, internal auditors should communicate, on a timely basis, the findings to the appropriate levels of management so that prompt action can be taken to correct or mitigate the consequences of discovered control discrepancies or weaknesses.[54]

It is perhaps a better idea to incorporate a review of the overall ERM framework within audit plans so that evidence from audits of individual parts of the business can be contrasted with a general evaluation of ERM. This book adopts this approach as the models in each chapter act as a way of evaluating key components of risk management in conjunction with various checklists in Appendix A. Together with the normal individual audits, auditing may obtain evidence on two levels. First, from one-off audits of high-priority areas that have been identified through risk-based annual audit plans. The other evidence will come from benchmarking the organization against ERM models such as those from this book. The auditor will look for evidence from one-off audits that support or add to the viewpoint secured from reviewing the overall ERM components, such as staff awareness levels, risk tolerance setting, or the widespread use of CRSA. Auditors are required to communicate the results of audit work:

> Communications should include the engagement's objectives and scope as well as applicable conclusions, recommendations, and action plans.[55]

And this communication should meet defined standards:

> Communications should be accurate, objective, clear, concise, constructive, complete, and timely.[56]

When we turn to the big picture in terms of delivering messages across the entire organization in the annual audit report, things can become complicated. The challenge is to take the evidence and develop meaningful reports for the board and audit committee:

> Senior management and the board normally expect that the chief audit executive (CAE) will perform sufficient audit work and gather other available information during the year so as to form a judgment about the adequacy and effectiveness of the risk management and control processes. The CAE should communicate that overall judgment about the organization's risk management process and system of controls to senior management and the audit committee. A growing number of organizations have included management's report on the risk management process and system of internal controls in their annual or periodic reports to external stakeholders. [57]

We return to the point that one way such reports can be furnished is through the use of models that are applied to assessing the state of play and isolating relevant gaps in the overall risk management and internal control arrangements.

SIC

The SIC at the bottom left of the model is about the Statement on Internal Control that is made by managers and executives as a way of certifying these controls and detailing any significant weaknesses. This comes out of the ERM process, and the auditor will want to express a view on whether these statements are worth the paper they are written on. The auditor will furnish reports that comment on what they expected to find, in terms of the way risks are being managed in these parts of the business in question, and what they actually found as a result of the audit:

> Engagement observations and recommendations emerge by a process of comparing what should be with what is. Whether or not there is difference, the internal auditor has a foundation on which to build the report. When conditions meet the criteria, acknowledgment in the engagement communications of satisfactory performance may be appropriate. Observations and recommendations should be based on the following attributes:[58]
>
> - *Criteria.* The standards, measures, or expectations used in making an evaluation and/or verification (what should exist)
> - *Condition.* The factual evidence that the internal auditor found in the course of the examination (what does exist)
> - *Cause.* The reason for the difference between the expected and actual conditions (why the difference exists)
> - *Effect.* The risk or exposure the organization and/or others encounter because the condition is not consistent with the criteria (the impact of the difference)

The various risk management models used in this book may help the auditor establish the "what should be" so that this may be compared to the "what is."

SUMMARY

The overall audit approach to reviewing the risk management process operates on several different levels. One way to consider auditing the risk management process is to go through the following five steps:

1. Use the audit charter to develop an approach to reviewing risk management that takes into account the board's ERM policy and the views of the audit committee. Within this charter, set out the level

of consulting work that will complement the most important core audit assurance services.

2. Use any work performed by the organization on ERM to support the risk-based audit plans after having judged whether this work is reliable.

3. Develop preliminary surveys in audit areas that have been prioritized through risk-based audit plans. CRSA workshops, interviews, and staff surveys may be used to clarify the terms of reference for the planned audits so that the resultant audit work may focus on real risks to achieving the set business objectives.

4. Review the risk registers in use in the areas under review and determine whether they can be relied on to support the business manager's reviews of internal control. Auditing should look for evidence that supports (or otherwise) the way risks are currently being managed in the areas under review. Where there are no registers in use, consulting work may be developed to assist the business to make the necessary progress, and meanwhile, the audit work may entail a complete assessment of risks and controls in the area in question.

5. Ensure that the audit work allows the chief auditor to report on the state of ERM and internal controls in the area that has been reviewed and also comments on the way that business management are certifying their controls as part of the wider controls disclosure infrastructure.

Note that Appendix A contains checklists that can be used to assess the overall quality of the enterprise risk management system and also judge the type of audit approach that may be applied to supporting and reviewing the ERM process.

NOTES

1. Institute of Internal Auditors, Standard 2100.
2. Hans Beumer, "Starting from Scratch," *The Internal Auditor* (August 2004), pp. 79–85.
3. Institute of Internal Auditors, Standard 2210.A1.
4. Institute of Internal Auditors, UK & Ireland, Position Statement 2004, *The Role of Internal Audit in Enterprise-Wide Risk Management*.
5. Institute of Internal Auditors, Practice Advisory 2120.A1-1.
6. Institute of Internal Auditors, Practice Advisory 2100-1.
7. Institute of Internal Auditors, IIA Standard 2120.A1.

8. Paul J Sobel, "Integrating Risk Management and ERM," *Auditors Risk Management Guide* (Chicago: CCH Incorporated, 2004), p. 3.01.

9. *Ibid.*, p. 3.06.

10. Institute of Internal Auditors, Standard 2010.A1.

11. Institute of Internal Auditors, Practice Advisory 2120.A1-4.

12. Institute of Internal Auditors, Practice Advisory 2120.A1-1.

13. "Organization for Economic Co-operation and Development," *OECD Principles of Corporate Governance*, 2004, p. 60.

14. Institute of Internal Auditors, Practice Advisory 2060-2.

15. Wes Scott, Audit Committee Chair, "The Good Side of Sarbanes-Oxley," *The Internal Auditor* (June 2004), pp. 36–39.

16. Institute of Internal Auditors, Practice Advisory 2060-2.

17. Lawrence B. Sawyer, Mortimer A. Dittenhofer, and James H. Scheiner, *Sawyer's Internal Auditing* 5th ed. (Orlando, FL: Institute of Internal Auditors, 2003), p. 34.

18. Institute of Internal Auditors, Practice Advisory 2100-1.

19. Institute of Internal Auditors, Practice Advisory 1000.C1-2.

20. Institute of Internal Auditors, Standard 2060.

21. Sam M McCall, City Auditor for the City of Tallahassee, "The Auditor as Consultant," *The Internal Auditor* (December 2002), pp. 35–39.

22. Institute of Internal Auditors, Standard 2440.C2.

23. Institute of Internal Auditors, Glossary of Terms.

24. Institute of Internal Auditors, Standard 2120.A4.

25. Institute of Internal Auditors, Practice Advisory 1000.C1-1.

26. *Ibid.*

27. Institute of Internal Auditors, Practice Advisory 2120.A1-2.

28. Institute of Internal Auditors, Practice Advisory 2010-2.

29. Institute of Internal Auditors, Practice Advisory 2120.A1-1.

30. Australian/New Zealand Standard: A Guide to the Use of AS/NVS 4360 Risk Management within the Internal Audit Process, p. 4.

31. Institute of Internal Auditors, IIA Standard 2010.

32. Institute of Internal Auditors, Standard 2110.A1.

33. Institute of Internal Auditors, Practice Advisory 2120.A1-1.

34. Institute of Internal Auditors, Standard 2010.C1.

35. Institute of Internal Auditors, Standard 2130.A1.

36. Institute of Internal Auditors, Practice Advisory 2120.A1-1.

37. Institute of Internal Auditors, Practice Advisory 2010-2.

38. *Ibid.*

39. Institute of Internal Auditors, Standard 2120.A2.

40. Lawrence B. Sawyer, Mortimer A. Dittenhofer, and James H. Scheiner, *Sawyer's Internal Auditing* 5th ed. (Orlando, FL: Institute of Internal Auditors, 2003), p. 36.

41. Institute of Internal Auditors, UK & Ireland, Position Statement 2004, *The Role of Internal Audit in Enterprise-Wide Risk Management*.

42. Institute of Internal Auditors, IIA Standard 2210.A2.

43. Institute of Internal Auditors, Practice Advisory 2100-1.

44. Lawrence B. Sawyer, Mortimer A. Dittenhofer, and James H. Scheiner, *Sawyer's Internal Auditing* 5th ed. (Orlando, FL: Institute of Internal Auditors, 2003), p. 331.

45. Institute of Internal Auditors, Practice Advisory 2120.A1-2.

46. Institute of Internal Auditors, IIA Standard 2200.
47. Institute of Internal Auditors, IIA Standard 2201.
48. Institute of Internal Auditors, Standard 2230.
49. Institute of Internal Auditors, Standard 2240.
50. Institute of Internal Auditors, Standard 2330.
51. Institute of Internal Auditors, Practice Advisory 2310-1.
52. Australian/New Zealand Standard: Risk Management Guidelines AS/NZS 436:2004, p. 39.
53. Institute of Internal Auditors, Practice Advisory 2120.A1-1.
54. *Ibid.*
55. Institute of Internal Auditors, Standard 2410.
56. Institute of Internal Auditors, Standard 2420.
57. Institute of Internal Auditors, Practice Advisory 2120.A1-1.
58. Institute of Internal Auditors, Practice Advisory 2410-1.

7

THE ILLUSION OF PERFECTION

Engagements should be performed with proficiency and due professional care.

IIA Standard 1200

INTRODUCTION

So far our models have been prepared with a view to establishing best practice in managing business risk. As each component of the models has been developed, we have been able to apply a benchmark to what organizations should be doing. This chapter is different in that the model used here is designed to demonstrate what should not be done, as opposed to what is good practice. There is a growing army of commentators who feel the emphasis on risk management and ERM is misplaced (i.e., it is creating a society where risks are seen in every dark corner and people start to become nervous about going to the stores). Some organizations start to play the risk game, in which they pretend their risk management arrangements create a perfect entity, where everything can be locked down and controlled. Meanwhile, other organizations simply ignore this risk industry and carry on as usual in the hope that, if anything goes wrong, someone else will take the blame. It has been jokingly suggested that there are people employed by some companies who are loosely referred to as "director in charge of going to jail" (i.e., someone who can take the fall, where there are significant problems).

Some CEOs invent hundreds of boxes that can be checked by various people in the organization in the hope that this evidence of good ERM can be used in their defense if the need arises. Managers may turn up at a risk workshop organized by the internal auditors and sit through the risk game, adding suggestions and comments much like a party game. Having chewed the fat, they get back to the real work and, after a day or two, forget most of what was discussed. The organization then reports on the widescale use of CRSA to underpin its ERM. The usual problem arises when the board insists on annual risk workshops, which are undertaken and then ignored until next year. This illusion of perfection is worrying. Any review of ERM will come across the various initiatives and consider some of the well-written documentation and reporting software that has been installed. Unfortunately, the hearts and minds of employees and corporate culture will not always have been won over. Any resultant report will describe how ERM is coming along but may well miss the point that there is no real belief in its value, outside of forming the basis for quarterly regulatory reports. Some of the signals of the illusion of perfection are included in this chapter as a warning for what the auditor must be on guard for, in assessing the risk that risk management is not really working.

POOR PRACTICE MODEL: PHASE ONE

The model used in this chapter focuses on risk management overload and the paper chase that some organizations embark on to protect their backs. Our first model incorporates the inherent conflicts between different groups of stakeholders in Figure 7.1.

Each aspect of the model is described below.

Figure 7.1 Poor Practice Model: Phase One

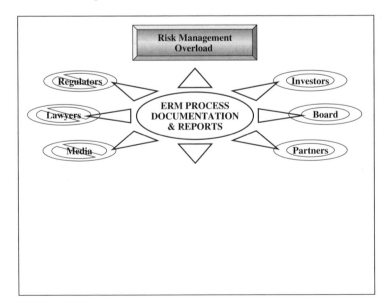

Risk Management Overload

Some organizations launch risk management in a way that can best be described as lurching into it, much as one might stumble into a muddy river. The consultants say risk management needs to be in place, professional journals contain a growing number of articles on this topic, and various regulatory agencies contact executive boards and tell them to start the ball rolling. The board then responds by asking something along the lines of, "What the hell do we do about this?" More often than not, the answer arrives in the form of, "Employ someone to do it. Anyone, so long as it's done." Hence, the risk industry swings into action, and in the worst-case scenario the risk police check every part of the organization to ensure that people are eating, drinking, and talking risk.

The great sway of risk activity is proudly reported back to stakeholders, and annual reports contain many contrived paragraphs describing the risk process that has been set up. A lone voice may be heard repeating, "Isn't risk management just about better management?" but this voice is ignored because people want to be seen doing risk stuff. After a few years, it becomes increasingly difficult to describe just what this risk stuff is and how it contributes to the business. In extreme cases, the management move away from ERM on the basis that they tried it and it did not work. For example, the role of management, in the context of corporate governance, has been described as follows:

> Broadly, management is responsible for the sustainability of the whole organization and accountability for the organization's actions, conduct, and performance to the owners, other stakeholders, regulators, and general public. Specifically, the primary objectives of the overall management process are to achieve:[1]
>
> - Relevant, reliable, and credible financial and operating information
> - Effective and efficient use of the organization's resources
> - Safeguarding of the organization's assets
> - Compliance with laws, regulations, ethical and business norms, and contracts
> - Identification of risk exposures and use of effective strategies to control them
> - Established objectives and goals for operations or programs

But, there is an argument that suggests that the second from last item, "Identification of risk exposures and use of effective strategies to control them," is part of the illusion of perfection, in that an organization should seek to achieve the stated objectives, but the risk management process is not an objective as such, but part of the way of promoting the achievement of the other objectives. When managers are asked to concentrate on the risk management process, they may well lose sight of the real business at hand. Risk management overload is associated with the following:

- Unclear concepts, where everyone has his or her own version of risk management
- No real methodology in place
- No buy-in from front-line staff
- No real tools in use
- No one on the board prepared to take the lead on ERM
- Chief risk officer complaining about the lack of interest from management
- Risk seen as an alien concept that is covered because senior management wants to feel safe
- No effort to assign a budget to the initiative
- A lack of good examples of how ERM has helped the business
- A stress on reports and detailed documentation with little attention paid to competence and understanding among employees
- A view that risk management needs to be done for a while until it is replaced by something more topical
- Poor attendance at awareness events, training, and risk workshops
- No attempt to explain the concept of risk appetite
- No link between ERM and statements on internal control
- No attempt to align risk ownership with responsibility for achieving business objective
- An attempt to assign risk management to the CRO or CAE and not locate it with business units and the workforce
- Some initial enthusiasm for ERM that starts to trail off after a while
- ERM seen as something that is done to keep the auditors happy

The risk concept can get hijacked by specialists who simply will not admit that risk management is just about doing things better. It is about getting people to take responsibility for their work, and not feeling victims to fate:

> The essence of risk management lies in maximizing the areas where we have some control over the outcome while minimizing the areas where we have absolutely no control over the outcome and the linkage between effect and cause is hidden from us.[2]

Regulators, Lawyers, and Media

The next part of our model concentrates on the growing presence of external players. While corporate society has shifted from the days of old when business success was a result of having some good old boys who keep the ship steady at the helm, things have moved on. The new societal dimension pays attention to the needs of stakeholders and the demands of the blinding spotlight that are often generated by the business media, who want to see quick returns with no room for failure. The steady-at-the-helm context has, for many businesses, turned into stormy waters and hazy horizons consisting of inconsistent and high-pressured demands from all comers. Corporate lawsuits can now be seen as the biggest threat to many organizations and the one thing that keeps the CEO awake at night. The Enron and WorldCom affairs culminated in pictures of corporate leaders handcuffed and facing criminal charges, which sent shivers up many an executive's spine. Many companies are developing a dialogue with the readers of their annual reports concerning their values, approach, and impact on society. Others endeavor to explain how they promote governance within their business:

> We have established governance as a high priority at Disney for one simple reason—it's the right thing to do. By investing in Disney, shareholders are placing their trust in the board to help shape the overall course of the company's business and to hold management accountable for its performance. In the end, governance is all about creating an environment that promotes informed, objective decision-making in the interests of all the shareholders.[3]

The problem lies in ensuring that these statements are translated into real-life corporate practices. The regulators, lawyers, and media want to see organizations that are well managed, ethical, fully compliant, and that grow at a respectable rate for the benefit of the economy and therefore the wider society, and they want each organization to publish strong messages on how this is being achieved. Formal risk management processes are a good way of ensuring that risks are contained and no one gets embarrassed, hurt, or simply misled. It would appear that standard risk management practice provides this magic formula:

> Any organization faces a number of uncertainties and risks which can both negatively or positively affect the organization. Risk can be managed in a number of different ways, including acceptance, avoidance, transfer, or control. Internal controls are a common method for reducing the potential negative impact of risk and uncertainty.[4]

Investors, Board, and Partners

Our model has a right-hand as well as a left-hand side. We have described the regulators and how they want big business to behave in a right and proper manner. The right-hand side contains stakeholders who want to achieve their income targets and ensure they can pounce on any opportunities to make quick wins. Investors achieve returns when this income is strong, whereas the board members have an eye on their bonuses, which are invariably linked to profit targets. Partners want the business to beat competitors and expand so that they can benefit from such gains. In this scenario, there is tremendous pressure to generate profits and constantly search for potential takeovers and partners. The selling point is that the company is prepared to take risks and lean forward to grow, expand, and seize new business opportunities. This dialogue with stakeholders is important:

> Risk management provides a structure to facilitate communication and consultation between external stakeholders, governing bodies, management, and personnel at all levels on defining and achieving organizational goals.[5]

But much depends on what is said and the extent to which what is said reflects the reality of what goes on in the organization. The standard risk model entails a systematic process for analysis, evaluation, and comparison, taking account of the views of all relevant stakeholders. Some boards see their success as being based on taking the biggest risks and then, as an afterthought, dress up the decisions in risk management jargon. Many argue that the right-hand model stakeholders have different perspectives from those on the left of the model. As mentioned earlier, some executives have learned to get on with the business and play the risk game to keep all sides happy. The regulators are told that nothing happens in the business without a carefully scored risk assessment aligned to the corporate risk appetite, while the investors are told that they will get great returns if they stick with a dynamic business, which has a feeling for the industry in question. The first point about the illusion of perfection is that it takes a great deal of time and trouble and some amount of good luck to satisfy all stakeholder groups all the time.

ERM Documentation and Report

The next item on our model is ERM records and reports. It is now not enough for organizations to say that they perform well and also behave well. They have to demonstrate that this is truly the case. The second point about the illusion of perfection is that just because an organization can produce a great deal of documentation regarding ERM, this does not mean that ERM is in place and working well. In fact, an excessive level of documentation may suggest that there is a focus on detailed analysis and not the basic principles of developing risk-smart people. Embedded risk management does not lead to the generation of lots of risk data. It leads to the use of standard business tools, systems, and techniques that incorporate the principles of good risk assessment and mitigation. In other words, there should be less documentation and reports that result from what can be called risk activity. People can get concerned that they are preparing risk data, or risk reports or risk assessments, when they know that this must be wrong. What they want to prepare and use is business data, business activity, and a criteria for good decision making. The use of risk as a principal product makes little real sense. It depends on what the organization and work teams are trying to achieve. Risk then should be implicit in how the business works, and there really should not be an amount of paperwork that relates to risk, rather than what people are trying to do. This is a strange environment for the auditor, who likes to see some documentation relating to the topic under review. At worst, the documentation is prepared mainly to ensure that something can be shown to the auditors. This is not to say that documentation is not important, as shown by the Australian/New Zealand risk standard, which argues that documenting each step of the risk management process is important for the following reasons:[6]

- To demonstrate to stakeholders that the process has been conducted properly
- To provide evidence of a systematic approach to risk identification and analysis
- To enable decisions or processes to be reviewed
- To provide a record of risks and to develop the organization's knowledge database
- To provide decision makers with a risk management plan for approval and subsequent implementation
- To provide an accountability mechanism and tool
- To facilitate continuing monitoring and review
- To provide an audit trail
- To share and communicate information

The risk standard goes on to describe what documentation should include at each stage of the risk management process:[7]

- The objectives of the stage
- The information sources on which the outcomes were based
- All major assumptions made in the process
- Who was involved
- The decisions that were agreed on

It takes a brave management and an even braver organization to tell the world about these issues, bearing in mind the scope for embarrassment and the way competitors depend on commercial intelligence to outdo their rivals.

POOR PRACTICE MODEL: PHASE TWO

We have had a go at describing the inherent conflicts in how an organization behaves and what it is prepared to tell the public. We turn now to other real-life factors that may operate to produce even greater conflicts within an organization. Our model continues in Figure 7.2.

Each new aspect of the model is described below.

Figure 7.2 Poor Practice Model: Phase Two

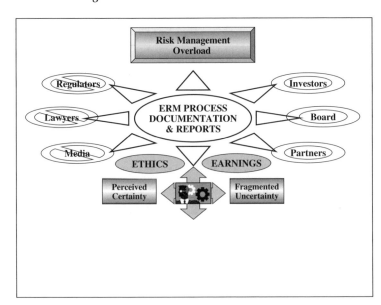

Ethics

We need to introduce the concept of ethics into the ERM equation. First and foremost, internal auditors have a clear ethical framework that guides their work in the sense that they:[8]

1.1. Shall perform their work with honesty, diligence, and responsibility.

1.2. Shall observe the law and make disclosures expected by the law and the profession.

1.3. Shall not knowingly be a party to any illegal activity, or engage in acts that are discreditable to the profession of internal auditing or to the organization.

1.4. Shall respect and contribute to the legitimate and ethical objectives of the organization.

These ethical values translate into a far-reaching role in the organization that is much more than simply checking financial transactions. Governance is mainly about the way an organization behaves, and in this context, the internal auditor has to keep several matters in mind in seeking to improve the governance process:[9]

- Promoting appropriate ethics and values within the organization
- Ensuring effective organizational performance management and accountability
- Effectively communicating risk and control information to appropriate areas of the organization
- Effectively coordinating the activities of and communicating information among the board, external and internal auditors, and management

Meanwhile, we would hope that the board and senior executives have the same considerations in mind, but ERM does not mean everything that the organization does is held out for public inspection. There is generally an opt-out clause where sensitive matters can remain in-house, even if these same matters constitute the highest-risk aspects of running the business:

> In some situations an organization may consider it not to be appropriate to communicate with stakeholders, for commercial or security reasons. In these circumstances the communication plan should document a conscious decision not to involve stakeholders but could still take their per-

spective into account through other means, for example, intelligence or business information.[10]

The auditor always has one eye on the ethical climate of the part of the business that is being reviewed. This is firmly enshrined in auditing standards:

> Significant engagement observations are those conditions that, in the judgment of the CAE, could adversely affect the organization. Significant engagement observations may include conditions dealing with irregularities, illegal acts, errors, inefficiency, waste, ineffectiveness, conflicts of interest, and control weaknesses. After reviewing such conditions with senior management, the CAE should communicate significant engagement observations and recommendations to the board, whether or not they have been satisfactorily resolved.[11]

ERM is based on people being open and honest about the way their business is being managed and ensuring that all material information is fully disclosed, including significant weaknesses in internal controls.

Earnings

Earnings management is a different aspect of managing a business, and the problem is that most managers are pretty good at understanding their revenue flows, but they are not always completely ethical. Many are driven by excessively high targets and work in a culture where mistakes are quickly punished. To fail to meet targets or to admit to error means the incumbent gets terminated. Some high-flying organizations are built this way to stay ahead of the opposition. In this environment, risk management becomes a game of cat and mouse, where managers ensure they keep their risk reports within the tolerances either because the risks are acceptable or because they have simply been kept off the balance sheet. COSO ERM recognizes that good performance is key to business success but also takes a long view of sustainable growth:

> These capabilities inherent in enterprise risk management help management achieve the entity's performance and profitability targets and prevent loss of resources. Enterprise risk management helps ensure effective reporting and compliance with laws and regulations, and helps avoid damage to the entity's reputation and associated consequences. In sum, enterprise risk management helps an entity get to where it wants to go and avoid pitfalls and surprises along the way.[12]

In theory this makes a lot of sense, but where executives are on short contracts and their bonuses are tied into maintaining the share price, there is always the temptation to massage the figures or cut corners to make short-term gains. This is why we have shown Ethics and Earnings on opposite sides of the model. At times the two factors are at odds, and ERM is manipulated to convince interested parties that all issues have been identified and contained (i.e., risks relating to irregularity and noncompliance as well as risks relating to poor performance and profitability). Because ERM demands that all relevant risks that concern stakeholders are addressed across the entire organization, this means the ERM process can be used to demonstrate that this has been done. Unfortunately, just because decisions can be traced back to a full risk assessment, this does not mean the decisions are always right:

> Researchers sought for ways of conducting a systematic analysis of the unexpected. Before the war they had concentrated on the inputs that went into decision-making. Now they recognized that the decision is only the beginning. The devil is in the consequences of our decisions, not in the decisions themselves.[13]

There will always be tensions between achieving results, behaving correctly, and being able to demonstrate that this is the case. ERM processes that are not sophisticated enough to deal with these tensions will become illusions (i.e., they will produce reports that tell investors what they want to hear, that tell regulators and law officials that all is well) and will allow employees and associates to feel comfortable working for such an organization. There is always great surprise when a large organization falls over or runs afoul of the public's expectations, even with a formal risk management process in place. This is why in the wrong hands and used in the wrong way, ERM can become a tool for creating an illusion of perfection.

Perceived Certainty

The next stage of our model builds on the theme we have been developing (i.e., the perception of certainty). The ERM process is simple in that it says that risks to objectives should be examined and mitigated, or they may be left if they mean exposures fall within stakeholder expectations. These expectations form what we have called the risk appetite:

> It is important to develop a communication plan for both internal and external stakeholders at the earliest stage of the process. This plan should address issues relating to both the risk itself and the process to manage it.[14]

The problem is that we have developed a message of perceived certainty within the risk tolerance that is made clear to all, but this defeats the first rule of risk in that we can never be certain of anything. In fact, a feeling of certainty is dangerous because it may give comfort where there really should be a state of alertness.

Fragmented Uncertainty

The perceived certainty stands at the left-hand side of the model and shows the regulators, lawyers, and media that they should concentrate on other organizations. The fragmented uncertainty is the image that is understood by the key investors, partners, and the board who know roughly how the business is doing. Many large organizations lurch from success to stagnation, through to restructuring and possible success or failure. This fragmented uncertainty is the reality of dealing with global markets in which market forces can change overnight as the price of oil fluctuates, or an important overseas region becomes volatile, or when exchange rates rapidly fall or rise. Many global markets can become fragile overnight, if the wrong factors come together at the wrong time, as in the following example.

CASE STUDY

A Worst-Case Scenario

A safety regulator's serious concerns raised over a leading cholesterol-busting drug wiped billions off the value of shares from several pharmaceutical companies after sending shock waves through the stock market.

Many board members spend their time tackling the next crisis that impacts next year's million-dollar bonus and have little time to wade through risk reports prepared for the last year's published financial report. A well-formulated ERM process has the ability to deal with the real issues that face any business, government body, or not-for-profit entity, and this reality is recognized in the COSO ERM:

While enterprise risk management provides important benefits, limitations exist. In addition to factors discussed above, limitations result from the realities that human judgment in decision making can be faulty, decisions on responding to risk and establishing controls need to consider the relative costs and benefits, breakdowns can occur because of human failures such as simple errors or mistakes, controls can be circumvented by collusion of two or more people, and management has the ability to override enterprise risk management decisions.[15]

POOR PRACTICE MODEL: PHASE THREE

We have described the forces that make it difficult to set up a worthwhile risk management process and the way the concepts can be abused to allow people to hear what the organization wants them to hear. One important factor that needs to be superimposed over these issues is the reliability of evidence to support ERM. It is here that the auditor has much to offer. Our model continues in Figure 7.3.

Each new aspect of the model is described below.

Figure 7.3 Poor Practice Model: Phase Three

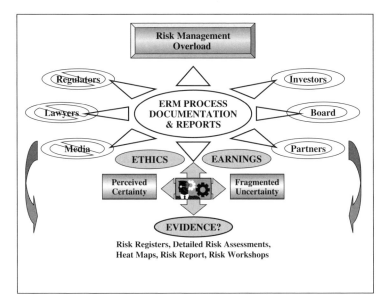

Risk Registers

We have discussed risk registers throughout this book. They are a simple device that seeks to capture the results of risk-assessed activities in a comprehensive database, so each part of the business is marked with its objectives, risks, scored risks, controls, a view on gaps, weaknesses, or any overkill on controls. Action plans to mitigate unacceptable levels of risk are fed into operational plans and performance targets for the respective risk owners. Big risks (e.g., red risks) are accelerated upward to fall into senior management's own risk registers until they hit the board's corporate register. This theory sounds pretty simple, but when considering the illusion of perfection, we need to focus on what can go wrong when introducing such registers through a series of examples.

CASE STUDY

Risk Register Deflecting Important Business Issues

A senior auditor turned up at the initial meeting with the business unit manager to discuss the terms of reference for the pending audit. After the usual opening pleasantries, the auditor set out a spreadsheet across the desk and explained to the business unit manager that this was audit's risk register for the business unit in question. Verifying the way risks were being managed would form the basis for the audit work. After glancing through the register, the manager thought to himself that this register should keep the auditor busy for the two weeks that had been allotted to the audit, and because none of the really vexing issues were on the register, the auditor would not interfere with the real issues facing the business unit.

CASE STUDY

Risk Bureaucracy

One organization interpreted risk management as the task of filling in an assortment of forms that fell into a risk register. Managers and staff embarked on a struggle to prepare detailed registers that became seen as tedious work. An automated database was bought to simplify the task, but this encouraged more data input. After a few years, most of the registers fell into disuse, and a change in focus paid much more attention to competence and developing what was called a risk-smart culture.

CASE STUDY

Risk Fear Tactics

Managers in one organization invented the phrase "the dreaded audit risk register" to describe the way that auditors would regularly arrive at the managers' office armed with a risk register that the auditor had compiled. The managers would then be subjected to a series of veiled threats from the lead auditor regarding any red risks or whether key controls over significant risk were being applied properly. Strangely enough, the auditors thought they were being quite progressive by using risk registers. It's just that no one told them that risk management is something that managers should do for themselves and not something that is done to them. The audit team was eventually dismissed and the work outsourced to real professionals.

Detailed Risk Assessments

The next facet of evidence relates to the analysis that is carried out before data is posted to the risk registers. A board can send out a directive that states: "all major decisions should incorporate a formal risk assessment before they are actioned" as a way of drilling risk management down into the business. This can result in masses of analysis that build up over time into an impressive mountain of evidence to support the way decision making is deemed clear, concise, and transparent—all good governance attributes. A further example helps illustrate the reality of corporate life.

CASE STUDY

Passing the Risk Buck

In one organization, the risk management team assumed a high profile and was known as the risk police, whose job it was to uncover big risks and sort them out. This meant that managers refused to take responsibility for managing risk in their areas of responsibility. Once this concept has set in, it is difficult to dislodge. The net result was a series of strange conversations during which managers passed on problems to the risk manager and could not understand why the issues were sent back to them for review and decision. To make matters worse, audit reports that had adverse comments were simply passed on to the risk manager for action. In the end, the back-office people had more power than front-line staff who were delivering the live products.

Heat Maps

Another way some organizations evidence their risk management process is to develop so-called heat maps of red, yellow, and green across the organization. This becomes a series of grids that are scoped through the business and can end up looking like a map that diagramatically represents the main business lines and support functions, with each aspect given a score along the lines that red is high impact/high likelihood while green is low impact/low likelihood. The idea is that senior management and the board can scan the organization and instantly see areas that need urgent action and close monitoring, while parts of the business that are soundly controlled can take a backseat. The main problem with heat maps as useful evidence is that they depend on how one defines red, yellow, and green. If red is bad, there is great temptation for business managers to ensure that nothing hits this grade either through thorough analysis and action or through simply fudging the scores. A portfolio view of risk is now becoming popular in many large and complex organizations:

> A portfolio view of risk can be depicted in any of a variety of ways. A portfolio view may be gained by focusing on major risks or even event categories across business units, or on risk for the company as a whole, using such metrics as risk-adjusted capital or capital at risk.[16]

Risk Reports

Another technique for providing evidential support for ERM is to install a detailed risk reporting infrastructure within the organization that reaches all parts of the business. The reports will detail the risk identification exercises, risk scores, action plans, and various risk triggers that can be established to alert management and risk owners that a problem needs resolving:

> All identified enterprise risk management deficiencies that affect an entity's ability to develop and implement its strategy and achieve set objectives should be reported to those positioned to take necessary action.[17]

The IT security officer may set up risk triggers for areas where red risks are emerging that affect the integrity of corporate and local information systems. The chief financial officer could impose further triggers where these risks affect the final accounts reporting systems. The problem arises when these reports are prepared mainly to show that a lot of risk activity is occurring, but not as a way of adding real value to the business. This potential misuse of risk reports can be illustrated in the following example.

CASE STUDY

Risk as Security

One transport company appointed a chief risk officer who had a security background and saw risk as anything that threatened the capacity to continue the business. This related to the main buildings, information systems, and infrastructure. The result of this narrow perspective was an obsession with contingency planning and stand-by facilities, with no attempt to consider risks to the business goals. Moreover, risk was seen as threats and not as a failure to reach out to new opportunities.

Risk Workshops

This is a bugbear. The illusion-of-perfection organizations boast about the sheer number of workshops that are held day in and day out. They argue that employees are stuck into risk management events and by definition are able to manage risk down to the risk appetite set by the board and implemented by the senior executive team. An example may help illustrate this point.

CASE STUDY

Risk for Risk's Sake

One newly appointed risk manager was told by the board to implement a program of risk-based events including workshops, awareness seminars, orientation sessions, sessions on risk registers, and interviews with key managers. She was instructed to perform at least 20 different sessions each month, and after delivering dozens of these events, realized that there was no standardized approach or overall aim to these sessions. After her first year, it became clear that the board was funding the program simply to sign off on the high level of risk management activity—and for no other reason.

POOR PRACTICE MODEL: PHASE FOUR

ERM is seen as an excellent device for encouraging an organization to perform and behave well and to explain how this has been achieved. Anything that gets in the way of this simple equation can be considered a risk and should be addressed by taking all reasonable steps. This means that the public image presented by the organization is derived from the reality of what goes on inside its offices, factories, units, and culture. Our model continues in Figure 7.4.

Each new aspect of the model is described below.

Figure 7.4 Poor Practice Model: Phase Four

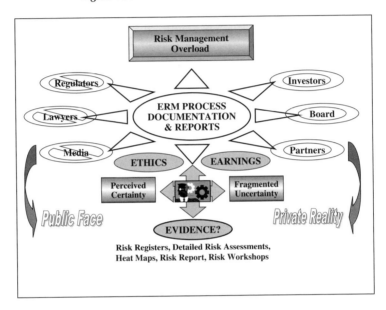

Public Face

The public face presented by an organization tends to look good, with its newly applied makeup on and having just returned from the hairdresser, but when one is choosing a partner, it is a good idea to see this person sans makeup. Some organizations work on the basis that if you look good, people will assume you are good, but ERM is about telling the stakeholders the truth—or at least telling them that you have a grip on the truth. For example, the Australian/ New Zealand risk management standard indicates that an organization needs to have a handle on the following key elements of risk management:[18]

- What is the source of each risk?
- What might happen that could:

- ○ Increase or decrease the effective achievement of objectives
- ○ Make the achievement of the objectives more or less efficient (financial, people, time)
- ○ Cause stakeholders to take action that may influence the achievement of objectives
- ○ Produce additional benefits
- What would the effect on objectives be?
- When, where, why, how are these risks (both positive and negative) likely to occur?
- Who might be involved or impacted?
- What controls presently exist to treat this risk (maximize positive risks or minimize negative risks)?
- What could cause the control not to have the desired effect on the risk?

Stakeholders would be satisfied if the organization they are concerned about had in place a process that sought answers to these and similar probing questions, but this public face can mask something underneath that tells a different story.

Private Reality

The private reality of some companies would surprise or even shock the public if it were widely known. Most corporate scandals result from organizations that have failed to meet a standard of behavior that is expected of them by the marketplace. The common theme is that they have let down all or some of the principal stakeholders and probably broken the law along the way. The illusion of ERM can be used to mask an enterprise in which officials and employees spend a great deal of time marching through their offices shouting out comments along the lines of the following:

- "I don't want excuses—just get the job done."
- "Don't mess up—or if you do, make sure it doesn't stick to me."
- "Whatever you do, don't make me look bad."
- "Don't get me into any more trouble than I'm already in."
- "Steal a march on others, anyway you like."

- "Open an escape route, so when we need to jump, we can have a soft landing."
- "Just make sure someone else is accountable."

POOR PRACTICE MODEL: FINAL

Our complete model is in Figure 7.5. Each new aspect of the final model is described below.

Figure 7.5 The Complete Poor Practice Model

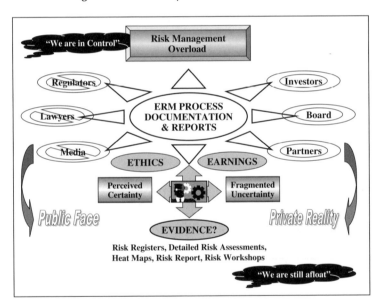

We Are in Control

The model is completed by adding two final elements that contrast with each other. Most organizations present themselves to the public as being entirely in control. Even where there are problems, a crisis, large losses, or a failing public service, the top people know that they have to appear calm and in control. ERM is essentially about being in control, even where there are concerns and areas that need improving. Adequate control, in this sense, is:

Present if management has planned and organized (designed) in a manner that provides reasonable assurance that the organization's risks have been managed effectively and that the organization's goals and objectives will be achieved efficiently and economically.[19]

But this air of calm may hide problems, much like the majestic swan who appears to be floating across the lake, while in reality the swan is paddling furiously underneath the water. The auditor is one of the few people in an organization who can give an entirely straight response when asked whether the entity is in control. Remarkably, the auditor has a formal facility for dealing with professional differences where the reality of control is different from the published position:

> When the chief audit executive believes that senior management has accepted a level of residual risk that may be unacceptable to the organization, the chief audit executive should discuss the matter with senior management. If the decision regarding residual risk is not resolved, the chief audit executive and senior management should report the matter to the board for resolution.[20]

One way of promoting the reality of control as compared to the illusion of control is to equip the audit committee to oversee the way the organization designs and manages its risk management and internal control process. In this respect, the auditor is once again in a key position to recognize and address this crucial matter:

> The CAE should assist the committee in ensuring that the charter, role, and activities of the committee are appropriate for it to achieve its responsibilities. The CAE can play an important role by assisting the committee to periodically review its activities and suggesting enhancements. In this way, the CAE serves as a valued advisor to the committee on audit committee and regulatory practices.[21]

We Are Still Afloat

The illusion of perfection that is created by a distorted ERM process contrasts with the reality of life in many big companies and government entities, where the executives need someone to help them as they occupy the hot seat:

> With management in the proverbial "hot seat," those at the top are looking for assurance that their organizations are addressing risks and

implementing controls that mitigate those risks effectively. Who better than the internal auditors to provide such assurances? Whether making sure the I's are dotted and the t's are crossed before management signs off on the financial statements, or checking to see that prescribed policies and procedures are being followed by all, the auditors' assurance role is steeped in organizational accountability.[22]

Although most organizations produce published reports that boast they are completely in control, many internal reports spend their time trying to find out whether the company is still afloat. As a company lurches from crisis to crisis, it may concentrate its risk management strategy on crisis management. Some organizations pride themselves on their ability to respond to a crisis as the carefully developed plans swing into action, to put out fires and keep the normal business systems going. Risk is seen as an assortment of external threats that have the potential to impact the information systems, buildings, and workforce. Many organizations employ chief risk officers who have a background in security and whose byline revolves around capacity, resilience, and recovery. In this environment, little attention is usually paid to the scope to establish risk management across all aspects of the business that line up with the variety of strategic and operational objectives found within the organization. Again, audit can come to the rescue. When ERM is not being applied to its fullest extent, the auditors can lead the way and show how risk can be built into the way the business is delivered:

> Management reporting and communication should convey risk management conclusions and recommendations to reduce exposures. For management to fully understand the degree of exposure, it is critical that audit reporting identify the criticality and consequence of the risk exposure to achieving objectives.[23]

For organizations that have a frightening reality, there is not much scope to talk about risk management as a surreal concept that should occupy the time of busy executives. More progress can be made when we tell our executives that the entire organization is itself the risk management system as it flexes to respond to external and internal forces. Selling ERM in this way leads to many more positives than getting involved in detailed debates on risk, risk concepts, and theoretical solutions to complex problems. In terms of building a real ERM as opposed to an illusion of perfection, it may be an idea to take the top people through various stages:

1. Start with basic management principles aimed at delivering the business in a legitimate manner.
2. Then add on risk management that is designed to protect the business by nailing down problems and significant issues.
3. Develop the scope of risk management beyond contingency planning as a way of both protecting and promoting the business.
4. Launch into ideas such as enriched management that are designed to grow the business but in a carefully managed way.

In this way, ERM can be applied in a way that merges with the business and gradually becomes part of the way people work. In terms of developing the cultural base, another idea is to develop the risk concept by moving through seven levels of thinking about risk in one's work:

1. It really is no big deal, we do it anyway.
2. It might be helpful to know a bit about this risk concept.
3. People keep telling us about risk management, and it sounds like it is happening in parts of the business.
4. Risk management is being fully developed as part of the corporate risk policy.
5. We are proud to say that we have an integrated ERM process in place that reaches all parts of the business.
6. Risk is being incorporated into our language and the way we do things.
7. It really is no big deal and we do it anyway.

If milestones are set for each level, then it is possible to plot the progress made by managers and staff. The single danger is to move straight into level seven, thinking it is level one—where people see ERM as no big deal because they do not understand it rather than because it has been carefully assimilated into the way they work. COSO provides much-needed help in making it clear that ERM does have several important limitations that reflect the fact that we live and work in the real world:[24]

- First, risk relates to the future, which is inherently uncertain.
- Second, ERM—even effective ERM—operates at different levels with respect to different objectives.
- Third, ERM cannot provide absolute assurance with respect to any of these objectives categories.

SUMMARY

Because auditing is about uncovering the reality of risk and control, there needs to be a recognition of the illusion of perfection that comes with an unrealistic application of risk management theory. One way to be on guard for the illusion of risk management perfection is to go through the following five steps:

1. Determine whether there is a state of risk management overload in parts of the organization where people have been bombarded with material that makes their life more difficult and less manageable.

2. Uncover any mismatch between messages given and sent back to different groups of stakeholders, where rigid regulatory disclosures are seen as a matter of doing the bare minimum to satisfy various legal compliance requirements.

3. Assess the extent to which risk management documentation is being produced to support the risk management process with no reference to the view that this documentation should help a business become and remain more successful.

4. Review the evidence that supports the business risk assessments and resulting view on internal controls to judge whether this has been developed in a way that reflects the commercial reality and the integration of risk into and inside the organization's business systems.

5. Produce audit reports that comment on the extent to which the public face presented by the organization matches the private reality of the way the organization works and ensures that it is able to meet earnings targets while maintaining an ethically sound position.

Note that Appendix A contains checklists that can be used to assess the overall quality of the enterprise risk management system and also judge the type of audit approach that may be applied to supporting and reviewing the ERM process.

NOTES

1. Institute of Internal Auditors, Practice Advisory 2100-1.
2. Peter L. Bernstein, *Against the Gods: The Remarkable Story of Risk* (Hoboken, NJ: John Wiley & Sons, 1996), p. 197.
3. Disney Corporation, *www.corporate.disney.go.com*, Chairman of the Board, October 2004.

4. Institute of Internal Auditors, Practice Advisory 2010-2.
5. Australian/New Zealand Standard: Risk Management Guidelines AS/NZS 4360: 2004, p. 11.
6. *Ibid.*, p. 96.
7. *Ibid.*, p. 96.
8. Institute of Internal Auditors, *Code of Ethics, Rules of Conduct*.
9. Institute of Internal Auditors, Standard 2130.
10. Australian/New Zealand Standard: Risk Management Guidelines AS/NZS 4360:2004, p. 21.
11. Institute of Internal Auditors, Practice Advisory 2060-1.
12. Committee of Sponsoring Organizations, *Enterprise Risk Management*, September 2004, Executive Summary.
13. Peter L. Bernstein, *Against the Gods: The Remarkable Story of Risk* (Hoboken, NJ: John Wiley and Sons, Inc., 1996), p. 217.
14. Australian/New Zealand Standard: Risk Management AS/NZS 4360:2004, p. 11.
15. Committee of Sponsoring Organizations, *Enterprise Risk Management*, September 2004, Executive Summary.
16. *Ibid.*, p. 59.
17. *Ibid.*, p. 80.
18. Australian/New Zealand Standard: Risk Management Guidelines AS/NZS 4360: 2004, p. 39.
19. Institute of Internal Auditors, Glossary of Terms.
20. Institute of Internal Auditors, Performance Standards 2600.
21. Institute of Internal Auditors, Practice Advisory 2060-2.
22. Betty McPhilimy, Chairman of the Board, IIA.Inc., "Seize the Moment," *The Internal Auditor* (August 2004): pp. 66–71.
23. Institute of Internal Auditors, Practice Advisory 2010-2.
24. Committee of Sponsoring Organizations, *Enterprise Risk Management*, September 2004, p. 93.

A HOLISTIC ERM CONCEPT

Value is provided by improving opportunities to achieve organizational
objectives, identifying operational improvements, and/or reducing risk
exposure through both assurance and consulting services.

IIA Glossary

INTRODUCTION

This short chapter summarizes aspects of ERM that have appeared so far
in the book. In this way, it is possible to assess the overall ERM process in
a holistic way that brings in many of the issues that have been addressed
in the earlier chapters. This wider view of risk is something that drives the
development of internal auditing:

> The sign of the future is the expansion from risk recognition to risk man-
> agement. It is an example of internal auditing leading the field in pro-
> viding a "value-added" ingredient to a time-honored function, the concern
> with risk and the use of risk-based auditing.[1]

ERM PROGRAM MODEL:
PHASE ONE

We need to bring together the three key forces that influence an organization: (1) stakeholders' expectations, (2) business risk, and (3) the rules that
are set by the various regulators. Our first model starts with the launch of
the risk management program in Figure 8.1.

Each aspect of the model is described below:

Figure 8.1 ERM Program Model: Phase One

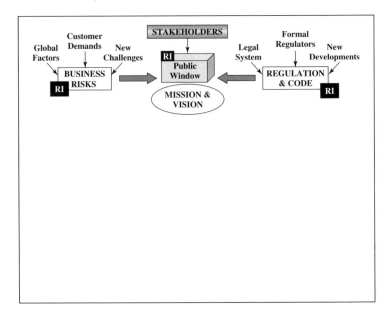

Stakeholders

We have already noted that organizations are increasingly being influenced by groups that have a voice in the way the management behave. This factor is at the top of the forces that steer the direction and pace of all larger organizations. The shareholder concept of people who looked for income and quick growth is gradually being replaced by the stakeholder concept where wider concerns about the effect on society and the need for sustainable growth are now being emphasized, as made clear in the following professional guidance:

> The chief audit executive (CAE) should include the environmental, health, and safety (EH&S) risks in any entity-wide risk management assessment and assess the activities in a balanced manner relative to other types of risk associated with an entity's operations. Among the risk exposures that should be evaluated are:[2]
>
> - Organizational reporting structures
> - Likelihood of causing environmental harm, fines, and penalties expenditures mandated by Environmental Protection Agency (EPA) or other governmental agencies

- History of injuries and deaths
- Record of losses of customers, and episodes of negative publicity and loss of public image and reputation

Business Risks

The next big factor relates to significant risks that impact the organization and that can make the difference between success and abject failure. The ERM process seeks to capture and manage these risks systematically across the entire organization. Our model analyzes these risks in terms of the following:

- Global developments—as world markets become increasingly inter-dependent, more and more organizations have to assess worldwide developments whenever they are faced with a strategic decision.
- New challenges, new directions, and opportunities that appear on the horizon, but only for a short time before they are captured and disappear.
- Heightened customer demand means that entities cannot simply keep on supplying what they believe is a good product. People are now deciding what they want and then going out and finding the supplier that best fits the bill.

Regulation and Codes

The side to ERM that is often forgotten revolves around understanding the risk of running afoul of laws, rules, and regulations. These kinds of risks can bring down even the most powerful corporate machines, and ERM suggests that they need to appear on the corporate agenda. Most regulations are based around fair play and transparency and should not be seen as a burden on corporate America. Regulations are part of the external context:

Establish the external context

This step defines the external environment in which the organization operates. It also defines the relationship between the organization and its external environment. This may, for example, include:

- The business, social, regulatory, cultural, competitive, financial and political environment
- The organization's strengths, weaknesses, opportunities and threats

- External stakeholders
- Key business drivers

It is particularly important to take into account the perceptions and values of external stakeholders and establish policies for communication with these parties.[3]

Public Window

The mechanism that handles the demands of stakeholders, business risk, and regulations is what we call the *public window*. This is the image, communication, and front office of the organization that greets the public. It is the PR machine that tells outsiders what is going on and what plans are in store. In terms of the ERM context, the public window gives the world an insight into the risk appetite of the organization by making clear what it sees as acceptable and what needs to be addressed. For the banking sector, the need for full disclosures on risk management is clearly spelled out:

> Banks should make sufficient public disclosures to allow market participants to assess their approach to operational risk.[4]

Mission and Vision

We turn now to the organization's internal processes, which starts with the mission. Rather than a corporate mission simply saying "we want to be the best at this or the best at that," it can result from the ERM context that takes on board all of the factors that have so far appeared on the model. Moreover, the mission results from an understanding of what different stakeholder groups expect and the need to balance strong performance with constraints posed by following the rules and regulations. ERM can help ensure that this goal can be achieved:

> Over the last few years, the importance to strong corporate governance of managing risk has been increasingly acknowledged. Organizations are under pressure to identify all the business risks they face; social, ethical and environmental as well as financial and operational, and to explain how they manage them to an acceptable level. Meanwhile, the use of enterprise-wide risk management frameworks has expanded, as

organizations recognize their advantages over less coordinated approaches to risk management.[5]

But the objectives in question have to have meaning and value in the first place and flow from the overall corporate mission in order for ERM to have a real impact on the business:

> Establishing the risk objectives that support and are aligned with the selected strategy relative to all entity activities, is critical to success.[6]

ERM PROGRAM MODEL:
PHASE TWO

The high-level aspects of corporate governance have been established, and now we need to turn to the remaining elements that set the context for good risk management. Our model continues in Figure 8.2.

Each new aspect of the model is described below.

Figure 8.2 ERM Program Model: Phase Two

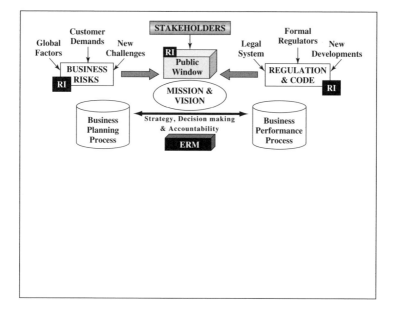

Business Planning Process

Planning propels most organizations toward their goals. The business planning models set out the constraints and drivers that allow the workforce to release their energies and get going. This is why the ERM process must attach itself to the planning process to have any real value. Risks inform the planning process and also pop up from the way planning criteria are assessed and analyzed. When developing ERM, it is essential that the planning process is revisited to assess the way it helps identify risk as well as how it in turn responds to risk. Good plans seek to reconcile the external and the internal context and respond effectively to both of them:

Establish the Internal Context

Before a risk management activity, at any level, is commenced, it is necessary to understand the organization. Key areas include:[7]

- Culture
- Internal stakeholders
- Structure
- Capabilities in terms of resources such as people, systems
- Processes, capital
- Goals and objectives and the strategies that are in place to achieve them

Establishing the internal context is important because:

- Risk management takes place in the context of the goals and objectives of the organization
- The major risk for most organizations is that they fail to achieve their strategic, business or project objectives, or are perceived to have failed by stakeholders
- The organizational policy and goals and interests help define the organization's risk policy
- Specific objectives and criteria of a project or activity must be considered in the light of objectives of the organization as a whole

Business Performance Process

The other side of the model contains the performance management system. Planning sets a direction for the organization, while performance management drives these plans into personal and team frameworks. This means that actions that develop from an assessment of current and emerging risks can be located within the way performance is managed by the organization.

Case Study

Adding Risk Management Objectives to Performance Targets

In a front-line business unit, the action plans resulting from risk management workshops were linked to personal targets for each of the assigned risk owners. The performance appraisal system involved reviewing the way all targets were delivered and also how risk management was employed by the employees in question.

Strategy, Decision Making, and Accountability

Many people argue that good risk management is essentially about employees being equipped and motivated to made good decisions, for the benefit of the organization. Following this line of thinking, the next part of the model combines strategic decision making with the need to ensure full accountability for these decisions at the very top of the business:

> When enterprise risk management is determined to be effective in each of the four categories of objectives, respectively, the board of directors and management have reasonable assurance that they understand the extent to which the entity's strategic and operations objectives are being achieved, and that the entity's reporting is reliable and applicable laws and regulations are being complied with.[8]

ERM

Having set the external and internal contexts, we can now turn to ERM and where it fits in, by asking what activities are included in ERM:[9]

- Articulating and communicating the objectives of the organization
- Determining the risk appetite of the organization

- Establishing an appropriate internal environment, including a risk management framework
- Identifying potential threats to the achievement of the objectives
- Assessing the risk (i.e., the impact and likelihood of the threat occurring)
- Selecting and implementing responses to the risks
- Undertaking control and other response activities
- Communicating information on risks consistently at all levels in the organization
- Centrally monitoring and coordinating the risk management processes and the outcomes
- Providing assurance on the effectiveness with which risks are being managed

Finally, the eight components of ERM should be included in the way that risk management flows from the contextual environment, as a response to the way an organization is set up to deliver its objectives:

> Enterprise risk management consists of eight interrelated components. These are derived from the way management runs an enterprise and are integrated with the management process.[10]

ERM PROGRAM MODEL: PHASE THREE

ERM is a response to the changing environment that demands that the private and public sector deliver their promises and behave properly in doing this. In our model we have so far been able to define ERM as the principal mechanism for achieving this difficult task. In essence, ERM asks that all parts of the business be on the watch for anything that affects the way they work, and then take all reasonable steps to work with these influences to make and maintain good progress. This is the high-level aspiration that has to be translated into front-line business processes. Our model continues in Figure 8.3.

Each new aspect of the model is described below.

Figure 8.3 ERM Program Model: Phase Three

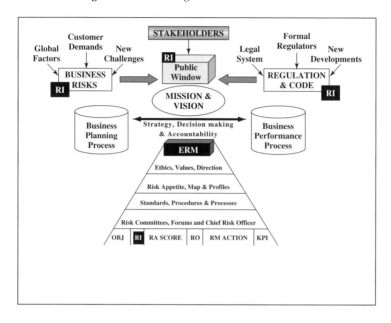

Ethics, Values, and Decisions

We have discussed decision making in terms of the way it relates to strategic planning and risk assessment. We turn now to an additional perspective of decision making that relates to corporate ethics and values. ERM argues that organizations need to address the risk of failing to meet the highest standards of conduct and that decisions need to be made in a way that promotes this concept:

> Because an entity's good reputation is so valuable, the standards of behavior go beyond mere compliance with law. Managers of well-run enterprises increasingly have accepted the view that ethics pays and ethical behavior is good business.[11]

The ethics advocate mantle has to sit somewhere in the organization to ensure this happens, and this is where the auditor may emerge as a worthy contender:

> Internal auditors and the internal audit activity should take an active role in support of the organization's ethical culture. They possess a high

level of trust and integrity within the organization and the skills to be effective advocates of ethical conduct. They have the competence and capacity to appeal to the enterprise leaders, managers, and other employees to comply with the legal, ethical, and societal responsibilities of the organization.[12]

Risk Appetite, Maps, and Profiles

The aim of the model is to expand the base that supports ERM, as it contributes to a crystal-clear public window. The next item on the menu is the way the organization defines itself in terms of a map that profiles the way risk affects its products. The profile needs to be illuminated by a bright light that picks up the peaks and troughs, that represent high and low levels of risk. This bright light is powered by the risk appetite that is set by the organization, in response to expectations from their key stakeholders. Keeping to our analogy, it is possible to isolate dangerous rivers, swampland, as well as firm ground and challenging hills, and this picture becomes what we have called the *risk map* of the organization. The CEO and the board are responsible for drawing up this complex map of the business:

> Because objectives relating to reliability of reporting and compliance with laws and regulations are within the entity's control, enterprise risk management can be expected to provide reasonable assurance of achieving those objectives. Achievement of strategic objectives and operations objectives, however, is subject to external events not always within the entity's control; accordingly, for these objectives, enterprise risk management can provide reasonable assurance that management, and the board in its oversight role, are made aware, in a timely manner, of the extent to which the entity is moving toward achievement of the objectives.[13]

Standards, Procedures, and Processes

We get closer to the real deal when clear standards and procedures are developed to support risk management. Each organization needs to explain how it sees risk management and how it will be applied to promote the business. This is no easy feat. It means documenting the approach to ERM and telling people how they can take a systematic approach to this important consideration. Such steps do not mean simply taking the published guidance and giving this out to managers and their staff. It involves a more detailed evaluation of how risks will be fed into the business to provide a better chance of success. The old saying "one size fits all" has been abandoned some time ago, because each entity, even within the same business sector, needs to assume an ERM process that makes sense for the way it operates. For example, the COSO ERM components have to be applied in a flexible manner:

> The eight components will not function identically in every entity. Application in small and mid-size entities, for example, may be less formal and less structured. Nonetheless, small entities still can have effective enterprise risk management, as long as each of the components is present and functioning properly.[14]

Risk Committees, Forums, and the CRO

We get closer to the final picture of ERM when we can get down into the structures that help move things along. An organization can produce a dozen policies, standards, and procedures to spread its vision of ERM. It can send these messages to its workforce and explain that it is important that all employees understand the risk profiles within which they operate, but the act of committing a budget to get ERM up and running makes all the difference. The best way to use such a budget is to employ or establish structures that lead the relevant initiatives and programs, and ensure that the new arrangements are up to the job. Before we go over the way a risk committee can be used to drive ERM through the business, the oversight role of the audit committee must be considered:

> The New York Exchange's Corporate Governance Rules require that a listed company's audit committee have a written charter that addresses the committee's duties and responsibilities, which must include discussing policies with respect to risk assessment and risk management.[15]

Some organizations go on to set up risk committees that may be used to report straight to the board on the way ERM is being established and applied. Various risk forums can be set up consisting of management teams, project leaders, and/or representative people from across the organization, who can take a lead on risks that cut through the business lines or help formulate the methodologies that support ERM. These groups are important because they represent the business lines and people who have an executive decision-making capacity, rather than simply oversight responsibilities.

As well as providing advice and guidance on ERM, the CEO will want to ensure that a monitoring process is in place:

> Monitoring can be done in two ways: through ongoing activities or separate evaluations. ERM mechanisms usually are structured to monitor themselves on an ongoing basis, at last to some degree.[16]

The final component is the so-called chief risk officer (CRO), who holds the post of risk champion. This person can act as a source of expertise on the way risk is addressed by the organization and the way procedures and processes come together to form a holistic whole. In one sense, the CRO may use models such as the one in this chapter to judge the way ERM is progressing. A summarized version of the COSO view on the CRO's responsibilities follows:[17]

- Establishing ERM policies
- Framing authority and accountability for ERM
- Promoting an ERM competence throughout the entity
- Guiding interpretation of ERM with other business planning and management activities
- Establishing a common risk management language
- Facilitating manager's developing of reporting protocols
- Reporting to the CEO on progress and recommendations

Objectives, RI, RA, RM, Actions, KPIs

The final part of this section is the basic risk cycle. Having set the context and put in place the required structures, it is possible to get both front- and back-office people to work through their operational positions in terms of managing risk. The equation is well known and is repeated here:

- Revisiting business objectives
- Identifying risks (risk identification, RI) to the achievement of these objectives
- Assessing these risks for their impact on objectives and the likelihood that they will materialize (risk assessment, RA)
- Developing risk management strategies (risk management, RM) to improve controls and create a reasoned response to high-level risks

- Establishing action plans to take forward changes and improvements required in light of the risk cycle
- Ensuring that actions are integrated into set key performance indicators (KPIs) so that progress may be monitored, particularly for strategically significant risks areas

The important thing is to ensure that the basic risk cycle is not forgotten when applying the global thinking and approaches that come with ERM. Meanwhile, a real-life example will bring home the way the risk cycle can be incorporated into working practices.

CASE STUDY

Risk Management Impacts a Culture of Communication

In one government office, workshops were a common feature of the way people connected. The workshops eventually became spontaneous breakout sessions in which people would get together and brainstorm an issue that needed to be pinned down. Many offices had a flip chart and a few chairs set in a corner, and work teams understood the risk assessment process, facilitating consensus and the need for good listening skills. Meanwhile, line managers had empowered their teams to bring up proposed system changes, which were presented by staff members and discussed at monthly management team meetings. Risk management was used as part of a culture change program to build more open communications and better ownership of processes and projects.

This focus on objectives is firmly built into the COSO ERM cube (see Figure 3.4):

There is a direct relationship between objectives, which are what an entity strives to achieve, and enterprise risk management components, which represent what is needed to achieve them. The relationship is depicted in a three-dimensional matrix, in the form of a cube.[18]

ERM PROGRAM MODEL: PHASE FOUR

We have provided many major components that need to be in place for ERM to have any chance of working up to its full potential. The bottom part of the model is about setting a firm platform for the initiative—something that is often missed out. Our model continues in Figure 8.4.

Each new aspect of the model is described below.

Figure 8.4 ERM Program Model: Phase Four

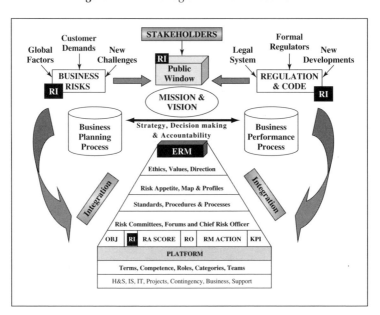

Platform

The ERM platform is based on a simple sentiment:

> Everyone in the organization plays a role in ensuring successful enterprise-wide risk management but the primary responsibility for identifying risks and managing them lies with management.[19]

Terms, Competence, Roles, Categories, and Teams

The thing that sets apart an organization that is able to reap the full benefits from ERM is the quality of its underpinning platform based on a simple sentiment (i.e., that the basic-grade employee is the single most important factor in whether an organization is able to grasp a new development). If the support office, divisions, project people, technicians, drivers, reception staff, production teams, local offices, head office, and all the other parts of the workforce are comfortable with the idea of risk and risk management, then there is hope:

> Virtually all personnel play some role in effecting risk management.[20]

It's a little like landscaping a new garden and using advanced technology to plan the work, appoint a designer, set out how the grounds will be developed, and all of the other high-level concepts that need to be addressed, but the act of planting seeds and allowing them to grow at ground level means the garden can actually flourish. Setting clear standards of staff competence is important to effective ERM:

> Competence reflects the knowledge and skills needed to perform assigned tasks. Management decides how well these tasks need to be accomplished, weighing the entity's strategy and objectives against plans for their implementation and achievement.[21]

H&S, IS, IT, Projects, Contingencies, Business, and Support

The next item is about mobilizing any expertise that already exists within the organization. Again, this can be missed when getting ERM in place. Rather than launch an ERM program and assume that everyone is at base one, it may be a better idea to search out those teams in the organization that have traditionally used risk assessments in their work to form a risk community, as seen in the following example.

CASE STUDY

Risk Community

One organization has developed the concept of a risk community of people in the front line of traditional risk management. This includes security, insurance, IT, projects, finance, safety, contingency planning, and business planning teams. Their view of risk was consolidated and rolled out across the business as terms, approaches, and basic tools that are then agreed on and used as standard practice by most employees.

This loosely networked group can then be used to help develop ideas, methodologies, and ways of spreading the risk message across the rest of the organization. The group may consist of the following:

- Health and safety people (H&S)
- Information systems (IS) and information technology (IT)
- Project managers
- The teams responsible for contingency planning, disaster recovery, and emergency business support
- Security personnel
- Corporate insurance officers
- External and internal auditors
- Any others who have developed their own risk language and techniques

Integration

The first point of call is to ask each member of the risk community how he or she sees risk and whether any common ground may be developed as a platform to the wider ERM process. To exclude these people may create bad feelings because they feel patronized by attempts to sell the risk concept as a simple risk cycle. It goes without saying that internal auditors will be leaders among the risk professionals and can take a lead in developing this approach to ensure the following principle can be applied:

> Enterprise risk management is not strictly a serial process, where one component affects only the next. It is a multidirectional, iterative process in which almost any component can and does influence another.[22]

Risk Identification

Risk identification (RI) is scattered across the model in an attempt to demonstrate how risk management is simply the way an organization responds to the risks that are spotted on the enterprise's corporate radar. In fully mature risk-based organizations, the risk cycle does not really apply. It is embedded within the organization and becomes more a case of ensuring that a horizon scanning mechanism is in place that is sophisticated enough to identify anything that impedes achieving objectives. This means a focus on risk identification, with the knowledge that, as long as we are best placed to spot each big or growing risk, our controls will be able to flex to provide a reasonable response. One major source of risk identification is the auditor, and the chief auditor has a distinct role in this matter:

> The CAE should consider whether it is appropriate to inform the board regarding previously reported, significant observations and recommendations in those instances when senior management and the board assumed the risk of not correcting the reported condition. This may be particularly necessary when there have been organization, board, senior management, or other changes.[23]

ERM PROGRAM MODEL: FINAL

We now arrive at the final three parts of the model to complete this holistic account of a dynamic and flexible ERM. Our complete model is in Figure 8.5.

Each new aspect of the final model is described below.

Figure 8.5 The Complete ERM Program Model

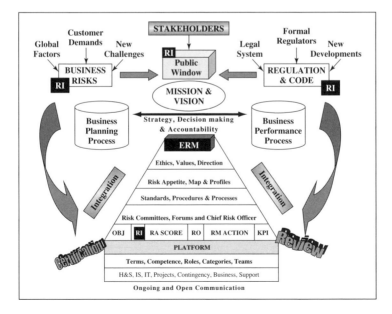

Certification

Having set up the context, platforms, and right culture to ensure that risk to the business can be spotted and tackled, it is time to attest to this effect. The certification item is pasted over the model to indicate that there needs to be a system in place to motivate, assist, and capture formal certificates published each quarter that explain how ERM has been operated and how this means internal controls can be focused and made right. This is particularly apt for controls that affect the financial reporting arrangements. Certificates should reflect efforts made by each management level to implement ERM, as the following example demonstrates.

CASE STUDY

Top Ten Risks

A design company concentrated on what it called the top ten risks. Here the board, management team, audit committee, divisional heads, and all parts of the business were asked to determine their top ten risks and use accelerated reporting to monitor the big risks where there were large levels of residual risk. The stoplight model was used, but there were three levels of yellow, as well as red and green. The three yellow levels encouraged managers to be highly selective when assigning residual risks to the various color codes. The entire risk management process was wrapped around business objectives and was based on defining the various risk owners (i.e., each person who needed to deliver specific objectives) throughout the organization. Red risks always made it on the agenda for the monthly board meetings. The corporate theme was based on sensible risk taking, overseen by a risk forum of key business managers. The risk cycle (and resulting risk registers) was then refreshed each month using short meetings, presentations, and workshops—and then programmed into the performance measurement framework. More detailed risk management effort was then applied to all new products, change programs, and larger business projects.

The management certificates may be aggregated into a formal published statement on internal control. There are three main approaches to this task:

1. A boilerplate certificate that follows a set series of phrases, normally on advice from the corporate lawyers

2. A description of some of the well-known strategic risks, such as an ongoing international restructuring project, along with some of the steps being taken to ensure these risks are contained

3. A full description of the ERM framework and measures that have been taken to ensure it is understood and embedded into the business

The third approach is starting to gain ground because it tells stakeholders how the organization is developing the right type of processes that underpin long-term success.

Review

Another matter that is sometimes missed from an ERM process is the review aspect. ERM is too important to design, implement, and then just leave up to chance. It must be subject to a constant evaluation to ensure it works and makes sense. In addition to built-in mechanisms for managers reporting upward about the way they are managing risk, the auditor has the most to offer in performing this review role:

> With our unique viewpoint as independent but inside observers, internal auditors play a vital role within governance processes by keeping the board, senior management, and external auditors aware of risk and control issues and by assessing the effectiveness of risk management.... Internal auditors must maintain independence, but we must go beyond just pointing out what is wrong; we need to be part of the solution.[24]

This point is echoed in the COSO ERM:

> Internal auditors play a key role in evaluating the effectiveness of—and recommending improvements to—ERM.[25]

Before we leave the audit process, external auditors should be put onto the radar because their contribution has also been recognized by COSO, bearing in mind that a major corporate risk relates to financial misreporting:

> External auditors provide management and the board of directors a unique, independent, and objective view that can contribute to an entity's achievement of its external financial reporting objectives as well as other objectives.[26]

Ongoing and Open Communication

Our final item goes to the heart of good ERM (i.e., communications across and around the organization), which will be making great progress if we can get people to buy into the risk agenda:

> Communication should convey:[27]
>
> - The importance and relevance of effective enterprise risk management
> - The entity's objectives
> - The entity's risk appetite and risk tolerances
> - A common risk language
> - The roles and responsibilities of personnel in effecting and supporting the components of ERM

This final point is very important, in that ERM involves adopting an inclusive approach to risk management:

> Every employee becomes a "risk manager" in the sense that heightened awareness of the impact of unwanted outcomes at all levels of the business provides an unsurpassed means of identifying new risks and refining the management of existing ones. Management remains responsible for the risk management process. However, by first training all employees in the importance of risk management to the future of the company and then ensuring that structures are in place to allow employees to participate in the on-going management of risks, a raised threshold of risk awareness is engendered and maintained.[28]

This is the real aim: To get a workforce that consists of risk managers at all levels and in all areas. When the risk tag eventually gets dropped and people start to talk about better business delivery, then we can move closer to an empowered workforce that refuses to believe things happen through fate but knows full well that people can take control of their work and produce results that meet, exceed, or even pleasantly surprise their key stakeholders. Much depends on sharing knowledge and seeing links between different parts of the business. Along with the review role, this is another area in which auditors can excel:

> By sharing knowledge and building bridges, internal auditors can educate and inform process owners, managers, and executive leadership about the ever-changing status of business risks and related controls throughout the enterprise.[29]

SUMMARY

A high-level review of the overall risk management process may be undertaken by the auditors annually, to reinforce individual planned audits of various high-risk areas of the organization and supplementary consulting projects. One way of performing these overall audits of the risk management process is to go through the following five steps:

1. Determine how the organization reports to stakeholders on its ERM framework and systems of internal control.

2. Assess the extent to which risk is assessed within the business planning and business performance processes to ensure that strategy, decision making, and clear accountability helps drive the business forward.

3. Assess each component of the ERM framework against a suitable model (e.g., the complete model used in this chapter) and judge whether a reliable and efficient system is in place to ensure that ERM achieves it goals to improve both business performance and conformance in the context of the corporate mission.

4. Ensure that various effective mechanisms are in place that enable the identification of existing, new, and emerging risks at all levels of the organizations before, during, and after strategy is formulated and implemented.

5. Produce audit reports that comment on the reliability of ERM in the organization along with details of any good practices, weak areas, and steps needed to ensure that ERM is able to meet the highest standards of quality (in the context of the risk maturity of management and the workforce).

Note that Appendix A contains checklists that can be used to assess the overall quality of the enterprise risk management system and also judge the type of audit approach that may be applied to supporting and reviewing the ERM process.

NOTES

1. Lawrence B. Sawyer, Mortimer A. Dittenhofer, and James H. Scheiner, *Sawyer's Internal Auditing,* 5th ed. (Orlando, FL: Institute of Internal Auditors, 2003), p. 122.
2. Institute of Internal Auditors, Practice Advisory 2100-7.

3. Australian/New Zealand Standard: Risk Management AS/NZS 4360:2004, p. 14.
4. BASEL Committee on Banking Supervision, Bank for International Settlement, February 2003, Principle 10.
5. Institute of Internal Auditors, UK & Ireland, Position Statement 2004, *The Role of Internal Audit in Enterprise-Wide Risk Management.*
6. Committee of Sponsoring Organizations, *Enterprise Risk Management*, September 2004, p. 36.
7. Australian/New Zealand Standard: Risk Management AS/NZS 4360:2004, p. 14.
8. Committee of Sponsoring Organizations, *Enterprise Risk Management*, September 2004, Executive Summary.
9. Institute of Internal Auditors, UK & Ireland, Position Statement 2004, *The Role of Internal Audit in Enterprise-Wide Risk Management.*
10. Committee of Sponsoring Organizations, *Enterprise Risk Management*, September 2004, Executive Summary.
11. *Ibid.*, p. 29.
12. Institute of Internal Auditors, Practice Advisory 2130-1.
13. Committee of Sponsoring Organizations, *Enterprise Risk Management*, September 2004, Executive Summary.
14. *Ibid.*
15. *Ibid.*, Application Techniques, p. 97.
16. *Ibid.*, p. 75.
17. *Ibid.*, p. 87.
18. *Ibid.*, Executive Summary.
19. Institute of Internal Auditors, UK & Ireland, Position Statement 2004, *The Role of Internal Audit in Enterprise-Wide Risk Management.*
20. Committee of Sponsoring Organizations, *Enterprise Risk Management*, September 2004, p. 88.
21. *Ibid.*, p. 3.
22. *Ibid.*, Executive Summary.
23. Institute of Internal Auditors, Practice Advisory 2060-1.
24. LeRoy E Bookal, past Chairman of IIA, Inc., "Internal Auditors: Integral to Good Corporate Governance," *The Internal Auditor* (August 2002), pp. 45–49.
25. Committee of Sponsoring Organizations, *Enterprise Risk Management*, September 2004, p. 88.
26. *Ibid.*, p. 89.
27. *Ibid.*, p. 71.
28. Neil Cowan, *Corporate Governance That Works* (Prentice Hall/Pearson Education, South Asia Pte Ltd, 2004), p. 43.
29. Nancy Hala, "Unlock the Potential," *The Internal Auditor* (October 2002), pp. 30–35.

APPENDIX A

APPLYING AN ERM DIAGNOSTIC TOOL

Each chapter of the book has described key aspects of risk management and the implications for internal auditing in terms of providing a suitable audit cover. Various models have been developed to help explain some of the issues at hand. Each chapter has been prepared to isolate key issues and describe the way various factors are interrelated to form a picture of the entire risk management concept. The final chapter attempted to pull some of the main issues together in a holistic and integrated framework. Appendix A takes on board a great deal of the material from the main chapters and builds a comprehensive checklist that can be used by auditors to assess where the organization stands in terms of implementing ERM. A separate checklist addresses the audit approach and may be used to judge where auditors stand in terms of auditing the ERM process. Together, the two checklists can be used as a general diagnostic tool or benchmark against which to judge the state of risk management and decide where to focus the audit resource for best results.

We start this appendix by setting out a comprehensive model that can be applied to auditing the risk management process. Each aspect of this model is addressed by the two checklists that follow the model. The more detailed checklist consists of 11 main elements with 150 questions and is designed to measure the effectiveness of the ERM process. The shorter checklist has 10 main elements and some 50 questions, and may be used to assess the audit approach that is applied to complement the ERM process. Note that each question on the two checklists would have to be answered by referring to a further list of more detailed subsidiary questions, which should be prepared by users to suit both the context of the organization or part of the business and the approach used by the audit department in question. Moreover, the checklists have been made fairly general to reflect the fact that they are applicable to all types of organizations in the public, private, and not-for-profit sectors.

Figure A.1   Comprehensive ERM Audit Framework

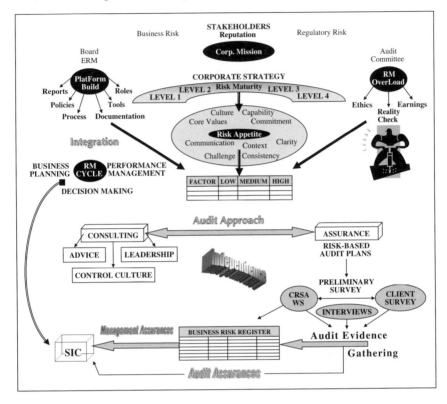

It is possible to assign a score of 1 to 10 for each of the items on the checklist:

1   Does not meet the criteria at all

5   Meets the criteria partially

10   Meets the criteria completely

The scores in between will reflect a best estimate of where the organization, business unit, or work area sits in terms of the two extremes (1 and 10).

ASSESSING THE ERM COMPONENT CHECKLIST

Stakeholders

A. **Stakeholders:** The interests of stakeholders should be built into the way risk is perceived and managed by the organization.	Score (1–10)	Evidence	Action
A.1 Is an effective procedure in place to identify stakeholders who have, or may have, a direct influence on the organization and to assess their expectations and any changes in these expectations over time?			
A.2 Is an effective procedure in place through which to identify stakeholders who have or may have an interest in the organization and to assess their expectations and any changes in these expectations over time?			
A.3 Is an effective procedure in place through which to identify groups of previously disparate stakeholders who may combine to exert leverage over the organization in a way that has not already been anticipated?			
A.4 Is an effective procedure in place through which to identify the risk appetite of different groups of stakeholders and whether this aligns with the risk appetite assumed by the organization as far as is possible?			
A.5 Is an effective procedure in place through which to identify the perception of different groups of stakeholders of the organization and whether there are any concerns regarding the perceived corporate reputation that may damage the organization in any significant manner?			
A.6 Is an effective procedure in place that enables a two-way dialogue between key stakeholders concerning the way risk is perceived and managed by the organization?			

(continues)

Stakeholders *(Continued)*

	Score (1–10)	Evidence	Action
A7. Does the organization have an effective procedure for managing the media in terms of responding to risks that have materialized to the detriment of the business that ensures there will be continuing confidence from the marketplace?			
A.8 Does the organization have an effective procedure for delivering key messages to stakeholders regarding the integrity, accountability, and transparency of the organization and the way decisions are made and implemented, which is inclusive and takes on board the risk perceptions of these stakeholders, and are staff fully aware of these messages and their importance as part of their interaction with customers, partners, and other stakeholders?			
A.9 Does the organization have an effective dialogue with its stakeholders regarding the top strategic risks and the way ERM is helping the business address these risks in the most appropriate manner?			
A.10 Is an effective procedure in place that allows the organization to scan the business press for matters of concern that impact on similar organizations and that may raise questions regarding the way these risks are being managed in the organization in question?			
A.11 Is the concept of stakeholders built into objective setting and risk assessment/management throughout the organization, particularly relating to internal customers, where one part of the business depends on other parts?			
Total score:	**Points:**	**Percentage:**	

Business Risk

B. **Business Risk:** The organization should have a clear understanding of the risks that arise from the business environment and be able to feed this information into the ERM in a way that is both appropriate and effective.	Score (1–10)	Evidence	Action
B.1 Is the organization able to identify global risks to its business resulting from changes in international market conditions and economic shifts?			
B.2 Is the organization able to identify all significant environmental risks to its business resulting from the implications of its products, employment policies, expansion plans, and other strategic factors?			
B.3 Is a process in place that involves comprehensive horizon scanning of all external factors and developments that could impact the ability of the organization to achieve its objectives, and is this process as good as (or better than) anything that is being applied by similar or competitor organizations?			
B.4 Is a formal capacity and resource strategy in place that ensures a dynamic response in the event of any developments and incidents that threaten or actually damage the business capacity (e.g., physical, knowledge, intellectual, or informational), and is this response adequately resourced and tested, in light of current, new, and potential developments?			
B.5 Is a formal process in place that recognizes and takes on board emerging trends and practices regarding fraud, abuse, and irregularity that may affect the organization?			
B.6 Is a formal process in place that recognizes and takes on board economic trends regarding interest rates, exchange rates, supplier positions, and commodity prices that may have a potential impact on the financial management of the organization?			

(continues)

Business Risk *(Continued)*

	Score (1–10)	Evidence	Action
B.7 Is a formal process in place that recognizes and takes on board any internal factors that may present a significant risk to the continuing business operations within the organization in terms of quality, efficiency, sustainability, and effectiveness of the business?			
B.8 Is a formal process in place that recognizes and takes on board emerging trends and practices regarding civil actions against similar organizations in the case of disputes over contracts and procurement projects, particularly relating to large information system developments and built software solutions?			
B.9 Is a formal process in place that recognizes and takes on board the need to ensure that employees have the right talents and competence to grow the business now and in the future, in line with current strategic directions and changes?			
B.10 Is a formal process in place that recognizes and takes on board best practice issues that are communicated within COSO ERM and other published guidance that impacts the organization and its business processes, in terms of optimizing the way these processes perform and respond to changing expectations from users, customers, and other stakeholders?			
B.11 Does the concept of business risk incorporate risk as opportunities that may be missed as well as factors that pose threats to the achievement of objectives?			
Total score: Points:	Percentage:		

Regulatory Risk

C.	Regulatory Risk: The organization should have a clear understanding of the expectations of regulatory bodies and statutory provisions and ensure that it responds appropriately.	Score (1–10)	Evidence	Action
C.1	Does the organization have a policy in place that embraces the spirit of regulatory/legal requirements in terms of responding in a dynamic and committed manner rather than a perception that rules should be seen as a matter for minimal legal compliance, that takes advantage of loopholes wherever possible?			
C.2	Is an effective procedure in place that ensures the organization is able to assume full responsibility for adhering to federal and state legislation and take on board new and tentative issues that arise from ongoing legal proceedings on matters that may affect the organization in question?			
C.3	Is an effective procedure in place that ensures the organization is able to assume full responsibility for adhering to specific rules and directives that impact the industry or service area that relates to the organization in question and takes on board new and tentative issues that arise from published guidance and draft provisions issued by authoritative and advisory bodies?			
C.4	Is an effective mechanism in place for ensuring that business strategies and processes are fully aligned to any regulatory or legal provisions in a way that promotes compliance and fully addresses the risk of failing to meet the expectations of regulators, inspectors, and other authoritative bodies?			
C.5	Is effective dialogue established between the organization and the relevant regulators that is designed to enhance the relationship and mutual understanding of both parties in a way that encourages good compliance and good working practices?			

(continues)

Regulatory Risk *(Continued)*

	Score (1–10)	Evidence	Action
C.6 Is there a good understanding of regulatory/ legal and procedural provisions among staff at all levels of the organization, which assists the ability of employees to adopt and adhere to all such provisions that affect their work?			
C.7 Is an effective procedure in place that allows and encourages all employees, associates, and partners to report any concerns they may have regarding the extent to which the organization is able to adhere to relevant rules, regulations, laws, and procedures and provides that any such reports of problem areas can be fully investigated and resolved in an open and competent manner?			
C.8 Do senior managers understand the need to respond to regulatory provisions and guidance in a way that encourages aspirations to discharge their obligation to act with profes- sionalism and accountability in a way that promotes integrity and leadership?			
C.9 Does the organization take steps to ensure that compliance issues are not seen as a burden on the business that is met by the completion of a vast number of detailed checklists that have no real value or benefit to the business?			
C.10 Has the concept of sound evidence to support ERM practices and resulting risk-mitigation decisions been fully explained to employees and the need to satisfy regulators and possible external investigations/reviews from appointed inspectors or compliance teams?			
C.11 Does the organization fully employ its ERM framework to address the risk of infringing on regulatory and legal provisions as well as business risks?			
Total score:	Points:	Percentage:	

Corporate Strategy

D.	Corporate Strategy: The organization's corporate strategy should be driven by the risk that stakeholder expectations, business issues, and regulatory factors impact the ability of the organization to achieve its objectives and be successful in the marketplace.	Score (1–10)	Evidence	Action
D.1	Does the corporate strategy take into account risks that have been identified at the board level?			
D.2	Is the strategy aligned to the risk policy in terms of taking on board the way risk is defined, identified, and incorporated into the way decisions are made and implemented?			
D.3	Is a process in place for ensuring that set objectives result from the corporate strategy and that this includes the assignment of responsibility for the delivery of these objectives to defined executives, which in turn allows these persons to become the designated risk owners for risks that impact the objectives in question?			
D.4	Does the strategy-setting process incorporate an informed understanding of the need to balance high-impact performance with the regulatory/compliance context for the organization in question in a way that fully recognizes respective obligations to different types of primary and other stakeholders?			
D.5	Does the corporate strategy take on board ethical considerations in terms of the need to ensure that opportunities for income streams, cost containment, and business growth do not infringe on the rights of others or impair the corporate reputation for fairness and integrity?			
D.6	Does the corporate strategy address the risk of not reconciling any inherent conflicts between the need to respond to stakeholders' expectations of quick returns with the wider need to ensure that business growth and market position are entirely sustainable now and in the future?			

(continues)

Corporate Strategy *(Continued)*

		Score (1–10)	Evidence	Action
D.7	Is there a robust system for communicating the corporate strategy to employees in a way that relates the key aspects and the key risks associated with the design and implementation of this strategy?			
D.8	Is the corporate strategy fully aligned to ongoing projects and information system enhancements in a way that takes on board the risks associated with these projects and the knock-on effect on the successful implementation of wider business strategy?			
D.9	Does the corporate strategy incorporate the language and sentiments of the risk strategy in a way that forms a holistic approach to dealing with the risk that the strategy will not achieve its stated aims.?			
D.10	Does the ERM flow from the corporate strategy in terms of being reliant on the effective management of risk, and in turn, is the corporate strategy informed by the ERM in terms of taking on risks that flow from the event identification element of the risk management framework?			
D.11	Do the corporate objectives acknowledge the need to formulate objectives at different levels in line with the COSO ERM dimensions of strategic, operations, reporting, and compliance objectives?			
D.12	Does the corporate strategy incorporate risk as belonging to various defined categories in conjunction with a formal model (such as COSO ERM)?			
Total score:		**Points:**	**Percentage:**	

Risk Maturity

E.	**Risk Maturity:** The organization should establish the degree of risk maturity that is in place among its employees and business processes and seek to develop a strategy that makes sufficient progress to achieve a satisfactory level of risk maturity, taking into account the expectations of key stakeholders.	**Score (1–10)**	**Evidence**	**Action**
E.1	Has the organization set out what it hopes to achieve through the use of an ERM framework in terms of an overall documented mission?			
E.2	Does the organization have a process in place through which it can establish where it stands in terms of the level of risk maturity that it has achieved in line with a set criteria and a formal survey of its position in conjunction with this criteria?			
E.3	Has the organization set out formal levels of risk maturity and established what needs to be achieved in terms of indicators for each of these levels?			
E.4	Has the organization put in place a formal project to drive the business through the various levels of risk maturity and enhancement that are sponsored by a board-level official and competent risk champion to act as project leader, along with a business case (relating to better business and internal control reporting) for the work that is seen as an important part of the overall business strategy?			
E.5	Has the organization defined an information system that acts to record the development of the project in terms of defining to what extent the organization has been able to move through the various set levels of risk maturity and promote the ability of the project sponsor to monitor progress and make decisions to assist with the task in hand?			

(*continues*)

Risk Maturity *(Continued)*

	Score (1–10)	Evidence	Action
E.6 Has the organization defined a formal budget for the ERM project that recognizes the need to ensure that the efforts are fully resourced, particularly at an early stage, notwithstanding the need to build the project into the current business processes and not invent new recording and reporting systems that suggest that risk management is removed from the actual business of the organization?			
E.7 Does the ERM project incorporate action points where steps need to be taken to get the messages and techniques into the workforce and the way business systems are being employed across the organization, and is the risk champion authorized and motivated to make decisions regarding the task of driving ERM into the business?			
E.8 Is a robust system in place to enable the board to monitor the success of ERM in terms of enhanced risk maturity across the organization, and is the board equipped to understand and endorse any necessary measures that the risk champion (project leader) may need to take to progress this matter?			
E.9 Does the organization use regular staff surveys to measure (and act on) the extent to which employees understand ERM and are able to employ the techniques and approaches of effective identification, assessment, and management of risk to the achievement of objectives?			
E.10 Is ERM seen as a framework that has to be implemented with care to ensure it is successful, including the use of pilot programs that enable a lessons-learned aspect to improve the way risk is incorporated into and inside the formal processes and informal cultures that operate within the organization?			

(continues)

Risk Maturity *(Continued)*

	Score (1–10)	Evidence	Action
E.11 Does the risk maturity project take on board and address the inherent difficulty in implementing new ways of thinking and new tools in an organization even where these changes are designed to lead to better business results?			
E.12 Is the ERM implementation project aligned with any culture change program that is designed to get people to take more responsibility for their work and view controls as empowering measures for improving their chances of success?			
E.13 Does the risk maturity project take on board the need to use time and resources carefully and ensure that an obsession with risk does not take over the real issue of getting people to build and account for better business decision making?			
E.14 Does the risk maturity project take on board the benefits of using simple devices such as color-coded reports (e.g., red, yellow, and green) to inspire management action only where it is required and appropriate?			
E.15 Does the risk maturity project take on board any extra investment in technology, such as reporting software, risk databases, and voting technology?			
Total score: **Points:**	**Percentage:**		

Board ERM

F. **Board ERM:** The Board should develop an ERM policy that addresses the key component of a suitable ERM framework.	Score (1–10)	Evidence	Action
F.1 Has a formal ERM policy been adopted by the board that sets out how the organization will develop and implement its ERM process, which takes on board all aspects of best practice, published guidance, external and internal auditors' views, but is set to fit the context of the organization in question?			
F.2 Does the risk policy use a definition of risk and a common language that captures the relevant issues in a way that best suits the organizational cultures in place and the way the business processes and workforce operate?			
F.3 Have the benefits of the risk policy been properly spelled out and attempts made to ensure that these benefits are fully realized, bearing in mind the costs associated with developing and implementing an effective ERM process?			
F.4 Does the risk policy fully spell out the roles and responsibilities of officials, managers, associates, partners, auditors, and all employees in respect to the way ERM is designed, applied, and reviewed in the organization?			
F.5 Does the risk policy directly refer to a suitable ERM framework such as the COSO model and a suitable internal control framework such as COSO or CoCo and make clear the link between ERM and disclosure responsibilities in respect to systems of internal control?			
F.6 Does the risk policy include all eight components of the COSO ERM framework in terms of living up to the standards set by this international model?			
F.7 Does the risk policy include a consideration of how ERM should be implemented with regard to a defined risk maturity model that best suits the organization?			

(*continues*)

Board ERM *(Continued)*

	Score (1–10)	Evidence	Action
F.8 Does the risk policy incorporate an approach to ensuring that the basic risk cycle (i.e., objectives, identification, assessment, and management) is built into the business processes to ensure that risk is duly considered and accounted for across the organization?			
F.9 Does the risk policy refer to the way ERM will be reviewed and assessed to ensure that the benefits are achieved and that it delivers its stated intentions, in a way that would satisfy the expectations of key stakeholders?			
F.10 Does the risk policy provide a reasonable attempt to embed ERM into the business in a way that ensures risk is dealt with in an efficient and effective manner, which includes the ability to flex and adapt to any change in direction or pace of the organization?			
F.11 Have the board members made clear their key priorities to their management teams along with a list of the top risks that they believe pose the most challenge to the business?			
F.12 Has the board established a clear set of documented standards covering the use of CRSA workshops, interviews, and staff surveys as a way of ensuring that the risk cycle is built into all parts of the business and that these standards are developed from international best practice in the use of these three techniques?			
F.13 Has the board endorsed a defined minimum documentation standard covering format, evidence, storage, and access for ERM activities acting on advice from the external and internal auditors?			
F.14 Has the board endorsed a defined minimum reporting standard covering clarity, conciseness, decision making, and priorities for ERM activities acting on advice from the external and internal auditors?			
Total score:	Points:	Percentage:	

Platform Build

G. **Platform Build:** The organization should establish a suitable platform on which to build, support, encourage, and maintain an effective ERM process.	Score (1–10)	Evidence	Action
G.1 Do reports that support major decisions within the organization acknowledge the concept of risk and seek to ensure that such decisions are made with regard to the risk appetite that is applied in the organization?			
G.2 Is the risk policy interlinked with other corporate policies in a way that means each is properly cross-referenced and made compatible with others to form a whole picture of the organization that fits with the holistic ERM concept?			
G.3 Do all key corporate and local business processes incorporate elements of the ERM components that promote an embedded risk management process?			
G.4 Does important documentation prepared across the organization to support management accountability include reference to risk assessment in a way that promotes ERM within all significant parts of the business?			
G.5 Are all suitable tools and techniques that may be used to support ERM understood by managers and their staff and applied in a way that helps the task of risk identification so that this information may be assimilated in the planning and decision-making mechanisms that are commonly applied in running front- and back-office business operations?			
G.6 Do the set roles and responsibilities of business managers and work teams across the organization take on board the need to implement the ERM policy and account for this task?			

(continues)

Platform Build *(Continued)*

	Score (1–10)	Evidence	Action
G.7 Does the culture of the organization support the open sharing of information wherever possible, with adequate steps taken to ensure that any so-called blame culture does not militate against the assignment of risk ownership in any meaningful manner?			
G.8 Are concrete steps taken to spread the messages from the risk policy throughout the organization in an inspired way so that all employees are able to buy into the concept of risk and risk management?			
G.9 Is the ERM process properly communicated to partners, contractors, and business associates in a way that makes clear the need to comply with the risk policy and ensure that it retains its integrity and reliability in all business transactions and ventures that impact on organizational objectives?			
G.10 Is the ERM process implemented in a way that is designed to help build trust among employees in that it encourages the sharing of information concerning risk down, up, and across the business units and structures?			
G.11 Do senior managers review the way risk management is being applied in areas for which they are responsible, and as part of this review do they have a corporately agreed-on benchmark against which to measure this progress?			
G.12 Is risk management built into change programs in a way that ensures all risks to successfully implementing such programs are understood, in terms of identifying these risks and assessing them for impact and likelihood, before ensuring that they can be properly managed?			

(continues)

Platform Build *(Continued)*

	Score (1–10)	Evidence	Action
G.13 Does the organization subscribe to national risk management forums and conferences that provide updates and insights into emerging issues in ERM?			
G.14 Is there a clear mechanism for recording near misses, accidents, and problems experienced by other organizations in the industry or business (or public sector) and building these concerns into the ERM process in terms of establishing alertness or learning lessons?			
G.15 Does the organization use all available in-house expertise on risk management from people such as those involved in health and safety, insurance, project management, and IT security to help spread risk messages and develop corporate risk standards that can be applied by nonspecialist staff?			
G.16 Where much reliance is placed on CRSA in front- and back-office parts of the organization, is a process in place that ensures these workshops are facilitated by people who are skilled in this task and that the reliability and impact of such workshops meets the highest of quality standards?			
Total score:	**Points:**	**Percentage:**	

Audit Committee

H. Audit Committee: The audit committee should have a clear oversight role in ensuring that the ERM is developed and applied in a meaningful manner that equates to the expectations of key stakeholders and is well placed to meet its stated objectives.	Score (1–10)	Evidence	Action
H.1 Do the terms of reference of the audit committee include a clear position regarding the organization's ERM process and make clear that it holds no responsibility for the reliability of risk management apart from providing an oversight of the process so as to report any concerns to the main board?			
H.2 Do the audit committee members possess a good understanding of ERM and ways that it can be developed and implemented within an organization that is supported by adequate orientation and ongoing update seminars both internally and through professional forums outside of the organization?			
H.3 Does the audit committee oversee the extent to which ERM is able to meet the requirements of specific industry, stock market, and/or public-sector regulators and general best practice guidance in a way that best suits the interests of the organization and its stakeholders?			
H.4 Has the audit committee considered and decided on the need and role of a specialist forum such as a risk committee and a designated chief risk officer to help meet its oversight responsibilities where this would be appropriate?			
H.5 Has the audit committee established a firm link between the corporate ERM and the internal control disclosure requirements that should also be part of the oversight responsibilities of the audit committee?			
H.6 Does the audit committee have the capacity to consider the extent to which the various roles and responsibilities established through the ERM process are being properly discharged and whether this fully contributes to the success of ERM in benefiting the organization?			

(continues)

Audit Committee *(Continued)*

	Score (1–10)	Evidence	Action
H.7 Does the audit committee have a formal mechanism through which it may promote, support, and encourage the ERM process, including the need to get employees to buy into the underpinning concepts and techniques and incorporate these matters into their day-to-day work?			
H.8 Does the audit committee have a robust mechanism that enables it to review and monitor the way ERM is performing in conjunction with an oversight of the way more significant risks to the business are being addressed?			
H.9 Has the audit committee established constructive links with the chief risk officer (or risk champion) as well as internal and external auditors in terms of their contribution to the effectiveness of ERM?			
H.10 Has the audit committee been involved in setting clear competencies and skills for the CRO or risk champion, which means the right person will be secured to design, implement, and sell ERM throughout the business units?			
H.11 Does the audit committee have suitable facilities to launch an investigation into any concerns, weaknesses, or reported problems that impact the ERM process or suggest that it is not able to tackle real concerns that impact the organization, including the need to ensure that any lessons are fed back into the way the risk cycle is being employed?			
H.12 Does the audit committee receive adequate support and information from a central resource (akin to a risk champion) in the organization who specializes in nurturing risk management throughout the organization, be it a chief risk officer or the internal auditor?			
Total score:	**Points:**	**Percentage:**	

Risk Management Overload

I.	**Risk Management Overload:** ERM should be integrated into the way the business works and the board should be on guard for signs that it is treated as a tedious paper chase that has little relevance to real work.	Score (1–10)	Evidence	Action
I.1	Is the board on guard for signs that risk management activities, such as an excessive number of drawn-out risk workshops, are overloading the business agenda and causing a noted amount of resentment among staff?			
I.2	Is the board on guard for signs that managers and work teams are paying lip service to ERM and creating detailed documentation such as risk registers that do not filter into their real work priorities?			
I.3	Is the board on guard for signs that risk management is being overlaid on the business and operations as something that is treated as a regulatory requirement that has to be performed with minimal effort for external review and no other reason?			
I.4	Is the board on guard for signs that risks are seen in isolation as a narrow concept relating mainly to one-off incidents and accidents that affect business continuity, which are treated through crisis management and contingency plans?			
I.5	Is the board on guard for signs that ERM is creating an entirely risk-averse workforce who are starting to adopt a fear of risk that they see as having unlimited potential to spoil the business, which is best addressed by taking no chances at all, even where good business opportunities present themselves?			
I.6	Is the board on guard for signs that risk is seen as anything that interferes with making more money without relating risk to other complementary objectives such as adhering to high standards of ethical behavior?			

(continues)

Risk Management Overload *(Continued)*

	Score (1–10)	Evidence	Action
I.7 Is the board on guard for signs that ERM is perceived as a matter of compliance with the risk policy with no real hope that in so doing there will be business benefits through more certainty, fewer surprises, and opportunities to reduce the number of cumbersome controls in place, after having assessed the level of risk in the business areas in question?			
I.8 Is the board on guard for signs that major decisions are being made entirely outside of the ERM framework on the premise that risk is seen as an audit issue that does not relate to real, and at times urgent, business situations?			
I.9 Is the board on guard for signs that ERM is not seen to relate to internal control in that managers are able to gauge the effectiveness of their controls by assessing the extent to which they are able to address unacceptable levels of risk to the achievement of their business objectives?			
I.10 Is the board on guard for signs that ERM is not able to drill down into the business reality where people, and the sometimes unpredictable ways in which they behave and relate to each other, are the main factor in achieving success?			
I.11 Is the board on guard for signs that a blame culture is in place in parts of the organization that mean ERM and the defined accountabilities that underpin ERM cannot be properly established?			
I.12 Is the board on guard for problems where external consultants supply prepackaged database and reporting software that may not suit the business context of the organization in question?			
Total score:	**Points:**	**Percentage:**	

Integration

J.	Integration: The board should ensure that the risk management cycle is fully integrated into the organization and its business systems.	Score (1–10)	Evidence	Action
J.1	Is there a central source of information and guidance to assist managers in dealing with ERM that also incorporates a help line and suitable intranet presentations on ERM and related matters?			
J.2	Is ERM built into business planning mechanisms, and does it take on board statistical information relating to risks, near misses, and operational issues that should be considered in developing and implementing plans at all levels in the organization?			
J.3	Is ERM built into the decision-making process for more significant decisions and properly aligned with authority and accountability arrangements for all levels of management in a way that ensures high-priority risks are addressed whenever options are appraised and selected?			
J.4	Is ERM built into the performance management system on the grounds that actions resulting from risk assessments should be reflected in performance targets to ensure these actions have more chance of being delivered?			
J.5	Are targets for ensuring that the organization progresses through the various set stages of risk maturity reflected within the performance targets for all employees?			
J.6	Is ERM part of staff competence in that suitable levels of competence in dealing with risk are deemed important and these skills and understandings should be examined during recruitment and promotion, and should also feed into staff training and development programs either on risk management concepts, tools, and approaches or as part of wider training seminars?			

(continues)

Integration *(Continued)*

	Score (1–10)	Evidence	Action
J.7 Does the organization work hard to produce a risk-smart workforce who are able to work within business units that have incorporated the ERM process into the general business systems?			
J.8 In furtherance of this risk-smart workforce, do all employees assume some degree of responsibility for risk management built into their role definitions at work?			
J.9 Do all parts of the organization understand the importance of building risks and the way risks cross over different systems and parts of the organization into the way they work in terms of promoting the principles behind ERM?			
J.10 Is risk management built into controls for new information systems in the sense that controls are established to mitigate all unacceptable operational risks where this is appropriate in terms of a properly costed business case?			
J.11 Do all major contracts, agreements, and joint ventures make clear the responsibility for defined risks and where this lies in terms of the parties to the arrangements, along with the process to be applied where new risks arise or where unforeseeable problems become evident?			
J.12 Are adequate structures in place to bring together people in the organization to feed risk into their respective work areas, such as a risk forum or risk working group, under the auspices of a chief risk officer (or internal auditor)?			
J.13 Has the way objectives are set across the organization been reviewed in light of their importance in the risk cycle, because objectives drive the identification, assessment, and management of risk?			

(continues)

Integration *(Continued)*

	Score (1–10)	Evidence	Action
J.14 In furtherance of clear and achievable objectives, has the organization reviewed its accountability arrangement to ensure that people are clear about their responsibilities and that these understandings are then able to support the concept of risk ownership?			
J.15 Does the organization hold regular risk-awareness seminars and ensure there are events, meetings, intranet presentations, newsletters, and other means to help employees understand and apply the principles of ERM?			
J.16 Are formal guidance and standard documentation available for use by managers and work teams covering the use of CRSA workshops and how risk information may be captured and processed in a consistent and professional manner?			
J.17 Are managers given incentives to update their documented risk assessments whenever there is a change in circumstances, in light of new information received and on a regular basis, which is at minimum undertaken each quarter?			
J.18 Do all business reporting systems across the organization incorporate ERM in that they highlight important areas for further action and deal with arrangements for monitoring areas where there is some concern or that are seen as high-risk parts of the business?			
J.19 Do all existing and proposed major business systems incorporate early warning mechanisms that report on activity or incidents that fall close to set tolerances and stimulate appropriate responses in terms of deficiency reports, tightening internal controls, and overall preparedness?			

(continues)

Integration *(Continued)*

		Score (1–10)	Evidence	Action
J.20	Have corporate reporting systems been reviewed to ensure that they are able to take on board information from various risk reporting systems across the organization so as to present a high-level view of key risks across business, possibly in the form of heat maps?			
J.21	Is a central mechanism in place that seeks to pull together any disparate risk activity to ensure that it falls properly within the ERM framework and report any problems to the board-level ERM sponsor, internal auditor, and the audit committee?			
J.22	Are all key performance indicators (KPIs) in use across the organization designed in a meaningful manner, with regard to an assessment of risks to the achievement of the underlying objectives in question?			
J.23	Is a formal board-sponsored process in place that is designed to promote continual improvement in the way ERM is developed, implemented, and reviewed?			
J.24	Where external consultants are used to kick-start ERM, is there a process to ensure the transfer of skills from these consultants to internal managers and staff?			
Total score:		**Points:**	**Percentage:**	

Risk Appetite

K.	Risk Appetite: The organization should establish and communicate a risk appetite that reflects the expectations of key stakeholders, which is used to drive risk tolerance set for all significant processes, projects, and performance systems across the business.	Score (1–10)	Evidence	Action
K.1	When setting the risk appetite, does the board take into consideration the core values of the business in terms of what is seen as acceptable behavior and the need to respond to the expectations of key stakeholders?			
K.2	When setting the risk appetite, does the board take into consideration the culture in the organization and the need to ensure that the way people work and relate to each other and their internal and external stakeholders fits with the definition of acceptable behavior and performance?			
K.3	When setting the risk appetite, does the board take into consideration the capacity of employees in that they are trained and equipped to deal with the levels of risk in their areas of work and recognize where residual risk is beyond, or may in future become beyond, acceptable tolerances?			
K.4	When setting the risk appetite, does the board take into consideration the commitment of the workforce and whether people are prepared to work hard to contain risk to acceptable levels?			
K.5	When setting the risk appetite, does the board take into consideration the clarity of objectives that people are working to and the extent to which they are able to measure the level of success and achievements?			
K.6	When setting the risk appetite, does the board take into consideration the context of the messages from the top, particularly relating to innovation and the search for new business, or the need to meet demanding targets?			
K.7	When setting the risk appetite, does the board take into consideration the consistency of message where the balance between risk taking			

(continues)

Risk Appetite *(Continued)*

		Score (1–10)	Evidence	Action
	and risk containment is provided to form a clear message of what falls within the range of acceptability and what falls outside of these limits?			
K.8	When setting the risk appetite, does the board take into consideration the challenge element where keeping within tolerances should not mean people refuse to take any risk at all and become risk averse by understanding the exposures but not understanding the risk of failing to grasp new opportunities?			
K.9	When setting the risk appetite, does the board take into consideration the communication systems where key messages relay the board's view of risk and reinforce the position that is supported from the top?			
K.10	When setting the risk appetite, does the board take into consideration the criticality of objectives, the risk category in question, whether upside or downside risk, authorization levels, control monitoring levels, and defined risk triggers?			
K.11	Has the board set out clear definitions of terms such as criticality, high-risk areas, unacceptable risk, risk triggers, board-level concerns, damage to the corporate reputation, excessive controls, and vulnerability and communicated these concepts to management?			
K.12	Has the concept of risk appetite been conveyed to partners, associates, and others involved in the organization in a way that makes clear corporate expectations regarding the degree of risk to which the organization is prepared to be exposed?			
K.13	Is the topic of risk appetite built into CRSA events in the form of a brief presentation on the subject and where the board stands on this matter?			
Total score:	**Points:**	**Percentage:**		

ASSESSING THE AUDIT APPROACH CHECKLIST

Audit Approach

A. **Audit Approach:** The CAE should establish a suitable approach in the context of the ERM process that makes the best use of the available internal auditing resource.	Score (1–10)	Evidence	Action
A.1 Have the available options for auditing's role in ERM been fully researched by reference to the IIA's Professional Practices Framework?			
A.2 Has the audit role in organizations that have an immature risk management process been defined with reference to the relevant IIA Practice Advisory?			
A.3 Has the audit role in organizations that have a mature risk management process been defined with reference to the relevant IIA Practice Advisory?			
A.4 Has the audit role in the ERM process been discussed at audit committee, aligned with the corporate risk policy, and formally documented within the audit charter?			
A.5 Have all suitable tools and techniques applicable to auditing the ERM process been identified and applied in the most appropriate manner by audit staff who possess the right competencies and skills to use these techniques?			
Total score:	Points:	Percentage:	

Consulting

B.	**Consulting:** A suitable range of audit consulting services should be applied by the audit department that reflects best use of audit skills to add value to the organization.	Score (1–10)	Evidence	Action
B.1	Has the audit department been able to apply a suitable level of advice to the board, audit committee, management, and relevant personnel regarding the design, implementation and review of the ERM process?			
B.2	Is the audit department able to provide leadership and a clear sense of direction on establishing a sound ERM process where there is no obvious resource that can fulfill this need?			
B.3	Has the audit department been able to measure the state of the control culture within the organization and use this information to help establish risk-based plans that tackle high-risk parts of the business?			
B.4	Has the audit department considered the extent to which it should facilitate the risk management process either at the local or corporate level, in terms of workshops and events that take personnel through the risk cycle?			
B.5	Is the criteria for accepting larger consulting projects based on an assessment of the most appropriate way to apply audit skills to promoting the ERM process?			
Total score:		**Points:**	**Percentage:**	

Assurance

C.	**Assurance:** A core assurance service should be applied by the audit department that reflects best use of audit skills to add value to the organization.	Score (1–10)	Evidence	Action
C.1	Has the audit department made clear that objective audit assurance services represent their most important role and that any consulting services should not unduly interfere with the ability to deliver these core services?			
C.2	Have the range of assurance services been explained to the audit committee and senior management in a way that makes clear how they impact the ERM process and seeks to provide an independent view on whether ERM is reliable and living up to its potential value to the organization?			
C.3	Does the annual audit plan reflect the importance of high-level risks that face the organization?			
C.4	Has the audit department incorporated a comprehensive review of the ERM framework either in its entirety or in terms of aspects that can be tackled individually using suitable diagnostic tools based on COSO ERM, other guidance, and/or relevant models from published material?			
C.5	Do individual audits incorporate an assessment of the way ERM has been applied in specific areas of the organization in such a way as to ensure that key risks are identified and addressed in conjunction with the risk appetite that has been defined by the board?			
Total score:		**Points:**	**Percentage:**	

Independence

D.	**Independence:** The audit process should be sufficiently independent to be able to have the optimum impact on the ERM process, business performance, and the overriding need to ensure that published disclosure requirements are sound and reflect business reality.	Score (1–10)	Evidence	Action
D.1	Has the audit department reviewed the underpinning concepts of audit independence in conjunction with the types of consulting and assurance services that are built into the audit plan and that result from requests from audit clients?			
D.2	Is consulting work performed with regard to the IIA's Professional Practices Framework, including the need to establish suitable safeguards where such work may potentially impair the independence of the audit process?			
D.3	When reviewing aspects of the ERM process, are sufficient steps taken to ensure that the auditors are not placed in a position where they are reviewing elements of ERM with which they have been intimately involved, in terms of helping to establish and revise the risk management framework?			
D.4	Has the CAE made sure that any close association with the ERM where the organization is starting to establish the relevant aspects of the required framework is reconsidered when such frameworks have been put in place and managers have a better understanding of ERM and their responsibilities for managing risk to the business?			
D.5	Has the audit department made clear to management that leadership, facilitation, help, and general advice on ERM is provided by the auditors in their capacity as consultants and that the assurance role involves a third party in terms of working for and on behalf of the board and its audit committee?			
Total score:		**Points:**	**Percentage:**	

Preliminary Survey

E. **Preliminary Survey:** Individual audit engagements should take on board all significant risks in the area under review and the extent to which the client has been able to manage these risks through a suitable risk management strategy and sound internal controls.	**Score (1–10)**	**Evidence**	**Action**
E.1 Has the auditor been able to develop the terms of reference for each audit, based on an initial assessment of the high-risk aspects of the area in question and the state of controls?			
E.2 Has the auditor considered the results of any CRSA events that have been undertaken by the client, or alternatively, whether there is scope to undertake an audit-facilitated CRSA event to secure a better understanding of the key risks so they may be incorporated into the resulting audit engagement?			
E.3 Has the auditor considered the results of any staff interviews that have been undertaken by the client, or alternatively, whether there is scope to undertake audit interviews to secure an understanding of the key risks so they may be incorporated into the resulting audit engagement?			
E.4 Has the auditor considered the results of any staff surveys that have been undertaken by the client, or alternatively, whether there is scope to undertake such surveys to secure an understanding of the key risks so they may be incorporated into the resulting audit engagement?			
E.5 Has the auditor been able to agree on the objectives, risks, and risk management strategy already undertaken by the client that will form the basis for the terms of reference of the resulting audit, before the detailed field work is performed?			
Total score:	**Points:**	**Percentage:**	

Audit Evidence

F.	**Audit Evidence:** The auditor should be in a position to secure reliable evidence that relates to the degree of reliability of the ERM process, either as a result of assessing the entire framework (or parts thereof) or from the results of audit work on individual audits that have been carried out.	Score (1–10)	Evidence	Action
F.1	Has the CAE set clear standards on the need to prepare audit evidence regarding the way risk is managed in areas that are being audited?			
F.2	Has the position on evidence produced by the audit clients regarding the state of their risk management process and internal controls been clarified in terms of the need to perform further work to ensure that management's view of their controls is assessed for the degree to which it is reliable?			
F.3	Is audit evidence sufficient, competent, relevant, and useful in terms of leading to an improved ERM process or in confirming that ERM adds value to the business and supports the quarterly disclosures regarding the statements on internal control?			
F.4	Is the evidence gathered from individual audits done in a way that means it can be aggregated to also comment on the wider aspects of ERM, at least as it affects the specific parts of the business and, where material, is able to encourage the auditor to expend further efforts to explore identified weaknesses in the ERM components?			
F.5	Has the auditor been able to form an opinion on the extent to which the level of risk tolerance achieved by the client can be satisfactorily aligned to the corporate risk appetite relating to the relevant part of the business (and risk categories in question)?			
Total score:		**Points:**	**Percentage:**	

Business Risk Registers

G.	**Business Risk Registers:** The auditor will need to form an opinion on the reliability and presentation of risk registers in areas where they are in use in the organization whenever this is possible.	Score (1–10)	Evidence	Action
G.1	Has the auditor assessed whether the risk register in the areas in question meet the standards set by the corporate risk policy and whether it is sufficient to capture all relevant information relating to risk management and internal control?			
G.2	Has the auditor assessed whether the risk register in the areas in question captures all relevant risk-mitigation strategies and supports any provisions in insurance policies relating to the need to mitigate losses in the event of a risk materializing that triggers a claim			
G.3	Where the auditor has been presented with a completed risk register by the client, have sufficient tests been applied to check whether there is adequate compliance with controls that are a material part of the risk management strategy in terms of mitigating risk to the levels consistent with the corporate risk appetite?			
G.4	Has the auditor been able to relate information prepared by the client to the evidence that has been secured during the audit in terms of forming an opinion on whether the risk register forms a reliable mechanism for recording the results of the operational risk management process for the area in question?			
G.5	Has the auditor assessed whether the risk register in the areas in question properly records decisions (as a living document) made by the client and staff working in the area in question regarding the impact and likelihood of risks that have been identified?			
Total score:		**Points:**	**Percentage:**	

Management Assurances

H. **Management Assurances:** The auditor should comment on the extent to which management's assurances on its risk management process and systems of internal controls is reliable and reflects a true position of the risks and associated controls in the area in question.	**Score (1–10)**	**Evidence**	**Action**
H.1 Has the auditor confirmed whether the concept of quarterly control disclosures reporting has been fully understood by managers and staff who are involved directly or indirectly in the preparation of the relevant documentation and reports in the area in question?			
H.2 Has the auditor confirmed whether the quarterly control disclosures reporting system in the area in question is robust and meets all corporate standards for such systems?			
H.3 Has the auditor confirmed whether the client managers have been able to perform a reliable review of their internal control over financial reporting and compliance in the area in question that is sufficiently robust to isolate all significant weaknesses and matters that should be made known to senior management?			
H.4 Has the auditor confirmed whether the ERM process and internal control reviews in the area in question have been sufficiently documented in line with set standards for record keeping and document retention?			
H.5 Has the auditor confirmed whether the application of the ERM process and internal control reporting in the area in question meets the expectations of key stakeholders, including the organization's regulators?			
Total score:	**Points:**	**Percentage:**	

Audit Assurances

I. Audit Assurances: The auditor should be in a position to prepare formal assurances to the board and audit committee regarding the organization's arrangements for ERM and ensuring that sound systems of internal control are in place and working properly.	Score (1–10)	Evidence	Action
I.1 Has the CAE agreed on an assurance reporting mechanism that enables the chief executive officer and chief financial officer to secure an important input into their own view on risk and controls as part of their obligation to certify their internal controls?			
I.2 Has the CAE agreed on a process for relaying disagreements to the audit committee about the level of risk tolerance that is accepted by the client manager?			
I.3 Has the CAE agreed on a system for grading audit report opinions in terms of the degree of reliance that can be placed on internal control in the area in question?			
I.4 Has the CAE agreed on an assurance reporting mechanism, which may involve providing a commentary on each aspect of the organization's ERM components?			
I.5 Has the CAE agreed on a process for monitoring high levels of residual risk that have been identified during an audit to ensure that they are suitably addressed by the risk owner in question, along with the ability to escalate any such concerns in the event that suitable action is not undertaken within a reasonable time frame?			
Total score:	**Points:**	**Percentage:**	

SIC

J.	SIC: The organization should be in a position to provide a statement on internal control (SIC) in the published report that forms part of the dialogue with all stakeholders regarding their relationship with the organization and that meets the needs of these stakeholders.	Score (1–10)	Evidence	Action
J.1	Has the CAE encouraged the CEO to formulate an SIC that moves beyond basic regulatory compliance but is used to enhance the standing of the organization?			
J.2	Has the CAE encouraged the CEO to enter a dialogue with the regulators to ensure that their intentions and desires are understood and applied wherever possible?			
J.3	Has the CAE encouraged the CEO to assume full responsibility for the internal control disclosures and not place excessive reliance on delegating controls reporting too far down the organization			
J.4	Has the CAE encouraged the CEO to establish a system for allowing managers to self-assess their risk and controls in a way that meets defined standards, which are acceptable to the external auditors and any relevant external review agencies?			
J.5	Has the CAE encouraged the CEO to drive the integration of ERM into the business in a way that provides a sound basis for reporting on internal controls?			
Total score:		Points:	Percentage:	

Scoring Your Assessment

ERM Process Scores				
Item	Title	Points	%	Action Plan Reference
A				
B				
C				
D				
E				
F				
G				
H				
I				
J				
K				
ERM Overall Score:				

(*continues*)

Scoring Your Assessment *(Continued)*

	Audit Approach Scores			
A				
B				
C				
D				
E				
F				
G				
H				
I				
J				
Audit Approach Overall Score:				

INDEX